THE
INTERPOL
CONNECTION

THE
INTERPOL
CONNECTION

An Inquiry into the
International Criminal Police Organization

by Trevor Meldal-Johnsen
and Vaughn Young

THE DIAL PRESS   NEW YORK

Published by The Dial Press
1 Dag Hammarskjold Plaza
New York, New York 10017

MANUFACTURED IN THE UNITED STATES OF AMERICA

FIRST PRINTING

Design by Judith Woracek

36 8 · 2
M 518

LIBRARY OF CONGRESS CATALOGING IN PUBLICATION DATA

Meldal-Johnsen, Trevor.
 The Interpol connection.

 Bibliography: p.
 Includes index.
 1. International Criminal Police Organization.
I. Young, Vaughn, joint author. II. Title.
HV7240.M44   363.2′06′21   79-17186
ISBN 0-8037-4089-1

ACKNOWLEDGMENTS

My particular thanks go to those who created the Freedom of Information Act and its supporters who have kept it alive. Grateful thanks also to Hugh Wilhere, Heber Jentzsch, Jeff Friedman, Bruce, Victor, Lisa, Jane, David, Linda, Artie, R., M., R.P., H., K.O., the Committee for Crime Reduction and Social Justice in the U.K., Simon Wiesenthal, the National Archives, especially the modern military branch, the Library of Congress, the UCLA library, a number of Congressional aides who spurred us on, other agency personnel, members of the media who helped, Resistance group members in France who remember, and our editor at The Dial Press.

—VAUGHN YOUNG

Many thanks to Heber Jentzsch, who first came to me with the incredible Interpol story and never lost faith. Also to Sylvie Herold at The Dial Press for her patience and skill.

—TREVOR MELDAL-JOHNSEN

To the Free Men of Tomorrow,
whose lives depend
upon what we do today.

CONTENTS

CONTENTS

FOREWORD

On February 9, 1977, one of the coauthors of this book became an intimate part of "The Interpol Connection" when an alert was sent to the police forces of 125 nations:

> Information has been received from Interpol Vienna that Young, Vaughn, was in Vienna on 1 February 1977 contacting police authorities . . .

The Telex also said Young was carrying a copy of a Congressional report.* It continued:

> The purpose of the alert is to insure protection of information in official police and criminal justice channels in the event some country may believe him to be a government official stop I repeat, Young is a private citizen and not an official of the United States government stop end Interpol Washington

Two days later a criminal investigation was initiated on Young for "possible impersonation." †

---

*The report was from the General Accounting Office (GAO), the watchdog of the Congress, about U.S. participation in Interpol. It is taken up later.

† Letter from Interpol Washington to Department of State, February 11, 1977. The request was made "on behalf of Interpol Vienna" but did not state

The search for "The Interpol Connection" began in the summer of 1974 in a small Hollywood library when Young found two books about the organization. Discarding the romantic tales of criminals captured in the best tradition of Dick Tracy and James Bond, Young concentrated on the history and structure of the organization. In order to clarify conflicting accounts about Interpol's activities during World War II, he traveled to Washington, D.C., to discover in the National Archives a secret Nazi connection. Subsequently he testified before the Senate subcommittee that opened the first probe of Interpol.

But it was the persistent rumors that Interpol officials were not combating illicit narcotics traffic but rather were actually involved in the movement of drugs that sent Young to Europe and Interpol after Young.

Because of his meetings with officials and private citizens in England, France, Belgium, Holland, Denmark, Germany, and Austria, it did not take long for Young's presence and line of questioning to come to Interpol's attention. Vienna was the first to put out an alert and query as to who he was, but it was Washington that fired a shotgun warning to 125 nations. In response, Vienna radioed Washington:

> We have the intention to supervise Young, Vaughn, when coming to Austria and so please send us exact personal dates and dates of passport of subject and verify please if identity is the same with the person registered in Vienna.*

Interpol's counterattack surfaced in Germany when police officials told the media that Young was a "swindler" (hochstapler) and in possession of either stolen or forged gov-

---

whom Young was impersonating. The investigation apparently fizzled when Young took his experiences back to Washington and related them in his second Congressional testimony.

*Radio message from Interpol Vienna to Interpol Washington dated February 11, 1977. The Austrian State Police had already found a Viennese who had traveled with Young as a translator and roused him from bed to find the American. However, Young had already moved on to Germany unaware of their search for him and Washington's alert.

ernment documents.* Learning of the story in Copenhagen, Young flew to Wiesbaden to demand a retraction but was told Interpol "didn't have time." Instead, they fired off another message to Washington:

> Please be advised that Young again pretended to be director of research National Commission on Law Enforcement and Social Justice Los Angeles, USA. Please send all information you may have on that institution especially whether or not it is an official agency or private institution. Thanks.†

Getting no assistance in Germany, Young traveled back to Vienna to confront the Interpol officials there. Not suspecting that he would later obtain copies of their messages under the Freedom of Information Act and document their involvement, he was told they knew nothing of the difficulties and could not help him further.‡

U.S. Embassy officials in Vienna said they would take Young's complaint but could not offer any assistance. "You

---

*It is still not clear if the allegation was totally fabricated or based upon the inability of Interpol officials to believe that many Americans come in possession of government documents. What is equally foreign to an American is the fact that European citizens cannot obtain such materials. Secrecy is so pervasive that to have an "official" report and not be an authorized official one must be a thief or a forger. The fact that the report in question was purchased from the GAO for $1.00 was completely incomprehensible to officials who were told. Additionally, Interpol also charged Young with impersonation of a government official because he said he had appeared before the Congress, not understanding that many private citizens so testify.

†The allegation that Young was pretending to this position is the most bizarre aspect, since he not only *was* the Research Director for the NCLE, which was sponsored by the Church of Scientology, but had been since 1974. He had testified before Congress and had made numerous Freedom of Information Act requests to various agencies, including Interpol Washington, under that title.

‡As Young later related, 'It was like being Alice in Wonderland. I explained how the Congress worked, how private organizations worked, and how many testify in the Congress and even how the GAO works and how we got the report for a dollar. After an hour, the head of Interpol Vienna smiled and said, through his translator, 'I understand! Now, which part of the Congress do you work for, the House or the Senate?' "

have to expect this working with Interpol," confided one official.

Despite the chilling effect on some of his sources, Young did manage to see some documentation naming Interpol officials involved in illicit drug trafficking. He took the information to a Congressional subcommittee overseeing the American funding of Interpol and testified for the second time. However, with a final touch of unreality, a subcommittee aide destroyed the lists of Interpol drug traffickers Young had presented.*

As 1979 began, the most powerful figure in Interpol resigned. Jean Nepote, the Secretary General for fifteen years, announced suddenly that he would retire and be replaced by his deputy, Andre Bossard. According to some sources, widespread media exposure of data uncovered by the NCLE was partially responsible for his decision to leave.

What began as casual research in a small Hollywood library ended in the exposure of an organization with a history and operation more dramatic than fiction.

From the Nazis, the CIA, and a key Watergate figure, to illicit drugs, there was certainly enough to keep anyone busy with "The Interpol Connection."

*The aide to Rep. Tom Steele, Chairman of the House Subcommittee on Treasury Appropriations, later told the *Sacramento Union* that he shredded the material because the Chairman "said we couldn't have all that stuff lying around and said to destroy it." Apparently it was done without the knowledge of the other subcommittee members.

THE
INTERPOL
CONNECTION

I think it was Hitler, and maybe I give him too much credit, who first conceived of the possibility of a world without reality.

———KEN MILLAR

(aka ROSS MACDONALD)

INTRODUCTION

This is not the first book written about Interpol. Others present the organization in a flattering light, using the "police story" style, with chapters featuring "The So-and-So Case" and "The Such-and-Such Caper," where archcriminals are brought to justice by dedicated, infallible supersleuths. These books were written either by ex-Interpol officials or by authors who, gathering their data from Interpol itself, became more interested in the glamour and adventure of the police-versus-criminal concept than in the workings of the organization. We too have presented some of Interpol's more notable cases, but they are not flattering. Through our research, which was done outside the regular channels, we have discovered a world of difference between what Interpol says it is, and what Interpol actually is.

The enormous amount of governmental secrecy in Europe became increasingly obvious during our research. One researcher went to Paris and worked for days to obtain information on the Nazi occupation of that city during the war. He was finally granted the most unusual favor of seeing a top-secret file. He got three pages concerning the sports activities of a

3

boys' school. English officials work under the umbrella of the Official Secrets Act, and nothing is released. In Germany it's just as bad. There is practically no way to get information except by talking to somebody who talks to somebody else, and so on. Strangely, most of our information on this Europe-based organization was obtained in the United States, either through persistent use of the Freedom of Information Act or through inspection of available official files and documents. In Europe, Interpol and other groups like it can operate under inviolable shields of secrecy because "everybody knows that nobody's supposed to know," as Vaughn Young puts it. Fortunately, the United States has a relatively open government compared to those of the rest of the so-called democratic countries in Europe.

A recent survey showed that the public's awareness of Interpol has been created by a combination of Interpol press releases and Hollywood films. Few, if any, of the people surveyed, including the U.S. police chiefs who were surveyed at their 1975 International Association convention, had the slightest idea about the true functions of the agency. As far as the public is concerned, the average Interpol agent is a character like James Bond, the archetypical global troubleshooter, the romantic international hero, just as the U.S. domestic spy is the dark man hiding behind his newspaper.

Writer Robert Walters has said, "In novels of international intrigue, Interpol is an infallible, high-powered, worldwide police department whose agents roam the globe in search of master criminals. But to many veteran law officers who have dealt with Interpol, whose headquarters is in France, it is a slow-moving, archaic bureaucracy which seldom performs useful work."[1]

It appears that truth today has become something found only in advertising. Public relations has become a sort of bodyguard for individuals and organizations who wish to create certain desired effects while at the same time hiding their true activities and intentions behind barrages of confusing and obfuscatory information.

4

Adolf Hitler, through his remarkable ability to manipulate, was able to control the ideas, minds, and destinies of millions of people. On every continent today, totalitarian governments maintain the status quo through a carefully applied blend of force and mental indoctrination. That is an easy thing when one has a captive audience, but even outside such closed environments, nations of sheep are being created on a far more subtle level through the use of both print and electronic media. These observations are by no means new, but they are pertinent to the image that Interpol, a quietly powerful organization, has managed to present to the public for over half a century.

The following composite of commonly accepted descriptions of Interpol contains thirteen fallacies:

> Interpol is a recognized intergovernmental police force whose task is to hunt down and arrest the international criminal. A multinational force, much like the United Nations, Interpol is made up of police of the Free World and is a bona fide law enforcement agency in its own right. Among the first to fight international terrorism and skyjackings, Interpol still leads the war on narcotics, while assisting a number of nations in the continuing search for wanted Nazi war criminals. One of the most highly respected groups in the world, Interpol, like any other police force, is under governmental control to safeguard the basic rights of every citizen. To this end it operates according to a strict code of behavior and adheres to the highest ethical standards.

Some of these fallacies have been consciously perpetuated through the years to create a desired image, while others have been allowed to persist, rarely, if ever, corrected or denied. We would like to set the record straight.

1. *Interpol is a recognized intergovernmental police force.*

Interpol is, in fact, a private organization. It has never been recognized or established by any international charter or treaty and has no police powers. Before 1971, it was classified by the

5

U.N. as a nongovernmental organization. Then, because of Interpol's cooperation with the U.N., particularly in the area of drugs, what the U.N. termed a "special arrangement" was entered into whereby Interpol was recognized as an intergovernmental organization. However, this expediency has little basis in fact. Interpol members are, for the most part, police and not governmental representatives, although certain governments have sent observers from their military, intelligence, customs, post office, and immigration departments.

In a letter to Vaughn Young on April 10, 1975, a U.S. Library of Congress legal specialist wrote that "Interpol appears to be a private nongovernmental organization with a special working relationship [general cooperation] with the ECOSOC [Economic and Social Council of the U.N.] as well as with a number of individual governments. The ECOSOC has stated that Interpol 'is now to be regarded as an intergovernmental organization' . . . The legal status of such a statement, in the absence of a General Assembly resolution, is questionable . . ."

2. *Interpol's task is to hunt down and arrest the international criminal.*

As a private corporation, Interpol does not have powers of arrest or any investigative rights. Its function is to disseminate *information*, although the line between information and intelligence is a very thin one.*

*Three terms—"information," "intelligence," and "intelligence information"—need to remain distinct. Information is made of raw facts whose relationship to other phenomena has yet to be considered or established. Information, until and unless it has been analyzed and evaluated, remains nothing more than a fact. Intelligence refers to the meaning of, or a conclusion about, persons, events, and circumstances that is derived from analysis and/or logic. Intelligence information consists of facts bearing on a previously identified problem or situation, the significance of which has not been completely established. The methods involved in acquiring information and/or intelligence information by any means and turning it into intelligence constitute the intelligence process or cycle.

The distinctions between these terms are important, because the hazards in blindly making the semantic leap from information to intelligence, or assuming they are one and the same, have been a root cause of the misadventures of most of American and other nations' organizations.[2]

3. *Interpol is a multinational force.*

The only multinational aspect of Interpol is found at its world headquarters outside Paris, where retired police from various countries have been hired, although today 80 percent of the permanent staff is French. Otherwise, Interpol is much like any large corporation with subsidiaries (bureaus) in various countries and with representatives from these offices also stationed at the main office. Information is exchanged between the many national bureaus, but the police forces themselves are subject to the laws and policies of their respective nations.

4. *Interpol is much like the United Nations.*

If Interpol is like the U.N., then so are any private international companies. It is not an arm of the U.N., and its decisions are not binding in any way upon its members.

5. *Interpol is made up of the police of the Free World.*

Police forces around the world have "joined" and pay dues as members, much as they have joined other police associations and fraternities. "Free World" is a misnomer, as both Rumania and Yugoslavia are members. Cuba, although supposedly inactive, is still listed as a member, and a number of police states and dictatorships in Africa, South America, and the Middle and Far East are also members.

6. *Interpol is a bona fide law enforcement agency.*

As a private company, it has no such status, although bona fide law enforcement agencies do subscribe to its services.

7. *Interpol was among the first to fight international terrorism and skyjackings.*

Interpol refused to even discuss the matter for several years, despite the pleadings of a number of countries. In 1969 it presented a secret study of the subject to its members, but the findings were never released publicly and the organization drew even more criticism. By 1973 the best it had chosen to do was pass an essentially meaningless resolution, *urging* "due enforcement of the law and observance of international obligations."

8. *Interpol leads the war on narcotics.*

This claim can be traced to Interpol's press releases. Occasionally, they are caught red-faced, as happened in August, 1974, when New York officials confiscated heroin valued at $12 million that had come through the still active "French connection." Only a few days before, Interpol had boasted in a release that the connection was no longer in operation.

9. *Interpol has assisted a number of nations in the continuing search for Nazi war criminals.*

Interpol, through a policy of labeling Nazi crimes "political," has succeeded in restraining itself from doing any such thing. They have publicly refused to help and were even charged by the World Jewish Congress in 1961 with lending an "unexpected sense of safety" to Nazis in hiding. Some of Interpol's top officials (before, during, and after World War II) have been Nazis or Nazi sympathizers.

10. *Interpol is one of the most highly respected groups in the world.*

Interpol has been wracked by scandal from Peru to Portugal. A high police official of one country called it "little more than a post office. It takes no initiatives of its own." Another estimated that in Europe, local police handle 95 percent of their enquiries among themselves, because of Interpol's inefficiency. The London *Sunday Times* reported that "far from being the slick and sophisticated organization of popular mythology,* Interpol is entering its 52nd year wracked by political conflict and short of money" and is considered "an irrelevance by many police forces" in the world.[3]

11. *Interpol is under governmental control.*

Interpol is not regulated, controlled, or supervised by any government or by the U.N. The French have access to its premises and archives, but its activities and financial affairs are entirely its own business.

12. *Interpol safeguards the basic rights of every citizen.*

Interpol's constitution makes no reference to the rights of

* Such normally reliable source books as encyclopedias and almanacs have, through lack of prior research and documentation, been obliged to perpetuate the myths of Interpol. The only sources available to them have been Interpol representatives and supporters. It is hoped this situation will now be corrected.

private citizens, let alone to the safeguarding of these rights. As the organization is not under the control of any government, citizens harmed by it have no legal recourse or protection, except against local officials, although many of its member police forces are from countries where the law does not allow citizens any rights. Late in 1974, bowing to public pressure, Interpol passed a resolution that "urges" that the privacy of the individual be taken into account. However, there are no provisions for enforcement.

13. *Interpol operates according to a strict code of behavior reflecting the highest ethical standards.*

Beyond its basic parliamentary procedure, Interpol's constitution makes no reference to any code or standard of behavior expected from its members, nor does it consider itself responsible to any degree for the actions of its members. Indeed, in 1973 Interpol's Secretary General Jean Nepote said,

> It is true that Interpol is not founded on an international convention in the usual diplomatic tradition. There is no parchment, red ribbon, or official seal. But its most recent constitution was adopted (in 1956) by an assembly composed of government-appointed delegates. Moreover, this constitution was sent at the time to the ministries of foreign affairs of all affiliated countries, and these authorities were given a period of six months to raise objections to any of the clauses of the constitution, on behalf of their country. Since no objections were raised, it can reasonably be argued that the organization's constitution was approved by the foreign ministries of all the governments involved.[4]

Although primarily an information conduit in its day-to-day operations, Interpol also serves a function as a coordinating and policy-making organization. It is, for better or worse, one of the few organizations in the world where law enforcement officers from many countries can meet together, discuss the problems they face, and come up with mutually agreeable solutions. Each year, Interpol holds seminars and meetings in various countries to discuss either general or specific crime in that area of the world, or a specific type of global criminal activity, such as drug traffic. Its annual General Assembly, attended by all of its members, is the official policy-making body of the organization, and committees from various member countries are also formed to study particular problems. The culmination of all this activity usually consists of resolutions that, although well-intentioned, are in no way binding upon member countries and thus do not necessarily result in the type of unified activity that might be desirable.

Interpol is divided into four main bodies—the General Assembly, the Executive Committee, the General Secretariat, and the National Central Bureaus (NCB's).

The General Assembly is composed of the delegates from each member country, and is the voting body of Interpol. It is the "supreme authority" according to Article 6 of Interpol's constitution. Article 7 states that national delegations should include high officials of departments dealing with police affairs, officials whose normal duties are connected with the activities of the organization, and specialists in the subjects on the agenda.

The General Assembly controls the policy of the organization. During its annual meetings it can alter the constitution, act on financial affairs, admit new members, and approve agreements made with other organizations. It also elects the president, vice-presidents, secretary general, and members of the Executive Committee. Only one vote is allowed per member country, regardless of the size of the delegation or the amount of dues paid.

The Executive Committee is a nine-member board made up of the president, two vice-presidents, and six delegates chosen by the General Assembly. Members are elected for a three-year term and are required by the constitution to belong to different countries. However, Article 21 of the constitution states: "In the exercise of their duties, all members of the Executive Committee shall conduct themselves as representatives of the organisation and not as representatives of their respective countries."

Their duties include supervision of Assembly decisions and the work of the Secretary General, agenda preparation, and the submission of proposals for the vote. Basically, the Executive Committee is something like a government elected by the General Assembly.

The General Secretariat, the permanent body, located at Saint-Cloud outside Paris, is Interpol's business division. It contains the "permanent departments" and, as a result, is both the workhorse and the most powerful section, in spite of the "supreme authority" of the General Assembly. Four of the Secretariat's departments specialize in certain crimes: one handles murder, burglary, assault, larceny, car theft, and missing persons; another deals with bank frauds and other types of embezzlement; a third with drug traffic and morals offenses; and a fourth deals with forgery and counterfeiting and also publishes *Counterfeits and Forgeries Review.* The departments also handle sex and morals offenses, identifications, "unlawful interference with civil aviation," and a vague category labeled "miscellaneous."

Other divisions are the general records department, where alphabetical and phonetical files are kept, and a special records department, where fingerprints and other methods of identification are used.

The Secretary General, the principal officer of this division, is nominated by the Executive Committee and confirmed by a vote of the General Assembly. He holds office five years and can be reelected.

The General Secretariat is the information center. It handles general affairs, finance, exchange of criminal reports, maintenance of the crime filing system, individual dossier files, collection of fingerprints and photographs, counterfeiting and forgery, a telecommunications system, and production of Interpol's magazine, the *International Criminal Police Review (Internationale Kriminalpolizei).*

The National Central Bureaus are the Interpol offices in various countries. Members are free to set up their NCB's as they see fit, but in practice the central police service of the member nation is chosen to operate the bureau. Each NCB is empowered to communicate directly with and exchange information with any other NCB.

According to Interpol, NCB's "can initiate within their own country, in accordance with their national laws, any police operation on behalf of another country . . ."[5] In other words, the Washington NCB is an arm of more than a hundred foreign police departments and, as far as Interpol is concerned, can act for that foreign agency in the United States.

The NCB's are also told by Interpol that it is their duty to "do all within their powers to ensure that the resolutions taken by the I.C.P.O. [International Criminal Police Organization] General Assembly are applied in their countries."[6]

If an organization such as Interpol handles information on criminal activities and then extends it to "suspected" criminal activities without qualifying the information—as Interpol does, in spite of its claims to the contrary—then it is leaving itself wide open to abuse, particularly if it is under no governmental control, as is the case with Interpol. The principles, ideas, and hopes under which Interpol was founded were basically sound and good, although its guidelines—which were really "gentlemen's" agreements and unregulated by any laws, and which have not been changed to this day—were extremely unrealistic, naïve, and vulnerable to political influence and corrupt practices. The gathering of information is a dangerous hobby in a world in which information is a useful and valuable commodity, and the danger increases as communication becomes faster and easier.

I swear loyalty and valor to you, Adolf Hitler, as Führer and Chancellor of the German Reich. I solemnly promise you and the superiors appointed by you obedience to the death. So help me God.

——THE NAZI S.S. LOYALTY OATH

Chapter One

DICKOPF: INTERPOL'S
NAZI PRESIDENT, 1968—72

Early on Wednesday, September 19, 1973, a message was carried around the world on the Interpol radio network: "Mr. Paul Dickopf, President of the I.C.P.O.—Interpol—from 1968 to 1972, has succumbed to a brief but fatal illness."

The Interpol journal reported that Secretary General Jean Nepote had attended the funeral in Muschenbach, Germany, on September 24 and that he had spoken briefly, "evoking the high esteem and friendship that the entire Interpol family felt for its former President." The magazine called Dickopf "one of the most outstanding figures in Interpol circles, and his election as President of the I.C.P.O. was greeted with approval on all sides and the conviction that he would never fail to give his firm support to all those who served the Organization through the world."

The platitudes were many and varied, and Dickopf's passing was lamented by police all over the globe. Germany's Minister of the Interior attended the funeral and added his praises. His career was called "exceptional" and his achievements were heralded, but no one mentioned the fact that before and during World War II, Dickopf had been an active Nazi officer in the

SS (*Schutzstaffel*—protection police), No. 337259, and a member of the *Sicherheitsdienst* (SD), the security service of the Nazi party. It could hardly have been expected. First, even in the Germany of today such things are not mentioned, and second, it was a closely kept secret.

Dickopf was elected to Interpol's Executive Committee in 1959, but his background was not discovered until late in 1974. At that time the German federal police (*Bundeskriminalamt*— BKA), of which he had at one time been president, immediately issued denials. The BKA said he had been a member of the Catholic Youth Organization in 1933 and, as such, had got into trouble with the Nazis. In 1939 he was allegedly persecuted by the SD, and in 1942 he escaped Nazi persecution and fled to Belgium. With the Gestapo on his tail, he crossed France and entered Switzerland as a political refugee in the summer of 1943. The BKA claimed that he then studied criminology in Lausanne and Berne. The embellishment that he had been drafted into the SS against his will was added later.

Paul Dickopf's SS personnel file tells a different story. In 1935, he became a member of the National Socialist German Student Organization (*National Sozialistischer Deutscher Student Bund*—NSDSTB), which had the same status and membership requirements as the official Nazi· party, the *Nationalsozialistische Deutsche Arbeiterpartei* (NSDAP). After voluntary army service in 1934–35, he began his police career in 1937 at the *Kriminalpolizei* (*Kripo*—criminal police) as a criminal commissar candidate. He spent the last three months in the SD *Reichsführers* SS. In 1938, he volunteered to join the *Führerschule* (leadership school) of the *Sipo* (*Sicherheitspolizei*—security police), to which only the most fanatical and loyal followers of Hitler and the Nazi party were admitted. Fifteen SS officers, from the rank of lieutenant upward, sponsored him. Otto Helwig, who in 1939 commanded the fake attack unit against Germany from Poland, was commander of the SD school and recommended Dickopf for officer's rank. He graduated as an SS-*Untersturmführer* (lieutenant), became a criminal commissar and member of the SD, the party's secret intelligence organization, whose duty was the establishment and maintenance of political control both in and out of Germany. (The Allies attached such importance to this organization that they ordered any member of the SD arrested on sight. It was expected that if an underground organization emerged to replace the old system, it would come from among the ranks of the SD.)

Dickopf enrolled in the General SS in 1939. There were basically two SS's: The *Allgemeine SS* (General) and the *Waffen SS* (Armed SS), the latter being in the military units. Later claims that he had been automatically enrolled do not hold water. The SS was elite, and requirements to enter were difficult. In a May 25, 1944, speech in Kochem, Himmler said that as early as 1934 he initiated a program to toss out the misfits. "It took me two years to eliminate from the SS all those who did not really belong to us, those who were not hard enough to stay with us, in other words, all the timeservers— and I did it by stepping up the requirements of the service, loading more and more on to it and making greater and greater demands."* According to Helmut Krausnick's authoritative book, *Anatomy of the SS State*, anyone who joined the SS later than 1934 must have known what he was doing.

By the mere fact of joining he was accepting certain principles and practices which could not but lead on occasions to culpable action . . . Entry into the SS, however, implied that a man accepted this risk with his eyes open . . . *Everybody*, however, who joined the SS was forsaking the sphere in which obligations were simply those of the normal loyal citizen and entering that in which the ideological order was paramount. By the mere fact of joining the SS *every man* was giving his ideological assent and declaring himself ready to do more than his duty . . . All this is equally applicable to the men who joined the political police subsequent to 30 January 1933 or some other police

* Krausnick, Buchheim, Brozat, and Jacobsen, *Anatomy of the SS State*, Collins: London, 1968, p. 392.

branch, primarily the *Sicherheitspolizei*, subsequent to 1936 . . .

Furthermore, Dickopf's personnel file states under "general assessment" that his character, posture, behavior, and knowledge qualify him to be suitable throughout as an SS *Führer*. His "Attitude to NS Philosophy of Life" reads "Positive." His attitude to life and judgment is "Good," his general racial picture is "Good," his behavior during and outside service is "Correct," and his willpower and personal hardiness are "Marked." In his own personal statement, Dickopf said that although his religion was Catholic, he did not believe in God.

The record of Dickopf's activities during the war is obscure, since his SS file for this period is incomplete.* His war records are omitted. Granted, thirty-year-old files cannot be expected to remain immaculate, but one would expect something in his file for the period after he left *Führerschule* through 1944. According to a BKA report sent to the U.S. Interpol office in 1975, Dickopf served "From 4/10/39 to September 1942 as head of the Police Liaison Office of Wehrkreis [Corps Area] V [Stuttgart] counter intelligence officer."

The BKA report said Dickopf deserted in September, 1942, and went to Belgium as a political refugee and then, in July, 1943, to Switzerland. However, the only indication his file gives of his disappearance is a brief entry, "Missing," dated 20/10/1944, and a letter of October 23, 1944, stating: "Against Paul Dickopf who was declared missing, exists at this time an arrest order." There is no arrest warrant in his file, although one would expect that if he had deserted, either the SD or the Gestapo (*Geheime Staatspolizei*—secret state police) would have issued one. There is also no record of court martial in absentia, either in his file or elsewhere.

Of course, these documents might have been lost from 1944

---

*Notations on the file, which we found in the Berlin Document Center, show that it had been taken out on the following dates: 17.2.50; 1.3.51; 15.12.52; 20.6.60; 14.8.61; 20/21.6.63; 5/13.5.64; 23/25.5.64; 21/23.5.65; 6.11.74. Photographs were missing and the corner of one page was torn off. Entire pages were also missing.

until 1974, but their absence becomes more curious when the German police system is considered. The customary police instrument for tracing missing and wanted persons is warrant notices, of which the German police had three kinds:

1. The *Deutsche Fahndungsbuch* (German Book of Wanted Persons) contained names of wanted persons in alphabetical order, their respective date and place of birth, and the name of the authority who wanted them. No description. It was issued every ten days. Paul Dickopf appears for the first time in issue No. 243 of April 16, 1943, nine months after his alleged disappearance, and for the last time in issue No. 284 of March 1, 1944.

2. The *Aufenthaltsermittlungbuch* (Book of Individual Residences and Personal Whereabouts) listed persons whose whereabouts were not known and who were wanted. Dickopf was not listed.

3. The *Kriminalpolizeiblatt* (criminal police papers) was the most detailed type of warrant. It was issued daily and listed in chronological order the crimes committed: property stolen, lost or found; persons missing, deserters, escaped P.O.W.'s, and escaped inmates of prisons and concentration camps. Whenever available, a full description and a photograph of the wanted person were given. Paul Dickopf was not listed, although the German authorities had full particulars.

The German police say that when Dickopf entered Switzerland in 1943, he studied criminology in Lausanne and Berne respectively. No record of his studies at either university has been located. Furthermore, Professor Methier, who taught at the University of Lausanne during Dickopf's alleged attendance, and who is currently the head of the Institute of Political Science and Criminology there, denied that Dickopf ever studied criminology there. However, he did say that Dickopf lived on a farm fifteen kilometers west of Lausanne at St. Saphorin sur Morges.

Although Dickopf's story of flight to Belgium and thence to Switzerland had obvious discrepancies, Interpol unhesitatingly promoted it. In 1975, the German police, answering charges against Dickopf, said that "Since he refused to serve as a German Intelligence Agent in Switzerland, he severed his connection with his unit and fled to Brussels, Belgium, where he remained as a political refugee until July of 1943."[1] It would have made no sense for Dickopf, as a Nazi SS officer, to flee to Belgium; Brussels had fallen two years before, and the country was by then occupied by the Nazis. It could hardly be called an ideal hiding place for a German intelligence officer who had deserted his post. Also, Dickopf was stationed at Karlsruhe or Stuttgart at the time. Neither place was much more than an hour's drive from Switzerland, yet, instead of merely accepting his assignment in Switzerland and then deserting to a neutral country, he chose to cross occupied Europe *twice* to get to Switzerland.

The German police said that after entering Switzerland, Dickopf contacted the American authorities well before the end of the war, informed them of his situation, and cooperated with them. This is entirely possible, since he was to have been sent to Switzerland in that capacity. But one also has to take into account that as early as 1943, Nazis were beginning to go underground and set up escape routes in countries like Switzerland.[2]

Polizei der BRD, a propaganda book on the West German police published in East Germany, says that Dickopf was "with the tale of alleged Nazi persecution, sent to a neutral country to engage in secret service activity in his special field—identification. He became, like thousands of other collaborators of the Gehlen Service (SD abroad, SD internal, and other criminal organizations), after 1945, an agent of the American secret service . . ." Although this can in no way be accepted as reliable, since the East German book was obviously published with the intention to discredit, some of the following facts tend to substantiate part of this theory.

On September 6, 1945, a "To Whom It May Concern" letter was written by an official of the American Legation in Berne, Switzerland, recommending Paul Dickopf "warmly" to the Allied authorities in his homeland, to which he was about to return. The letter stated: "Mr. Dickopf has been of great service to me," particularly during the period following the German surrender. The testimonial was written by Paul O. Blum. Blum was not listed as a member of the staff in the American Legation records in the State Department, although he was one of Allen Dulles's right-hand intelligence men in the Office of Strategic Services (OSS), the organization that would later give birth to the Central Intelligence Agency (CIA).

When interviewed in Tokyo on April 7, 1976, Blum remembered Dickopf immediately. He was reluctant to specify Dickopf's role in working with him, but he emphatically denied that Dickopf could possibly have been a double agent. "I had faith in him." Blum said. "He established as far as I was concerned his bona fides with us." Blum said it would be indiscreet for him to indicate other people who might have information on Dickopf, but he concluded that Dickopf "was one of the few ex-Nazis whom I learned to respect." Blum reportedly moved into the CIA when it was formed in 1947. Some speculate that Dickopf moved with him.*

Further evidence of Dickopf's being employed by the Allies is contained in a preliminary repatriation list that was prepared by the British Foreign Office for Switzerland. The list was divided into categories, such as A = German Intelligence Service Officials, C = Commercially Undesirable Germans, and so on. There were 176 names on the list. Number 28 was DICKOPF, Paul. He was listed under category A, German Intelligence Service Officials. Probably a lot more about Dickopf

---

*Highly informed confidential sources in both Germany and France told us that Dickopf had served the CIA until his death in 1973. Apparently while not a full-blown operative in the usual sense of the word, Dickopf met with CIA officials in the American Embassy in Bonn while president of the BKA, and in Washington, D.C. According to our sources, one of the things that Dickopf was called upon to do was to help the CIA establish a drug intelligence network independently of a proposal that had been put forward by Interpol Secretary General Jean Nepote, who has apparently never suspected Dickopf's relationship with the American spy agency.

could be learned from the Swiss Foreigners' Police in Berne, who have a thick file on Dickopf but have refused to release it for inspection.

After the war, Dickopf returned to Germany and joined the police again, and his rise under the mentorship of Globke and Dullien was meteoric. Both Hans Globke and Herbert Dullien were exposed as Nazis. Dullien was a member of the SS and NSDAP as early as 1933. His party number was 1853922. During the war he was chief of Department III in the General Commissariat of Wolhynia and Podolia and Reichskommissar of the Ukraine. His department was in charge of the looting of the occupied areas. Globke was co-author of the dictatorship laws and the racial laws of Nazi Germany and thus shared the burden of responsibility for the Final Solution.

When West Germany became a member of Interpol in 1952, Dickopf became head of the German NCB. By that time he was also deputy president of the BKA. In 1965 he became president of the BKA, and three years later he was president of Interpol.

To help finance new offices, Interpol had instituted an "Extraordinary Building Budget," and during Dickopf's tenure as president, Interpol became more affluent. In February, 1970, the I.C.P.C. journal reported that "exceptional contributions had been paid" by Venezuela and Switzerland. Another large contribution came from Brazil. At the 1969 convention in Mexico City, Interpol reported that "More than twenty contributions of this kind have already been received." When questioned about this in 1975, Interpol Secretary General Nepote denied his own magazine's story completely, saying, "South American countries did not give special contributions to Interpol." As a private organization, Interpol does not have to disclose the source of its funds to anyone.*

---

*Up to and including 1967, the audit of Interpol's accounts was done by three delegates and two deputies appointed by the General Assembly, who "verify that expenditure is undertaken reasonably, in accordance with instructions of the General Assembly and that it is correctly accounted for . . ." and report to the General Assembly. The United States was dissatisfied with this arrangement, and at the 1967 General Assembly in Kyoto its delega-

Simon Wiesenthal, the famous Nazi-hunter, has said that Dickopf's career in the German Federal Police was marked by his refusal to support the German authorities of justice in persecuting Nazi criminals, and that in the German NCB under Dickopf there are "also other persons with an SS past."[3]

Not surprisingly, Interpol's attitude toward Nazi war criminals did not change while Dickopf was president. Ladislas Farago, who spent a number of months traveling through South America while researching a book, cited an incident involving one of the most wanted Nazis, Klaus Altmann alias Barbie: "At least two Interpol chiefs stationed in South America had to be dismissed summarily for blatant corruption. One was so 'influenced' that he refused to act in the extradition case of Klaus Altmann-Barbie, even when the Peruvian Government lodged a complaint with Interpol headquarters in Paris, pointing out that the case involved 'common-law crimes' (the smuggling of currency and suspicion of murder) and not Barbie's Nazi past in France."[4]

When the Dickopf story first broke in 1974, with the release of a file listing a man with an SS number, and the same name, birthdate and birthplace as Dickopf, Secretary General Nepote insisted that not only was it false but that it was probably the wrong man. He resented the assertions that Dickopf was a

---

tion drew attention to the need for improvement. Its position paper for the meeting noted for the report showed assets "in a form which would never be countenanced by a United States company or agency," since it gave only "approximate value" of property "calculated on a somewhat arbitrary basis." The paper concluded, "It appears that what has been done here is to make a horseback estimate."

In the months following the Kyoto Assembly, James Pomeroy Hendrick, special assistant of the Treasury, to the Secretary, corresponded with Nepote about the need (in the U.S. view) for a private firm of accountants to audit Interpol, in an attempt to reach an agreement. With the support of the Canadian delegation, the U.S. discussed the subject at the Executive Committee meeting in May, 1968. At the Teheran General Assembly in July of the same year, the by-laws were amended to allow the accounts to be audited by an independent private accounting firm and two auditors appointed from the General Assembly to see that expenditure was reasonable and justified. This is the procedure still used today.

Nazi but did not try to alter the story in any way. He merely denied it outright. Dickopf had never been a Nazi.

When researchers began to come up with more proof, Interpol Paris changed its story. They said that Dickopf had been in the army but had deserted. Then they admitted that Dickopf had been in the SS, but he had been "automatically enrolled." Finally, in an interview with Vaughn Young on December 12, 1975, in Paris, Nepote insisted that Dickopf had been drafted.

> Dickopf, oui. I knew him very well. Very, very well, Dickopf . . . he was, you know the history of Dickopf . . . he was the . . . before the war, studied the law in Vienna, in Austria. Not in Germany. In Austria. He studied law in Austria, in Austria, and he came to the police as a criminal commissar, which is more or less in England, for instance, a chief inspector, something like this, a lieutenant in the army, in Stuttgart. You see he was in Stuttgart. In the local police in Stuttgart. And when the German army was mobilized, you see, they called all men in the army. Dickopf, German citizen, was called to the army. And he received a rank of assimilation in the SS, which is not the Gestapo. You know, it is quite different. In the SS, which is more or less the Sicherheit Security Service, or something like that. And he was appointed in the counterespionage, in Stuttgart, in the city where he was working, in the city criminal police. He stayed there. I have seen some documents saying he was in the SS school or something like this. Possibly, I don't know. But I'm not astonished because they did not ask him if he would like to go or not. Because, you see, he was in the machine . . . When he realized what was happening in Germany with the political system, he deserted his post . . . and I know because he told me personally many times . . . Never. Never. Never. I never heard one word from anyone about his background. And if he had been a Nazi before the war, he would have been judged. I don't think he would have been promoted, you see. I don't

think so. It does not mean that he had not perhaps to sign some paper or to write something under pressure, you know.

The French police did not emerge without disgrace from the German occupation either. During the war the Germans followed the same pattern of concentrated centralized control and intensified militarization of the police in France as they had elsewhere. Police officers were screened for political reliability and those found unsympathetic were deemed "dispensable." France did not have an overly large number of "dispensables." The French police, groomed in a tradition of policing and prohibition as a method of crime prevention, were generally receptive to the idea of a police state, perhaps more so than in many other countries. Once the French collaborators' reliability was secured, they were able to maintain a limited autonomy as long as they upheld the Nazi regime.

Jean Nepote was appointed a superintendent in training in the Director General's office of the Sûreté Nationale in 1941, and served during the Nazi occupation of France. When interviewed in 1975, Nepote discussed his activities after the completion of his general education.

After that I studied laws and graduated in law, you see, from the University of Lyons and I worked since 1935 in the provincial police in the city of Lyons which is a big city of France, a big province of France . . . as a civil servant, a civil servant. I was called in 1936 to fight a certain Mr. Hitler, you see, in the French Army. I stayed in the French Army from October '36 to July '40. And when the French Army was collapsed, I came back to my job and I considered it was a very . . . work of civil servant. I don't like it very much. I like something more concrete, more. And I came in the French police, French Sûreté Nationale, in the free-zone of France in the beginning of '41.* I was appointed in the headquarters of the police,

* France fell to the Nazis on June 14, 1940. In 1941 the Sûreté Nationale was under Nazi control, and the head of the Paris Gestapo was Boemelburg, "one of the shining lights" of the Nazi Interpol office.

you see. And after the liberation of France, came back to Paris. I was appointed to the CID, to the French CID, in the headquarters of the CID. And one day the commissions, the organization was moved from, it was not moved, but rebuilt. It was destroyed to ribbons and the headquarters were installed in Paris. I was asked by my chief at that time if I would like to work for the international organization.

Nepote was irate over speculation that he had been a Nazi collaborator.

It has been said on Dutch television by somebody, see, that M. Nepote was a collaborator, he was appointed in Paris at his request during the war. During the war I never put one foot in Paris [banging desk]. And secondly, at the end of the war, I was one . . . I had an exceptional promotion because of the services I gave to the Resistance and virtue of the decree which appointed me to the administration of the new Republic, after the end of the war, to promote those who helped the Resistance. And secondly, I have received a decoration from General De Gaulle for the action I took in the network of Resistance which was called Ajax.

"You see," Nepote added, "this is a type of stupid things which we're told about Interpol without any knowledge of the facts."

Ajax, named inappropriately after the suicidal Greek hero of the Trojan war who killed himself because the armor of Achilles was awarded to Odysseus, was actually an umbrella organization, formed out of London to work in France. It had four relatively small Resistance groups underneath it: Zadig, Micromegas, Candide, and Stuart. Ajax itself was not a Resistance group; it was much like a corporate structure embracing several other organizations within it. Ajax was founded by Achilles Peretti, a Corsican who was an ordinary policeman during the war. Today he is the mayor of Neuilly, the richest suburb of Paris.

Ajax was formed in about 1941. It was designed in part as an

26

umbrella for French police who wanted to be with the Resistance, but it was also to supply, from its subordinate parts, information about a possible Nazi invasion of England and similar intelligence.

Probably the most interesting fact about Ajax, as it applies to Jean Nepote, is that it served as a diploma-mill at the end of the war. According to one official source, there were approximately two hundred members in Ajax at the end of the war. By 1947, twelve thousand members were listed. Another source, who had been an Ajax member during the war, said that only about five percent of the Ajax members "really resisted," and the rest were part of "Peretti's Corsican and freemason Mafia." The same Ajax member said he did not know Nepote in the network, but that he had been declared a member in 1945, when Peretti had returned from London. He said that many of the real members in Ajax had held a grudge against Peretti for having, in 1945, established certificates of membership in Ajax for "reasons of protection and promotion."

Peretti, conveniently enough, was also a member of the "purification" committee after the war to determine who had collaborated and who had not.

A woman who had typed up the network's reports for London during the war said she knew of Nepote, but was surprised to hear that he had been an Ajax member. When she heard that he had received a citation for being an Ajax member since its inception, she exclaimed, "It's a little too much!"*

Peretti's assistant during the war, Simone Catoni, also helped Peretti with his smuggling for the Vichy government. According to Phillip Bernart's book, *Roget Wybot et Bataille la DST*, Wybot, who headed up the DST (*Direction de la Surveillance du Territoire*—the French equivalent of the FBI)

*It has also been claimed that Marcel Sicot, Interpol's second Secretary General after the war, was a member of Ajax, but several people have denied this. One high-ranking official said that he had a document to show that not only did Sicot not belong to Ajax but that he was unreliable and an opportunist. The document was not available. Another man, today a high-ranking Sûreté official, said that Sicot was definitely not in Ajax, but it is interesting that Peretti appointed both Nepote and Sicot to their Sûreré positions.

after the war, said that "strangely Catoni and Peretti, simple police commissars in 1942, seem now to have a lot of money." Without spelling out the connections, Wybot also said that "Ajax after the war will be famous for the incredible proliferation of its members after the flight of the Germans."

At least two other recent Interpol officials were possible Nazi collaborators. Serge Langlais, today an important Interpol official, worked for the judicial police in Nice during the war. During the administrative purge of collaborators of 1944, Langlais, then a police inspector, third class, second echelon, was relieved from duty for a period of two years. He was one of a number of people who, when the Gaullist government took power, were disciplined for assisting the enemy, either "by their deeds, their writings or their personal attitude."

Now retired, Henri Joseph Feraud was, until recently, head of Interpol's Division of Judicial Studies. During the war, he was stationed as a superintendent of the judicial police in Marseilles and, like Serge Langlais, was a victim of the 1944 administrative purge. On July 23, 1945, he was suspended from duty and his pay was cut in half. When interviewed in Paris in October, 1974, about former Interpol President Dickopf's Nazi background, Feraud said, "I cannot understand that such things have been said. Of course, it would have been very unthinkable to elect a president of Interpol . . . We have so many countries which have suffered, the election of a Nazi would have been impossible."

After the war, friction developed between the French Resistance groups, among Communists and non-Communists, as to who was going to control Paris. The theme at the time was that whoever would control the police would control the peace. In the struggle as to who would control agencies such as the DST and the Sûreté, Peretti tried to put his assistant Catoni in charge of the DST. However, Wybot got the job and Catoni was made his deputy. Peretti, meanwhile, became Deputy Director of the Sûreté Nationale under Director General Pierre Boursicot, the man responsible for bringing Interpol headquarters to Paris under Secretary General Louis Ducloux.

During Peretti's and Catoni's brief tenure at the Sûreté, a number of people were appointed to posts in the DST and the Sûreté, and interestingly enough, well over 50 percent of those appointed to high positions carried Ajax diplomas. Peretti and Catoni, both Corsicans, were developing an empire.

Peretti left after two years to enter politics, and Catoni left after two years to go into the hotel and real estate business on the French Riviera. Boursicot left the Sûreté in 1950 and became head of the SDECE (*Service de Documentation Extérieure et du Contre-Espionage*), the French equivalent of the CIA. France, like the United States and England, had an "old boy network" that emerged out of the war and would continue to wield influence and exercise great power for a long time afterward. Ironically the French were the first to attempt to organize international police cooperation.

A policeman learns from bitter experience to look at his environment with a somewhat sceptical eye. What he likes to see is order—a solid, definable kind of order in which the pattern of society can be expected to produce the minimum constabulary difficulty.

——HARRY SODERMAN,
A Policeman's Lot

Chapter Two

BEGINNINGS IN EUROPE AND THE UNITED STATES

The crime rate increased at the turn of the century, and, because of the development of swift methods of transportation, foreign borders that were once barriers became sanctuaries for criminals. A man could commit a crime in Paris, board a train, and be safely in another country in a matter of hours.

European criminologists saw a solution in greater international cooperation. The French, in particular, were keen to establish some kind of European central police office, and from 1904 on made a couple of abortive attempts in that direction. But it was not until 1914 that the first concrete steps were taken when, probably at the urging of the French, Prince Albert I of Monaco convened the First International Congress of Criminal Police.

The president of the meeting was Monsieur Lainarde, dean of the law faculty at the University of Paris. Twenty-four nations attended, but plans to organize an international association were interrupted by the tumult and confusion of World War I, which swept Europe for four years.

When the defeated Austro-Hungarian Empire was disarmed and split up into a number of smaller nations, all police files remained in Vienna. Law enforcement officials in the new countries directed their enquiries there, automatically making it a center for "international" police affairs.

In 1923, Johann Schober,* the president of Vienna's police, invited police departments in Europe, South America, and the United States to an international police congress to be held in Vienna.

A month before the meeting, it was announced that the following questions would be discussed:

The organization of rapid and direct means of intercourse between the police authorities of all countries; the institution of a vigorous campaign against international criminals, involving fuller cooperation between police authorities and the adoption of the most modern methods of crime detection; the extradition of arrested criminals; the expulsion of criminals who have served their terms; the introduction of an international language for police; the combating of drunkenness and drug habits in so far as the latter came into the competence of the police authorities; the study of criminal signs of intent and especially criminal tactics and statistics.

On September 3, 1923, the International Police Congress opened in Vienna. By some counts there were 138 delegates of police and judicial authorities from 20 countries and states, by others there were 120 delegates. Most of the delegates came from various European countries.

There was no shortage of proposals. They included one to establish an international police bureau, either attached to the League of Nations Secretariat or, if inappropriate, an independent institution representing all the countries.†

*Schober was Chancellor of Austria in 1921 and 1922.

†Major General Ralph H. Van Deman, known as the "father of U.S. military intelligence," had also once sought international cooperation. While chief of Allied counterintelligence for the Paris Peace Commission in 1918–19, Van Deman proposed an internationally backed League of Nations intelligence agency. But nobody he spoke to saw the need for such a service. He wrote to Brigadier General Marlborough Churchill, saying, "How under the sun they

The League of Nations, it turns out, was embroiled in problems of its own, leaving the way open for the creation of an organization that would later be known as Interpol.*

Another proposal made at the Congress was that police be attached as members of their diplomatic representatives in the manner of the extant commercial, military, and press attachés,† but the head of the Vienna police proposed that, if possible, diplomatic channels be abandoned and that police authorities themselves maintain direct contact.

The Congress adopted English, French, and German as official languages‡ and recessed on September 7, after agreeing to create the International Criminal Police Commission (I.C.P.C.). To avoid political rifts, it was decided that Vienna, since it straddled both east and west, would automatically serve as the new seat of the organization and that the head of the Austrian police would also lead the group, a decision that would have disastrous consequences.

The initial formation of the Commission was not without confusion. Delegates did not sign documents on behalf of their

---

expect to function without it, I can't imagine and am sure they will have to come to it in the end. Just now, however, they seem to have exceedingly vague ideas of what the organization of the League is going to be."[1]

*The Commission changed its name in 1956 at the Twenty-Fifth General Assembly in Vienna and became the International Criminal Police Organization. Members felt the "commission" designation had a limiting and temporary connotation and changed it to "organization" to give the institution broader status and create a public image of permanency. The name "Interpol" also came into being around this time, although its sources are more obscure. One story says it was coined by a Fleet Street newspaper reporter, but Michael Fooner, in his book Interpol, is probably closer to the truth. He says that the radio units had been using the organization's cable address as part of their on-the-air signature, with "This is Radio Interpol calling." This was picked up by the head of the Italian Interpol bureau, Dr. Giuseppe Dosi, who, together with Secretary General Marcel Sicot, made frequent references to it during press conferences. "Reporters began to pick up the word Interpol and use it in their stories," Fooner wrote.

† J. Edgar Hoover brought this idea to fruition about 20 years later when he had FBI agents, acting as "Legal Attachés," stationed in U.S. embassies around the world.

‡ The Congress had even considered adopting Latin as its official language.

countries, as they did not possess the authority to commit their governments, and thus the Commission's status and authority were questionable. It appeared legally to be a nongovernmental organization.

The London *Times* cautioned the police against premature euphoria. "Unfortunately," it said,

> many of the proposals adopted are at the moment of hardly more than platonic value, seeing that the police have not the final word in the adoption of certain new courses of procedure when such are not in accordance with the existing laws of the countries. For this reason certain resolutions relating to the extradition of criminals, the cost of their transportation to their own countries, and elimination of the diplomatic channels in the intercourse of police establishments of the various countries in certain matters, and so forth, can only be accepted subject to confirmation by the several Governments.[2]

The Commission, having no resources of its own, functioned under the authority of both the International Congress of Criminal Police, which had established it, and the Austrian government, which financed and regulated its daily activities.

The Austrians were in a majority on the Executive Committee, and its president was automatically an Austrian. The president and two vice-presidents of the Congress held identical positions in the Commission, even though they were two different bodies.

The first Secretary General was Dr. Oscar Dressler. Some say that Johann Schober was the guiding genius in the early years, but Dressler was invaluable. He had joined the Austrian police in 1902, serving in a number of capacities, and he both spoke and wrote French, English, Spanish, Italian, and German, an obvious asset to an organization with "international" aspirations.

The International Bureau, which was set up in the Vienna Police Directorate, housed a roster of departments, including the International Register (information service on international criminals), the International Register of Prosecutions, the International Register of Persons Dangerous to Society, as well as departments that handled counterfeiting and passport forgery. The only foreign office was the Bureau for Long Distance Identification, located in Copenhagen, which Europe's police used for its fingerprint technology.

In an initial effort toward financial independence, the Commission first published its official journal, *International Public Safety*, in 1924, at a subscription price of fifty-five Swiss francs a year. Subscribers were offered all reports on the work of the I.C.P.C. and were automatically enrolled as members of the Commission.

Harry Soderman, a Swedish policeman who worked for the Commission for almost twenty years, beginning as an expert on forged passports and other documents, claimed that a few years after its formation, the Commission was already proving indispensable, serving as a center of information about international criminals. It had departments dealing with international search warrants, forged documents, drug traffic, and other crimes involving the crossing of borders. It also undertook the responsibility of asking its members for quick arrests of criminals, pending extradition, "avoiding the slow, diplomatic channels."[3]

Each year the delegates of member nations met for a convention in some European capital. According to Soderman, they "were gay and festive occasions, with much display and pageantry." But, he hastened to add, "they served a more important purpose than to furnish opportunity for talk and eating at banquets. They fostered personal relationships between the police chiefs, and this is all-important."

Explaining the value of these personal relationships, Soderman went on to say,

If Herr Banzinger, chief of the Federal Police of Switzerland in Berne, received a telegram from Police Chief Mustapha Pasha in Cairo asking him to arrest a certain Spaniard called Ramon Gonzales for having committed a fraud in Egypt, Herr Banzinger would know that Mustapha Pasha was a thoroughly reliable person, that he need not worry about whether Gonzales was being accused of some special sort of crime for which he could not also be arrested in Switzerland, and that he could be certain the Egyptian authorities would eventually ask for his extradition.

In its early years, the Commission's conventions were of superficial importance. They functioned as a social club, a sort of "old boy network" where one could meet one's peers and form judgments of individual as well as national characters and intentions. But business was conducted as well. Delegates from twenty-nine countries attended the 1926 conference in Berlin, the majority representing European countries, although China, Cuba, Argentina, and Egypt also took part. At that meeting, Johann Schober, who was at that time still the president of the Vienna police and thus President of the Commission, undertook the chairmanship of the convention. Responding to the delegates' hopes of creating an international criminal police force, Schober advised all those attending that the agenda under discussion should pertain to matters of practical usefulness only. He believed that the creation of a truly international criminal police force was at that time something too far removed from reality to be pertinent to the Commission's business.

In 1928 the Commission achieved financial independence by instituting a membership fee for participating nations, at a rate of one Swiss franc per 10,000 population, and by 1929 the Commission seemed to be approaching an organization that was truly European, if not international in scope. In that year, the Commission had its own radio network, with Germany, Austria, Poland, and Czechoslovakia linking up first, followed by Hungary, Belgium, France, Switzerland, Rumania, and the Netherlands.

In 1930, at the Commission's sixth session in Vienna, the organization officially separated from the Congress, and by 1932, the Commission had developed its own departments, independent of the Vienna police and with its own radio code.

. . .

In the late twenties, a fascinating figure from the United States entered the international police scene. Baron Collier, born in Tennessee, described himself as a capitalist in *Who's Who in America*. Collier had made a fortune in advertising, banking, real estate, transportation, and as a corporation executive in a number of companies, but his real interest was police work. He held the honorary post of New York City's Special Deputy Police Commissioner in Charge of Foreign Relations, which entitled him to display a badge and use a siren on his personal car, all of which gave him innocent pleasure.[4]

Collier was also a moving force in another private police organization, the International Police Conference, which had been formed in New York in 1921. Collier wrote that "Its world-wide membership brought international matters into discussion, and its many conferences showed conclusively the necessity of as close international cooperation as had already been attained nationally."[5]

In 1929 Collier attempted to organize an International Police Conference in Paris. The French agreed in principle but changed their minds at the last minute and refused to give their approval. Collier, who was paying the expenses of the delegates, several of whom were already on the way to Paris when notice of the cancellation was received, lost about $30,000. The French change of heart was prompted by a letter from Schober, the president of the International Criminal Police Commission, to the prefect of the Paris police, in which he strongly objected to the president of the Conference, former Police Commissioner Richard E. Enright of New York. Enright and some of his associates, who had visited Europe earlier in the year, had made a bad impression on various European police officials, and the unofficial character of the Enright organization, which had no official sponsorship from the American government, alienated Schober.[6]

Schober's opposition was finally overcome when Enright was dropped and a new president was elected to the International Police Conference. In 1931 a joint meeting of the Conference and the International Criminal Police Commission was held in

Paris, and Collier called for the creation of a new organization, the International World Police. He said the International Criminal Police Commission represented "a perfected international clearing house for police matters in so far as the various countries in Europe are concerned."[7] But Collier pointed out that European police operations were federal or national in scope, unlike the U.S. system, which was divided into municipal and state divisions, and he considered the United States Division of Identification (the future FBI) incapable of fully meeting the needs of the U.S. police. Collier did not propose his new organization as a successor to any existing groups. "It is to be simply a clearing house—a central bureau—a 'main office' for the handling of any and all international police matters, other than those which pertain directly to established federal bodies, for the benefit of all existing and recognized police institutions."[8]

Resolutions approving the creation of a world police organization were passed by both organizations, although, except for the fact that the United States was not a member, the I.C.P.C. was already performing a similar function, at least in Europe.

So in fact the convention was merely a token effort, since Schober was much more interested in having official United States membership in his own organization.

In 1933 Collier organized an International Police Congress in the United States, paying the fares and expenses of all the delegates. The heads of various European police forces attended, but for them it was more for the free holiday than for the opportunity to share Collier's dream and make it a reality. According to Soderman, ". . . the International Police Commission of Vienna was in operation and Collier's idea of a World Police did not appear to be necessary. The only outcome of the Congress (except for a beautiful volume containing all the proceedings and the speeches of the delegates, paid for by Collier) was that he received some continental decorations. For several years, however, one of the rooms on the first floor of the New York Police Headquarters on Center Street continued to serve as the office of the World Police, with a full-time secretary."[9]

So went the dream of Mr. Baron Collier. Unrealized, perhaps unfortunately so, in view of the disastrous fate that was to befall the International Criminal Police Commission in Europe.

The United States became involved with Interpol early on, but did not make any commitments for more than a decade. In 1923, when Schober called for an international police congress in Vienna, the police departments of Washington, Chicago, and New York were invited. As far as can be ascertained, only New York was represented,* but the U.S. police did not join the Commission.

By 1924 the notorious Teapot Dome oil case had cast a pall over President Warren G. Harding's government, and the administration's corruption had spread into many levels, including the Department of Justice. Attorney General Harry M. Daugherty left office in disgrace after being implicated in the oil deal, one of a long line of scandals that had occurred over the previous three years in the Department of Justice and its Bureau of Investigation.

Begun in 1908 as a small Justice Department force under Chief Examiner Stanley W. Finch, the Bureau of Investigation had considerably expanded its operations during World War I, but when J. Edgar Hoover took the Bureau over in 1924, it was in shambles. It had barely survived a long series of scandals involving politically motivated agents with criminal records and others without qualifications.

Hoover had first started to work for the Justice Department in 1917 at the age of twenty-two. World War I had created a

---

*According to Marcel Sicot, former Secretary General of Interpol, the Congress was attended by New York City Police Commissioner Richard Enright. However, a State Department telegram to Vienna on August 21, 1923, said New York would be represented by Samuel G. Belton, the deputy chief inspector.

suspicion toward certain foreigners, then called enemy aliens, and to handle the supposed threat, the Attorney General had created the War Emergency Division and had placed John Lord O'Brian in charge. O'Brian hired Hoover to review aliens who volunteered for military service and wanted to become citizens.

In 1919, at age twenty-four, Hoover had become head of the Bureau's General Intelligence Division (GID), and he soon directed his zeal at rooting out alien spies, saboteurs, and draft dodgers. The "Red Menace" of Woodrow Wilson's second term was in full swing. Hoover, who had been reading Marx, Engels, Lenin, and Trotsky, formed perceptions of conspiracy that would stay with him throughout his life. His duties were to determine the scope of the Communist plot in the United States and the appropriate means with which to prosecute the participants. His brief, which was given a lot of press attention, proclaimed the development of a massive conspiracy that was attempting to undermine all non-Communist governments. As a direct result of the press Hoover's brief received, Attorney General A. Mitchell Palmer invoked the War Sedition Act and launched the "Red Raids" by authorizing special agents to conduct authorized massive dragnet arrests in thirty-three cities. Without special authorization, federal agents were not to carry arms or to make arrests and had to rely on local laws and local police or a U.S. marshal to make their arrests.[10]

When the Ohio gang took over in 1921, Hoover was promoted to Assistant Director (GID), a post he held for three years while the Bureau became the most corrupt and incompetent agency in Washington. After President Harding died, President Coolidge forced the resignation of Attorney General Daugherty and appointed Harlan G. Stone in his place. Stone was instructed to clean up the Bureau.

Hoover, who had agonized over the Bureau's corruption, was appointed acting director in 1924, accepting the job only on the condition that he would be able to avoid any political meddling and that he would have sole control over merit promotions. Hoover cleaned out the deadwood, and his Bureau lay low during the rest of the twenties. In the early thirties, criminal gangs were on the rise (there were 282 kidnappings reported in 1931), and in 1932, when the Lindbergh baby was kidnapped, Congress authorized the Federal Government to act against crimes of violence committed in jurisdictions other than on government reservations. In 1933, gun battles were an almost daily news item, the headliners including Pretty Boy Floyd and his gang, Machine Gun Kelly, Baby Face Nelson, Arvin Karpis, Ma Barker and her sons, Clyde Barrow, and John Dillinger, who became Hoover's most important prize.

Homer Cummings, Attorney General from 1933 until 1939, worked very closely with Hoover in pushing through all the legislation that Congress passed in the "Hoodlum Era," the years from 1932 to 1934 when law enforcement in the United States underwent its most radical change in history. Cummings was strong on law enforcement and on strengthening the Bureau. Ugo Carusi, who was executive assistant to six attorneys general from 1925 to 1945, said of Hoover, "During those years he was building . . . a terrific case with Congress and they were helping him all they possibly could. I suppose some Congressmen thought it was good politics, but I think most of them thought it was the right thing to do, and that's where he got his big start . . . from then on they took him pretty much at his word when it came to appropriations or authority of that kind." [11]

This kind of willful blindness and all-accepting Congressional attitude would prevail for more than thirty-five years, at least as far as the activities of Interpol would be concerned— whether Hoover was involved or not. Congressional naïveté not only would keep Hoover's pockets full but would enable Interpol quietly to gain an undeserved respectful reputation that was self-perpetuating. Funds would not be questioned, and fear of investigation would be nonexistent.

By 1934, the special agent had the power of arrest and also the right to carry any kind of arms, making him a roving police-man. As a result of Hoover's Red Raids, the local police forces around the country had by that time developed their own intelligence units, called red squads, as part of their regular crime combative programs. So, while the regular police took on investigative capabilities, Hoover's Bureau took on crime combative capabilities, and the still extant interchangeable relationship between the local and federal police was established—something that would prove very valuable to Interpol.

Since Interpol's Secretary General Dressler regularly used diplomatic lines to send invitations to American authorities, Hoover was undoubtedly aware of the organization soon after its inception. Interpol had begun actively to court United States membership in May of 1924 by making overtures to the Department of Justice through the Department of State, but the Department of Justice felt that the Federal Government had limited jurisdiction over the areas in which Interpol operated and could therefore gain little by joining the group. The Assistant Attorney General directed Interpol's attention to the Criminal Identification Division in the Department of Justice's Bureau of Investigation, since the purpose of that division was "to acquire, maintain, and exchange with criminal law enforcement agencies at home and abroad, any data which will be of assistance in the identification of criminals."[12]

On April 17, 1935,* the United States was formally invited to attend the Interpol Conference in Vienna.[13] The State Department referred the invitation to Attorney General Cummings for his opinion, stating that there was "no record of this government having been represented" at any of the Commission's previous meetings.[14] Apparently, Cummings in turn consulted Hoover, who advised against attendance since the United States had not had prior representation. Although Hoover was "already familiar with the work of the International Criminal Police Commission,"[15] and although accepting such an invitation would seem to be a natural course of action, the real reason for Hoover's reluctance to join was probably be-

* In April, 1935, Hitler broke the Versailles Treaty by introducing compulsory military service into Germany. That year, the anti-Semitic Nuremberg Laws were proclaimed, and in October, Italy attacked Abyssinia.

cause he was too busy investigating the Nazis at home to consider expanding his operations overseas.*

Since 1933, the local and federal police forces in the United States had been investigating pro- and anti-Nazi organizations throughout the country. In 1934, when Adolf Hitler became Chancellor and Führer of Germany and when the armed forces oathed to Hitler (at that time, Jewish shops were already being boycotted in Germany), President Franklin D. Roosevelt had launched an intensive investigation of the Nazi movement. In spite of this feverish preoccupation with Nazi threats in the United States, Hoover probably was not very aware of the turmoil that was building up in Austria and Germany. William C. Sullivan, who worked closely with Hoover from 1933 until his retirement in 1971 (as Assistant to the Director in Charge of all Investigations, Criminal, and Security, and Foreign Operations), has described Hoover as "very conscious of the fact that he was not educated. He never read anything except the memos and investigative reports that passed over his desk. He had no interest in any kind of culture. He was not interested in plays, not interested in poetry, not interested in political science or history or biography. He never read anything that would broaden his mind or give depth to his thinking."[16]

The first volume of Hitler's *Mein Kampf* was published in 1925, the second in 1926, and by 1933 it had sold over one million copies. Robert Payne said that, "except for the Bible, no other book sold as well during the Nazi regime . . . had more non-Nazi Germans read it before 1933 and had the foreign statesmen of the world perused it carefully while there was still time, both Germany and the world might have been saved from catastrophe . . . Few people read attentively, and there is no evidence that Baldwin, Chamberlain, Churchill, Roosevelt, Stalin, or any of the political leaders most directly affected did any more than glance at it. If they had read it with the attention it deserves, they would have seen that it was a blueprint for the total destruction of the bourgeois society and

---

*The Bureau, which was later renamed the Bureau of Investigation, became the Federal Bureau of Investigation in 1935.

the conquest of the world."[17] Hoover must not have read *Mein Kampf* either, for even when he was in the midst of the Nazi controversy at home and, later, abroad, he blithely continued to maintain a disaffected stance toward the Nazi threat unless it was a question of enhancing the reputation of the Bureau or of filling the Bureau's coffers.

In Europe, the pleasant social atmosphere of the Commission continued for the twelve years after its inception, but in 1935, the Copenhagen conference signaled a different and far less simple era.

That year, Germany's delegate was a young, flashy Nazi named Kurt Daluege, who said of his mission, "My chief qualification for the job is that I have been in almost every cell in the Moabit prison in Berlin."[18] SS *Gruppenführer* East Kurt Daluege had lost a secret battle with Heinrich Himmler, his great rival, the year before. Daluege had been made a general of police by Hermann Göring and had controlled the ordinary uniformed police as well as the security police of the Reich and Prussia. He had also wanted to head the Gestapo, but being a protégé of Reich Minister of the Interior Wilhelm Frick, and a rival of Göring's, fulfillment of his ambition eluded him. Although his allegiance to the Nazi cause was never in doubt, Daluege's appointment as Gestapo head would have given Frick access to information Göring would have preferred to remain concealed and because of this, on April 20, 1934, Göring chose Himmler as leader de facto of the Gestapo.

During the basic reorganization of 1936,* when Himmler was named supreme commander of all the German police forces, Daluege was given responsibility over the ORPO (*Ordnungspolizei*), the ordinary police, which included the urban police, the administrative police, the police of the waterways, the coastal police, the fire service, the passive defense and its technical auxiliary police. At that time, Reinhard Hey-

---

*In 1936, Hitler occupied the Rhineland, received 90 percent of the national vote in a referendum, and established the Rome-Berlin Axis.

46

drich, already chief of the SS, was made chief of the Gestapo central office. The *Kriminalpolizei* (*Kripo*—criminal police), headed by Himmler, was then called upon to become the guardian of national "strength" as interpreted by the Nazis.* To change the traditional role of the police and endow the *Kripo* with the necessary powers to carry out their new duties willingly, the Nazis introduced a flexible new concept called *Verbrechens-Vorbeugung*, loosely translated as "crime prevention," which allowed the *Kripo* to track down and arrest not only criminals but also *potential* criminals.

To further achieve these ends, Himmler, who was also the commander in chief of the SS, formed the *Sipo*, or security police, by linking the Gestapo, the secret state police, with the *Kripo*. He reorganized both branches and established close ties with the SS.†

While all this was going on, Interpol invited the United States to send representatives to its meeting in Belgrade, Yugoslavia, from May 25 to May 31. The State Department again asked Attorney General Cummings for his views and, in the event of a favorable reply, to suggest suitable delegates.[21] Although Cummings and Hoover had received previous invitations for FBI attendance from Dressler and Dr. Kristian Welhaven, the commissioner of police in Oslo, Cummings replied that although he thought it would be "highly worth while for delegates to attend the meeting . . . ," the busy schedule and cost of acceptance would not enable the FBI to attend.[22] When the State Department then asked whether to appoint a delegate from the American Legation or Consulate, Cummings re-

---

* As early as 1936 Hitler had plans to use the police of Europe as a "counterintelligence ideological front to combat Bolshevik infiltration,"[19] and captured Nazi documents show that, together with Spain, Germany planned to form an organization of police forces for counterintelligence and propaganda purposes.[20] In November, Germany and Japan signed the Anti-Comintern Pact.

† In 1939 the Gestapo and *Kripo* were merged with the intelligence systems of the SS and the Nazi party, forming the SD (security service). The SS was formed in 1925 to protect Hitler—an extension of his personal bodyguard.

plied that he thought it "advisable." His budget would not be taxed, and Hoover would get a report on the meeting.

On May 14, 1936, the State Department instructed its legation in Belgrade to designate a delegate, and John L. Calnan, vice-consul at Belgrade, was subsequently appointed.

Evidently Calnan was not strongly impressed by the meeting, as it "brought forth nothing that is not already known to the American police." However, he saw it as an opportunity for the "chiefs of the various criminal police of the world" to foster "an esprit de corps in the Commission and, at the same time, to enable them to discuss in a friendly but business like manner methods which may eventually be developed into a simple and uniform international system for combatting and controlling crime."[23]

Calnan did not remark upon the presence of Nazi Lieutenant General Daluege, then director of the regional police in Berlin, except to say that Daluege had objected to a French proposal that prostitution and traffic in women and children be placed under the control of a League of Nations special committee. Daluege had taken the prevalent German position, saying he could not agree with any system that could be controlled by the League of Nations—an extremely political issue for a nonpolitical organization—but Calnan offered no comments. Calnan reported that the group had discussed "Repressive and preventive measures against the preparation of crime or any other kind of dangerous conduct that indicates criminal designs," but he made no further comment here either. He did say, however, that Dressler had approached him and expressed the hope that the United States would eventually become a member of the Commission.

In 1937 the United States was again invited to Interpol's annual meeting, this time to be held in London.* In a note to the Secretary of State, the British Ambassador invited the United States to send a delegate, saying that although the United

---

*In November, 1937, Hitler outlined his plans for future wars in his *Hossbach Minute*.

States was not formally represented on the Commission, "both the British Delegate and the members of the Commission generally feel that this need not necessarily debar them from formal participation on this occasion."[24]

In a comment probably directed at the Germans, even though it was sent to all who were invited, the Ambassador said that His Majesty's Government desired that uniforms not be worn at a meeting of this character, since they were "inappropriate . . ."

The Ambassador cautioned further that "there has been a tendency to give undue prominence to the social side of these gatherings" and that in order to "preserve the practical utility of the meetings, the entertainment program represents a very considerable reduction on that accord to the delegates on previous occasions."

Hoover, never an enthusiastic supporter of frivolity, appointed W. H. Drane Lester, the Assistant Director of the FBI, as his delegate, and in an unusual move, even sought permission for Lester's appointment from the President.[25] Assistant Secretary of State Wilbur J. Carr informed Lester that the President had approved his appointment, but Carr directed that, in the absence of specific instructions from the Secretary of State, "you are not authorized to enter into any oral or written agreement which may be construed as committing this Government to any definite course of action."[26]

Although Kurt Daluege, Germany's delegate to the 1936 conference, was a vice-president of the I.C.P.C., Germany did not attend that London conference. Germany had decided to hold its own conference in Berlin, to which fourteen foreign police agencies sent representatives, many of them having also sent delegates to the London meeting.

The Berlin meeting was held from August 30 through September 10. Belgium, Bulgaria, Brazil, Finland, Greenland, Holland, Italy, Japan, Yugoslavia, Poland, Portugal, Hungary, Uruguay, and Switzerland attended. As the Gestapo was the moving force behind the conference, Heydrich, Heinrich Müller, Karl Böemelburg, and other top Gestapo leaders officiated. Daluege, Germany's Interpol delegate, was also there.* Most of the delegates attending were chiefs of the political police in their respective countries, and the discussion centered around "preventive" methods against Bolshevism.

Lester reported directly to Hoover on his return and only later sent his confidential report to the State Department.

Without going into great detail, Lester noted that

There was considerable acrimonious discussion among the various delegates concerning an Austrian report titled "Suppression of the Preparation for a Crime or Any Other Dangerous Conduct Revealing Criminal Intentions" with the Italian, Austrian, Hungarian, French and Belgian delegates leading the discussion . . . the friction between the Austrian and French delegates was particularly noticeable . . . Germany sent no official representative to the conference and . . . there was more or less animosity between several representatives of Austria and Hungary and those of Italy, France and Belgium.[27]

Lester did not speculate any further on the absence of Germany or on the internal conflicts.

In the "General Comment" section of his report, Lester noted that the conference was actually of greater practical importance to European countries than to Great Britain and the United States. The conference was dominated by Austrians, but the French, Belgian, Italian, and English delegates had taken an active part. He speculated that England's involvement was mainly a goodwill gesture, rather than for immediate practical benefits, but that "the organization will play an increasingly important part in the detection and apprehension of criminals in Europe and in cooperating with the British Isles and Possessions as well as with the United States of America, in criminological matters generally." Like Calnan, Lester de-

---

* Just three weeks earlier, Hitler and Austrian Chancellor Kurt von Schuschnigg had met in Berchtesgaden, where they signed a ten-point agreement, one of which was that all police powers were to be placed in the hands of Hitler's nominee, Artur Seyss-Inquart.

termined that, although the United States might not receive any immediate practical value from membership in the Commission, the opportunity to meet foreign law enforcement officials and obtain scientific criminological data would be of benefit.

In formal discussions about U.S. membership, Commission officials had bent over backward to lure the United States into a formal relationship, and were even prepared to violate their own rules. On the subject of fees, Lester had pointed out that the Commission's system of basing a country's contributions on population rather than proximity to the seat of activities was disproportionate in the case of the United States, but the officials assured Lester that no country would be called upon to contribute more than 7,000 Swiss francs annually, and that in the case of the United States, the Commission would be willing to accept any reasonable amount. Lester concluded his report by recommending permanent membership and that a U.S. delegate, appointed by the Attorney General, be sent each year to attend the Commission's conferences.

On February 26, 1938, FBI agents in New York arrested three people who were involved in what was believed to be an extensive Nazi espionage ring.* Leon G. Turrou, who had been a special agent in the FBI's New York City field office since 1929, had, along with Major Joe N. Dalton of the army's intelligence division, unofficially begun the investigations in 1935 and had secretly gotten U.S. Customs and Post Office officials, as well as the British secret service, involved in the case. Hoover, who was not informed of the investigation until early in 1938, saw the event as one that would further enhance the reputation of his organization. He asked no questions and gave his complete blessings to the operation, hoping that the arrests, which soon made headlines across the country, would lead to more power for the FBI.

*The Bureau averaged about 35 espionage cases a year between 1933 and 1937, but in the fiscal year 1938, the number multiplied dramatically to 250 cases.[29]

Turrou was placed in charge of continuing the investigations and, in addition to getting confessions from the arrested spies, enlisted several of them to return to Germany to spy for the United States. On the advice and direction of Hoover, whose views about expanding U.S. intelligence services were supported by officials in the intelligence divisions of the Army and Navy, Turrou played up his investigations to the press, after which a conflict developed between Hoover and the Attorney General. Cummings was concerned that the issue might develop into a political debate over counterespionage and American relations with Germany.[28]

Despite obvious concern over Nazi infiltration into the United States, despite the State Department being aware that Kurt Daluege, a Nazi officer, was a vice-president of Interpol (and that Germany had held its own separate conference the year before), in March, 1938, a bill proposing U.S. membership in the International Criminal Police Commission, "as advocated by Director Hoover," was presented to Congress.* The wording was similar to that which Lester had used in his report to the State Department, and, as Lester had done, the bill proposed that the Attorney General be designated to hold the Interpol membership. The bill assured Congress that the Commission's activities "do not in any manner affect the diplomatic relations or political matters but are restricted solely to the exchange of information relative to the technical and scientific methods of crime detection."[30] The bill passed and the United States became a member of the Nazi-dominated organization.

*In 1938 Hoover submitted a report to the President on the activities of the German-American Bund and its attempts to influence favorable policy toward the Nazis.[29]

The soil exists for the people which possess the force to take it . . . and what is refused to amicable methods is up to the fist to take . . . The new Reich must obtain by the German sword sod for the German plow and daily bread for the nation.

——ADOLF HITLER,
Mein Kampf

Chapter Three

THE NAZI TAKE-OVER

ANSCHLUSS *

At 8:00 A.M. on March 12, 1938, the main body of the German Eighth Army crossed into Austria along the whole line between Scharding and Bregenz. By midday, the German units had reached Innsbruck. At 9:15 A.M. Luftwaffe units landed in Vienna. There was no resistance.

Detachments of the army occupied Vienna on March 13, and on March 14 the Austrian Army took the oath to Hitler. At 4:00 P.M. on March 13 a short cabinet meeting was held. The business did not last long. In a few hours Germany had taken control of Austria, its government, its wealth, and its institutions. Austria become a province of the German Reich and Hitler became the Austrian head of state.

Dr. Michael Skubl, chief of police and President of Interpol at the time of the German take-over, was one of the officials who went to the airport to meet *Reichsführer* SS Himmler and his entourage during the night of March 11–12, 1938. After

---

* Anschluss is a German word meaning literally union or accession. It is used to denote the union of Austria with Germany.

that unsettling experience, Skubl entered the Federal Chancellery at noon on the twelfth and received the news that Himmler had demanded his resignation. "He can have that very cheaply," he answered, "because I have already decided on that in the early hours of the morning."[1] Vienna lost its chief of police and Interpol lost a President.

Testifying at the Nuremberg trials on June 13, 1946, Skubl told how he was then made prisoner. "First of all, I was held prisoner in my official apartment under SS and police guard and then, on 24 May, two officials of the Kassel Gestapo conducted me to a forced residence in Kassel, where I remained until my liberation by the Allies." Skubl was one of 36,000 Austrians held in political arrest between 1938 and 1945.[2]

The Germans quickly released a friend of theirs from the penitentiary where he had been incarcerated for several years. Otto Steinhausl, a former Austrian police official and a Nazi, became the new President of the International Criminal Police Commission.*

The Commission, it turned out, had made a grave error at its inception. Ironically, the decision that the head of the Austrian police would automatically become the head of Interpol was originally made to avoid political rifts, but now it left the way open for the Nazis to take over the organization.

Hoover received an invitation in May to Interpol's 1938 conference in Rumania, but an officer of the FBI informed the State Department that the FBI would have to decline, since "no plans had been made for participation in this session."[3] The State Department then informed the Royal Legation of Rumania of the FBI's scheduling difficulties.[4] There was no mention of the Nazi take-over.

The State Department, meanwhile, was deliberating the Justice Department's request for membership in the I.C.P.C., and, on June 10, a resolution was passed and the United States became an official member of Interpol. The Germans had

---

* Steinhausl was in bad health from his sojourn in prison, and a year later he died of tuberculosis.

marched into Austria almost three months before the State Department okayed the bill. To all intents and purposes, and as later events proved, the Commission was under German control, a fact not mentioned in any correspondence relating to passage of the bill, nor did any discussion take place on the floor of the House.*

On June 20, eighteen people, of whom only four were subject to U.S. jurisdiction, were indicted by a federal grand jury on charges of spying for Hitler's Reich. The same day, Leon Turrou, the FBI official who had headed the investigation, submitted his resignation to the FBI, and it was revealed that Turrou had signed a contract with the *New York Post* to do a series of articles about spy activities in the United States. Cummings had been able to silence Hoover in his efforts to keep the public's knowledge confined to what was contained in the charges against the arrested spies, but it was clear that if Turrou went to the press, the information that he had could set off a major domestic and international crisis. It became necessary to meet Turrou's challenge head-on by acknowledging the seriousness of the spy threat and by expanding the U.S. intelligence services.[5]

On June 24, President Roosevelt held a press conference on which *The New York Times* reported that the President favored "larger appropriations for the Army and Navy intelligence services for the expansion of counterespionage activities within the United States . . . however the President wanted it clearly understood he would not sanction espionage by American agents abroad . . . President Roosevelt was reluctant to discuss the government's attitude toward the part of the Reich government in the espionage activities credited to it in the grand jury investigation . . ."

The *New York Post*, which had agreed to withhold publication of the articles pending completion of the trials, reported on June 24 that it believed that "nothing in this series of ar-

---

*According to a letter dated March 24, 1938 (twelve days after Anschluss), from the State Department to the Bureau of Budget, the State Department had "no objection to the proposed legislation."

ticles would have, in any way, interfered with the course of justice," and that "the purpose of these articles was to awaken the American public to the danger of spies and the necessity of enlarging the FBI, as well as the intelligence services of the Army and Navy."

It was clear that Turrou had forced the President's hand, but whether Hoover remained behind Turrou's activities until the end remains uncertain. In light of Hoover's desire to expand the FBI's espionage capabilities, cooperation between the two men does not seem unlikely, although Hoover covered himself by voiding his previous acceptance of Turrou's resignation and by backdating a letter that dismissed Turrou from the FBI "with prejudice."[6]

The result of Turrou's actions was that the FBI, the Army, and the Navy were able officially to increase their domestic espionage and counterespionage activities by increasing appropriations, personnel, and by recruiting the services of local law enforcement officials in carrying out their investigations. However, the FBI was not as successful as the military agencies in staking out approved jurisdictions for its intelligence activities. Officially, the FBI was confined to the United States, but perhaps Hoover was not overly concerned about the restriction since the FBI did have a leg into Europe through its Interpol membership, although that organization adamantly professed that it would have nothing to do with activities of a political, religious, military, or racial nature (a tenet difficult to take seriously considering that the Nazis controlled the organization).

Soon after Anschluss, the Commission convened in Bucharest for its last prewar international convention. The Commission's president, secretary general, treasurer, two of its permanent reporters, and its agents were all either German or German supporters. Its radio station now belonged to the German police. English and French delegates felt that the organization was international only in name. According to Harry Soderman, "Several times events had come near to open disaster, for the patience of many of us was tested to the utmost in that first week."[7]

A proposal was made by a French inspector general to move the bureaus to a neutral country. Switzerland, the traditional haven of neutrality, was proposed but the General Assembly showed its sympathies by voting the proposal down. It was decided that the Commission would continue for at least another year under the old system.

The gathering had its compensatory moments, though. "In Rumania," Soderman wrote, "the hospitality was lavish, to use an understatement. Since such a show was staged for police chiefs, what must have been done for visiting royalty? First we all spent a week in Bucharest. Then there was a second week on the royal yacht, going slowly down the Danube to the Black Sea. I imagine this trip was arranged by our benevolent and astute host, Beanu, the head of King Carol's secret police, with the idea of escaping the tense proceedings of the Commission in the city."

During the final week, delegates were showered with champagne, caviar, and beautiful gypsy dancers. Recreation even included a sturgeon-fishing expedition. Small wonder, as Soderman says, the delegates "fell into a sort of agreeable madness." The delegates shakily patched up their differences, and the Fourteenth General Assembly meeting ended with the promise to meet the following year in Berlin, where the fifteenth meeting was scheduled.

In spite of Hoover's activities against pro-Nazi sympathizers at home, documents obtained under the Freedom of Information Act reveal that the FBI actively cooperated with the Nazi Interpol for a year and a half after Europe had fallen to Hitler, and that Hoover consistently maintained the fiction that the I.C.P.C. was an "independent" organization.

On March 28, 1939, the State Department telephoned the FBI to ask if Germany had taken over control of Interpol "or whether [the FBI] had any information along that line whatever." Hoover replied that, "the meeting (in Berlin) merely is being held in Germany this year . . . the organization is an independent entity which holds its meetings in different countries at different times." Of course, this was after Germany had taken over Austria and Interpol, imprisoning some of its officials and installing its own puppet Steinhausl as President, after releasing him from jail in Vienna.

During this time Hoover's relations with Interpol officials were extremely cordial.* For example, W. Fleischer, a Third Reich criminal police commissioner and a Hoover admirer, wrote to the FBI chief on June 26, 1939, thanking him for the FBI's annual report and proudly informing Hoover that the Reich's fingerprint division had 772,371 fingerprint records. He enclosed a photograph of Berlin's new police laboratory and concluded by saying, "May I ask a personal favor? I should be deeply grateful to you if you could send me a photograph of yourself with a little dedication."[8] Hoover sent him an autographed photograph. This was after the fall of Czechoslovakia.

Hoover's almost obsessive concern for the prestige of the FBI was substantiated in part by some internal FBI correspondence from 1939. On July 20, 1939, a year after Congress had authorized the FBI to join Interpol, FBI official N. H. McCabe wrote to Hoover deputy Nichols expressing concern that the FBI had not yet formalized its member status.

McCabe's worry was that if the FBI failed to join, "the Secret Service or some other Federal Agency may seek to become a member, and the FBI might thereby suffer in international prestige." He went on to acknowledge that "a very delicate political situation has developed in Europe," noting that since Germany controlled Austria and Austria controlled Interpol, the "principal objection" to joining the group was its "distinctly Austro-German atmosphere."

Nevertheless, McCabe recommended that "if we fail to join

---

*On March 14, 1939, German troops entered Prague, and on March 23, Hitler and Italian dictator Benito Mussolini signed the "pact of steel." On April 15, President Roosevelt appealed to Hitler for peace, and on April 28, Hitler rejected Roosevelt's proposal.

at this time after we have already indicated a willingness to join and after obtaining the necessary funds for membership . . . it might be construed as an act of unfriendliness."

On July 5, 1939, the United States received an invitation from the German Embassy to attend the Interpol conference scheduled for August 29 through September 7, which was being presented "under the patronage of the Reichsführer SS and Chief of the German Police Heinrich Himmler." Members were asked to send their replies to Oscar Dressler, the Commission's Secretary General since 1923.

The purpose of the conference, the Embassy said, was to help develop further and to render "still more successful the cooperation of the criminal police in the domain of the international war on crime." As an extra incentive, the Nazis announced that "For those who take part in the Conference and for accompanying members of their families, a number of privileges are contemplated (such as reduction in hotel rates, free sightseeing tours, etc.)." [9] Teas were also planned for the ladies. The offer was later changed to *free* hotel accommodations in an effort to bolster what must have been disappointing responses.

While Germany's intentions had become painfully evident by the summer of 1939, the State Department actually gave the matter of attendance serious consideration. On July 15, they passed the invitation on to the FCC, as the conference was to feature a special program with an International Police Radio Technical Committee. The following week, State sought the advice of the Attorney General "as to the desirability of accepting the invitation." It gently noted that "very careful consideration should be given before sending any American representation to an International Conference held in Germany at this time." [10]

On July 28 the Federal Communications Commission (FCC) informed the State Department that it was declining the invitation to the Berlin conference, explaining that the meeting had "only a secondary interest" because of the wide difference between American and European police systems. [11]

The Attorney General had also decided not to accept, not

because of Nazi involvement, but, because, as his office stated, they "did not believe this Conference would involve matters which would make it necessary for this Government to send a delegation," and that the "procedure followed in the European countries on these matters was completely different from that followed in this country . . ."[12]

The Attorney General confirmed this in a letter dated August 21, 1939, to the Secretary of State, in which he explained that "Careful consideration has been given to the advisability of accepting such an invitation. I am of the opinion that the invitation should be declined and that no American representative should be designated to attend this International Conference to be held in Germany at this time."[13] The German Embassy was duly informed that it would not be practicable for the United States to participate.

The U.S. High Commissioner in Manila had received an invitation to the Berlin conference and on August 1 wrote to the Secretary of State for information on the Commission, "so that they may take intelligent action on future invitations from this body." On September 16, after France and England had declared war on Germany, the State Department sent them a description of the Commission and its purpose taken from the 1937 Lester report, noting only that the United States did belong to the organization but had decided not to attend the meeting.

But the meeting was never held. By 1939 the Nazis had already invaded Poland and started their jackbooted march across Europe. The Commission, however, was by no means inactive, according to its own present-day claims.

Interpol's official organ, *International Criminal Police Review,** began to reflect a German point of view immediately after Anschluss.

*The I.C.P.C. was also responsible for the creation of the noun code used by the dense German network of police radio stations, according to an army intelligence report.[14] In the same report, U.S. Army Intelligence (G-2) also listed the I.C.P.C. magazine as one of the "most important periodicals" put out by German police.

The Interpol journals published criminal statistics that classified criminality according to race and attributed the causes of crime to racial differences, according to the Nazi philosophy in which criminals and all those classified as antisocials were genetically inferior. Jews and gypsies were determined to be genetically inferior and were automatically branded as criminals. The Nazis established the Criminal Biological Institute to deal with antisocials and criminal "kinships" within the borders of the Reich. The purpose of the Institute was to protect the German people from "parasites" and to discover methods to prevent the growth of antisocial kinships at the root of the hereditary level. Thus, through their magazine, I.C.P.C. members were introduced to the Nazi racial hygiene program.

The June, 1938, issue, in its report on the Biological Criminal Congress held in Munich the previous year, stated that "The guilt will be established according to biological research of the personality of the perpetrator. Not only the act marks the habitual criminal, but also his way of life and his slow but continued descent into the antisocial state. The criminal biology will also establish the extent of the hereditary disposition of the perpetrators."[15] The same June issue included a discussion of sterilization, in which a Dr. Schutt of the Reich Ministry for Health was quoted as saying, "Only those should be rehabilitated who are found genetically healthy and worthy."

The July, 1938, issue included a review of *New State Law*, a book by Wilhelm Stuckart, one of the main contributors to the infamous Nuremberg Laws. Dressler reviewed the book, praising it as an excellent description of the National Socialist reconstruction of the state. In the same issue, a criminal wanted for crimes committed in Brussels was described as "Jewish."

The August issue described a criminal wanted in Poland as "Jewish." The December issue announced that Switzerland wanted a man of "Jewish type."

By January, 1939, the Germans had their crime prevention program in full swing, and the magazine printed an article on repressive and preventive measures against the preparatory criminal activities and against other dangerous behavior that indicated criminal will. Casting aside the principle that one is innocent until proved guilty, a number of delegates were reported as being in favor of repressive and preventive methods. The delegate from Finland mentioned that sterilization laws had existed in his country since 1935.

In February, 1939, preventive *arrest and internment* was mentioned as being effective against the "habitual and professional" criminal.

In the March, 1939, issue, Secretary General Dressler praised Stuckhart's brochure about the racial and hereditary care of the Third Reich. He recommended it to readers in countries where racial and hereditary laws did not exist, saying that "racial care is of immense importance for the combat [sic] of criminals."

By September 16, 1940, a month after Germany began to bomb London, Hoover was still friendly with Nazi Interpol officials. After receiving materials on passport standardization from Interpol in Berlin, Hoover politely acknowledged their receipt and, as a routine matter, with no mention that anything was out of the ordinary, forwarded a copy of the passport data to Adolf A. Berle, Jr., Assistant Secretary of State. Furthermore, FBI wanted notices appeared in the I.C.P.C. journal until near the end of 1940. That year, four of the wanted notices described the criminals in a uniquely un-American way: "Jewish Race."[16]

In 1940 the head of the German Security Police, Reinhard Heydrich (later known as the Hangman), consolidated his position by becoming President of Interpol. Steinhausl, whom the Germans had placed as the head of Interpol after the Anschluss, had died from tuberculosis a year after taking over as head of Interpol, and Heydrich announced that "Since the adoption of a resolution in 1934, the head of the Vienna Police has been the President of I.C.P.C. Austria is now an integral part of Germany, and the resolution concerned should therefore apply to the Director of the Sicherheitspolizei of the Third Reich!"[17]

According to the I.C.P.C. magazine, the resolution was unanimously accepted, as was a vote to move the Commission's headquarters to Berlin. However, it appears that the vote was conducted by mail, and those who did not reply were considered in favor of the proposal.*

On April 15, 1941, the organization and all of its permanent administrative machinery was moved to the Berlin suburb of Wannsee.[18] Secretary General Dressler and some of the other staff also made the move, but staff members who refused to relocate were jailed for their insubordination.

The Interpol journal No. 5 of June, 1941, announced that the Norwegian delegate to Interpol, Dr. Kristian Welhaven, had "retired," but all involved knew the true story. Welhaven, who had refused to become a tool of the Nazis, had been sentenced to hard labor in a concentration camp. After some time, he was removed from the camp to a basement cell in one of the Gestapo's buildings in Wannsee. He was eventually released and exiled to a small Bavarian village, where he was joined by his wife—possibly as a result of pleadings by some of the Interpol members from "neutral" countries.[19]

Jonas Lie was then appointed to replace Welhaven as Norway's official delegate. Lie's association with the Nazis dated back to 1934, when he struck up a friendship with Josef Terboven, the man who became *Reichskommissar* (governor) of Norway during the war. In 1941 Lie, together with Terboven and Himmler's agent, Rediess, established an imitation of the *Allgemeine* (general) SS in Norway. Himmler personally arrived in Oslo for the oath ceremony of the Norwegian SS, which swore loyalty to both Hitler and Vidkun Quisling, and Lie was appointed *Standartenführer* (colonel). Later, in recognition of his service and devotion, Himmler presented him with the *Totenkopfring*.† During the war, when capital punishment was reintroduced, Jonas Lie, as Minister of Justice, exercised his power over life and death. On his orders, the chief of

---

*Decades later Nepote would say the Interpol constitution had been approved by the legislative bodies of all member countries because he had mailed it to them and no one had objected, thus giving approval. Still, he called Heydrich's tactic a "fraud" in an interview with Vaughn Young, although he had clearly duplicated the Gestapo chief's tactic.

† Death's-head ring.

the civil section of the Oslo police was shot for failing to arrest a woman who had defied the labor mobilization order.[20] Lie committed suicide after the war.

In Denmark, another man who had been a delegate to Interpol before the war did well under the new masters. In mid-1941 Eigil Thune Jacobsen was appointed Minister of Justice. He strengthened police power and established a branch of secret police to deal with political crime and sabotage.[21]

In Berlin Interpol's General Secretariat was established in a Jew's confiscated villa, and the personnel was expanded fourfold almost immediately, a forewarning which gave some indication of Nazi intentions.

Organizationally, Interpol was located in the RSHA (*Reichssicherheitshauptamt*—National Department of Security), the combined national headquarters of the SD and *Sipo*, the new branch of the German police that linked the Gestapo (Secret State Police) and the *Kripo* (Criminal Police). An October 4, 1944, G-2 report discusses the *Kripo* as "an integral part of the Nazi machine of repression, and as such makes fullest use of the racial laws of the Third Reich. The arrest of deserters and escaped prisoners of war should be noted among the *Kripo's* duties." The SD was the intelligence system of the SS and Nazi party. The RSHA consisted of eight *Amter* (bureaus), but it was regarded as a single department rather than a collection of separate offices. The three branches—Gestapo, *Kripo*, SD—were closely connected.

Interpol's section was *Amt V* (Bureau V), also known as the RKPA (*Reichskriminalpolizeiamt*—Office of State Criminal Police). According to Allied intelligence, the RKPA, "under the Nazi regime, has not only expanded the concept of 'combatting' to include 'prevention' in the most ruthless sense; it also plays an important part in the investigation and prosecution of what are today called 'political crimes,' but would formerly have been regarded at the most as venial offenses. The line dividing cases of interest to the Gestapo and those within the field of the Kripo has in many instances become rather vague."[22] The RKPA, controlling the network of criminal police offices, developed out of the old Prussian criminal police headquarters, whose functions consisted only of the combating of crime in the normal sense of the term, but ordinary crime, it is apparent, was not *Amt V's* only concern. It contained a bureau for the suppression of gypsies. Medicine, criminal biology, and the attempt to prove race were carried out under its auspices. *Amt V* also had indexes of all antisocial and criminal "family groups" in Germany.

On December 1, 1941, the FBI's nine-man Executive Conference recommended that "no further communications be addressed to this organization." The recommendation was prompted by a September 23, 1941, letter to Hoover from I.C.P.C. Secretary General Dressler, who was responding to Hoover's request that Interpol locate any possible criminal records of a suspect the FBI was seeking. Noting the address on Dressler's letterhead, FBI aide J. F. Buckley, questioned whether the letter should be answered, since to do so "might be said to tacitly recognize the fact that Germany has taken over the International Criminal Police Commission" and that Hoover's correspondence would give "foundation for criticism of the Bureau."[23]

On December 4, 1941, just three days before the United States entered the war, Hoover issued the following memo: "It is desired that in the future no communications be addressed to the International Criminal Police Commission, whose present location is Berlin, Germany."

Hoover's motivation throughout this entire 1938–41 period is obscure. One generous interpretation was that he was using his ties with the Nazi organization to gather data or to spy on the Nazis. However, none of the thousands of documents on this period released by the FBI remotely hint at such a possibility, and the real reason probably lies in Hoover's character. An autocrat of extreme degree, Hoover never gave up power once he had acquired it. An undated Allied Control Authority memorandum relating to an inspection of the I.C.P.C. files discovered in Berlin in 1945 or early 1946, said that "Despite its close connection with the *Reichskriminalpolizeiamt*, the IKPK apparently tried to maintain international contacts and implications to the end. In 1942 (!) (*sic*) the United States Federal Bureau of Investigation was still carried in a report as a cooperating agency."* There were no further details.

On January 20, 1942, the now infamous Wannsee Conference was held. There, sixteen top Nazis, including Adolf Eichmann, were called together by Heydrich to lay out the "final solution to the Jewish problem." Although the conference has been the subject of nearly every history of the era, only one writer noted that the "final solution" was planned in I.C.P.C. offices.[24] Although less has been written about the Nazi persecution of the gypsies than of the Jews, Europe's gypsy population was severely decimated during the Nazi era. The "Final Solution Conference" also handled the gypsy problem—its third decision was to sweep up 30,000 gypsies together with the Jews and send them to death in Poland. From Interpol's point of view, the results of the conference were fast in coming. In a 1943 issue of the I.C.P.C. magazine, Dressler reported that criminality in Bohemia had decreased after preventive measures had been taken against such antisocial elements as "professional criminals, vagrants, gypsies, and other light shunning individuals" by placing them in internment camps.

In November, 1943, French collaborator Jean Felix Buffet was listed as an Interpol official on the masthead of the magazine. Buffet, the chief of the criminal police in German-occupied Vichy, is remembered mainly for his stirring appeal to his men in 1944, just before an expected Allied invasion and the anticipated French Resistance uprising. "Public order is being increasingly threatened," he said,

---

*IKPK stands for the *Internationalen Kriminalpolizeilichen Kommission*. Except where it has been quoted in its German form, we have used the English version ICPC, International Criminal Police Commission. In 1956 the group changed its name to the International Criminal Police Organization to rid itself of the transitory connotations of the word "Commission." It then became the ICPO.

and criminals masquerading under political or patriotic labels are increasingly indulging in brutal and cruel attacks on the persons and property of the peaceful population. Nothing can justify homicidal violence. Nothing can justify the murder of the defenceless.

As a regular police officer like yourselves, I guarantee all of you who remain loyal complete security for yourselves and your families. As a regular police officer I tell you: Do your duty and you will have nothing to fear.[25]

Sturmbannführer (Major) Karl Böemelburg, chief of the Gestapo in Paris until 1943, was another "experienced policeman" who had become familiar with the chiefs of the French police while working with Interpol in Vienna. When King George VI visited France in 1938 he had been delegated by Interpol to study, with the French services, the problems of security and the measures to be taken against international terrorists. As one authority said, "He had thus been able to make direct contacts, which he did not fail to renew as soon as he settled in as head of the Gestapo at the rue des Saussaies."[26]

The Sûreté Nationale was also located at the rue des Saussaies.* According to the Commission's journal (No. 11) of October 30, 1943, the Sûreté's political police activities were further streamlined when ordinary criminal matters were transferred to the office at the rue de Monceau.

One writer's description based upon interviews gives a more practical insight into the supposedly streamlined activities of the Sûreté.

In the rue des Saussaies, there were cells in various parts of the building. The largest one was in the basement, while various little box rooms on all floors were summarily transformed into barred cells. Five or six prisoners were sometimes herded together for hours on end in a small,

---

*The Sûreté, a French political police organization, was the counterpart of the German SD during the war. It dealt with the suppression of political undesirables, members of the French resistance, Jews, socialists, and the like. It was also a member of the Nazi Interpol.

airless cupboard, handcuffs were left on their wrists the whole time and some were chained to a ring in the wall. Then the moment came for them to appear before their inquisitors. The first replies brought a hail of blows in their wake. If the unfortunate man, still chained, fell to the ground, he was kicked to his feet with such violence that fractured ribs or limbs were commonplace.[27]

During the war years, the *International Criminal Police Review*, under Dressler's direction, printed more articles on criminal biology, castration, and preventive measures against criminals and antisocial persons. On at least one occasion, its wanted notices even included "criminals" who had escaped from concentration camps. Dressler was also responsible for the production of a book called *The I.C.P.C. and Its Work (Die Internationale Kriminalpolizeiliche Kommission und Ihr Werk)*. A fairly normal public relations type of book, it contained a foreword by Dressler and an introduction by Ernst Kaltenbrunner, who was to be the next president of Interpol. The book described the work of I.C.P.C. and laid out its history and purpose in a rather innocuous way, the only jarring note being the mention that the Commission had declared a "war on the gypsy plague" as early as 1934. The fact that Dressler moved to the Nazis' side was never fully acknowledged by Interpol in subsequent histories, for that would be to admit that the group existed under the Nazis. But in 1960, when he died, an obituary in a magazine admitted that Dressler's "attitude during the period of 1938–45 has raised some criticisms and doubts in regard to his character," but he was still "the moving spirit of the I.C.P.C."

When Heydrich was assassinated by Czech patriots on June 5, 1942, Dressler lamented his passing and, in 1943, he congratulated Kaltenbrunner on his position as the new president of I.C.P.C.

Ernst Kaltenbrunner was a giant of a man, almost seven feet tall, with a brutal face. He was born in Austria and joined the Austrian Nazi party in 1932. A lawyer in the town of Linz, he

70

soon played a leading role in the camouflaged SS and became a party spokesman in Upper Austria. He was arrested and imprisoned in January, 1934, and again in May, 1935. On his release he worked for Anschluss and was one of the party that welcomed Himmler to Vienna. He succeeded Heydrich as leader of the RSHA in January, 1943.

Kaltenbrunner was a man who enjoyed his work. On many occasions he went to the camps to watch the extermination of the "fodder" he had supplied. In 1943 he went to Mauthausen to see an experiment to test methods of execution. Prisoners were killed by hanging, a bullet in the neck, and the gas chamber. "The prisoners and employees of the camp have related that Kaltenbrunner arrived in excellent humor, laughing and joking all the way to the gas chamber where these experiments took place, and while waiting for the victims to be brought in."[28] Kaltenbrunner was executed in Nuremberg prison on October 16, 1946.

The head of *Amt V* was Artur Nebe, who was also a vice-president of Interpol. Before the war, Nebe had been a German delegate to the Commission and became a close friend of Soderman's. Soderman, in *Policeman's Lot*, described Nebe as a professional policeman and a "very mild Nazi, and even that Nazism wore off in due time." However, Nebe personally directed some of the "mobile killing units" and assisted in the Nazi "medical experiments."[29] He was also responsible for putting Göring, one of the greatest butchers in history, into power by supplying Göring with material that was used to blackmail the Minister of War, Field Marshal Werner von Blomberg, into leaving Germany in 1938. Göring then became General Field Marshal, the highest military dignitary in the nation.

Nebe is also well known for the part he played in the formation of Heydrich's "Kitty Salon," the brothel that was set up to get information from both foreign diplomats and indiscreet party members. Nebe, who had headed the Berlin criminal police, had once worked for the vice squad. With this valuable experience under his belt, he was the perfect choice to recruit the girls. Based on the proposition that men talk more freely without their clothes on, the "Kitty Salon" was a valuable source of intelligence data for the SD.

Perhaps though he is best remembered in Czechoslovakia. In 1942, after the assassination of Heydrich, Nebe was called to Prague to head up the investigation. He found that villagers of Lidice, about thirty kilometers from Prague, had "helped with perpetrators of the crime." Despite denials by the villagers, the entire village of Lidice was dynamited and razed to the ground. First, however, all the men were shot and all newborn babies and infants had their throats cut. Some of the women were killed and the remainder were sent to Ravensbruck concentration camp. Children were sent to another camp in Poland.[30]

Nebe was later reported as executed for taking part in the plot to kill Hitler, but this is possibly false, and Nebe may still be at large.[31] He was apparently seen in Ireland in 1960 in the company of Otto Skorzeny, a man who helped plan escape routes for Nazis at the end of the war.

Yet another area needing closer inspection is the role Interpol played in the Nazi plan to wreck the British economy by flooding the world with counterfeit pound notes. The program was carried out by SS *Sturmbannführer* (Major) Frederick Schwend at Sachsenhausen concentration camp. The Nazis efficiently rounded up as many convicted forgers and counterfeiters as they could get from the jails and police records of Europe.[32] The criminals had a choice of working for the glory of the Third Reich or going to the gas chambers. Considering that all the convicted forgers were neatly indexed in the Interpol files at Gestapo headquarters, the Nazis had a good start on their project.*

Interpol's offices were linked with the *Sipo* telephone and teleprinter network, and the files, fingerprints, and photo-

---

*Nazi-hunter Simon Wiesenthal expounded upon Interpol's use of files to recruit counterfeiters and forgers, as well as spies, in the 1977 film *Dossier Interpol*, produced by Studio 22 in Amsterdam.

graphs of international criminals were under the authority of the chief of the German criminal police office. Soderman, an acknowledged world expert on forgery and counterfeiting also worked for the German Interpol, although there is nothing to connect him with this project. The final irony is that archforger Schwend was jailed in West Germany in 1976 because he did not have enough money to meet a hotel bill of eight dollars a night.

It becomes obvious that Interpol not only continued to exist during World War II, it hummed with activity. The Nazis found it a valuable tool, not only in Germany but, as a G-2 military intelligence report said, for "the control of the Criminal Police Departments in the various satellite nations."[33] The assenting attitude of many of its members toward Nazi thought years before the outbreak of war made the German take-over easy. It is not a proud chapter in the history of the organization. But there is another reason why Interpol has steadily claimed, to this day, that the organization ceased to exist during the years 1939 to 1945. An admission of its busy role during the war could have led to the discovery that a number of the men responsible for its "re-creation" in 1946 were Nazi collaborators.

Whenever possible, we buried our failures and publicized only our successes, and, hell, anybody can look gigantic if they can get away with doing this.

————WILLIAM C. SULLIVAN
Assistant to the Director of the FBI
in charge of all Investigations Criminal and
Security and Foreign Operations.

Chapter Four

"RECONVENING" AFTER THE WAR

Harry Soderman, the Swedish policeman who was an early member of the I.C.P.C., protested vehemently against charges that the Nazis had used Interpol politically. "In the immediate postwar hysteria," he claimed, "it was said that the Nazis had used the Commission for their own purposes. I don't think that this is fair. As far as I can judge, they kept up its outward seeming (*sic*), at least, for the sake of vanity, and scrupulously avoided mixing any politics into its remaining activities."[1] Considering that Soderman became a permanent member of the Commission in 1942, it is perhaps in his interest to make such a patently false claim.

In 1946 Soderman arrived in Brussels to meet with Florent E. Louwage, an old friend and head of the Belgian police force. They decided to call a meeting of former members of the International Criminal Police Commission in an effort to renew the organization's network. To win as much official sanction as possible, Louwage persuaded the Belgian Government to send invitations through its diplomatic channels.

Disregarding the war years, the conference called itself the twenty-fifth ordinary session of the I.C.P.C. According to Sir

77

Ronald Howe, then head of the Criminal Investigation Department (CID) at Scotland Yard and an Interpol supporter since 1934, the Brussels meeting was "presided over by what might be termed another 'Big Five.' Florent Louwage of Belgium, Harry Soderman of Sweden, Wernher Muller of Switzerland, Louis Ducloux of France and myself."[2] Other important individuals behind the rebirth of the Commission were Colonel Van Houten of Holland, Agostino Lourenco of Portugal, and Francisco I de Echalecu y Canino of Spain. All, except for Ronald Howe, had collaborated with Interpol, to one degree or another, during the Nazi reign. The Big Five were all old friends, a kind of inside circle who, Soderman says, "knew and trusted one another," and together they led the reinstated organization.

Louwage was elected President because he was apparently "the only prominent member of the old Commission who had come untainted out of the ordeal [the war]."[3] Closer inspection of his activities indicates otherwise. His failings during World War II were overlooked by some and undiscovered by others.

Florent Louwage was born in Caloo, Belgium, the son of a police official. He first enlisted in the Belgian Army, but in 1909 he joined the Ostend police, where he was soon promoted to assistant superintendent of the Brussels police. In 1914 he rejoined the army and served as an infantry officer up to August, 1915, when he transferred to the army's intelligence and detective department. By 1919 he was Judicial Officer in the Brussels public prosecutor's department, and in 1925 he became the Belgian delegate to the International Criminal Police Conference in New York.

When World War II broke out, Louwage became *Inspecteur General de la Sûreté de l'Etat*, and continued to work for the new Nazi masters of Interpol. His name appeared on the masthead of the organization's magazine throughout the war, and in 1943 he was personally congratulated by Ernst Kaltenbrunner for helping translate into French the new German-produced book on Interpol, with Kaltenbrunner's introduction and Dressler's preface. By his own admission, Louwage was a member of the Commission's permanent staff in Brussels during the war. In 1943 and 1944 he wrote books on criminal psychology in which he listed himself as an active member of the Nazi Interpol.*

Louis Ducloux was elected the first Secretary General of Interpol.† During the war he had served in the headquarters of the Sûreté Nationale in Vichy. In the thirties he had been implicated in the Stavisky affair, a scandal that exposed corruption in the Sûreté, which had been covering up for big-time swindler Serge Alexandre Stavisky—a man who made fortunes by numerous fraudulent enterprises and who had been a secret agent for the Sûreté Generale. At that time, Ducloux was one of the directors of the Sûreté Generale and directly in charge of all the investigations of Stavisky. There was a strong suspicion that Ducloux, on three separate occasions, intervened to protect Stavisky by hiding documents that could have exposed not only Stavisky's operations but also the involvement of high-ranking government officials and senior officers of the Sûreté Generale. The Stavisky affair heavily discredited the Sûreté, and the court of inquiry that was appointed to investigate the case was severely criticized for not taking action against Ducloux.[4]

In addition to the appointments of Louwage as President and Ducloux as Secretary General, the rest of the Big Five, Howe, Soderman, and Muller, were elected members of the Executive Committee and Reporters General by the delegates from the seventeen member nations present at the conference.

A number of changes were also made in the original constitu-

---

* Louwage's successor as President of Interpol was Lourenco of Portugal. He, in turn, was succeeded by Franssen of Belgium. They both had collaborated with the wartime Interpol.

† Ducloux's successor as Secretary General of Interpol was Marcel Sicot, general secretary of the Sûreté Nationale headquarters during the war. Sicot publicly denounced the weeding out of Nazi collaborators from the French police that took place between 1944 and 1948 in France. Jean Nepote, the present Secretary General of Interpol, also came from the headquarters of the Sûreté Nationale. He became Commissaire de Police à la Direction General de la Sûreté Nationale in 1941.

tion. The President was to be assisted by an Executive Committee whose members came from a number of different countries, to give the operations a "truly international flavor."[5] The President and Executive Committee were to be, at least on paper, completely independent of the country in which the headquarters were installed. However, the Secretary General would belong to the host country. The President was to be elected for a period of five years and could reside anywhere.

When the delegates and committee proposed Paris as the new seat of the I.C.P.C., the French Government, acting through Pierre Boursicot, Directeur General de la Sûreté, decided to provide the Commission with free lodgings at the Sûreté's headquarters, use of Sûreté personnel, and some initial financial support. Subscriptions were to be levied on member countries on the basis of five Swiss francs per 10,000 inhabitants of each country. The I.C.P.C. was to be given a subsidy amounting to two million French francs (about 65,000 Swiss francs) which included France's subscription (14,000 Swiss francs), as well as a sum to help with the setting up of the French National Office as the material organization of the 1947 session.

In June, 1946, the "new" Interpol moved into its modest little office at rue Alfred-de-Vigny and later moved into 11 rue des Saussaies—home of the Gestapo and the SS during the war, then the offices of the French Ministry of the Interior and of the Sûreté Nationale.

After the Brussels meeting, Louwage wrote to the Allied Control Authority on June 11, 1946, requesting that certain funds being held in a Berlin bank be released to the new Commission. Louwage claimed the funds consisted of contributions made by governments that had been members of the Commission before the war. In order to give his letter official sanction, he added that Interpol had been instructed "by the delegates of governments attached to the I.C.P.C. to request authorization to dispose of the funds in question."

The slow-moving Allied Control Authority investigated the matter. A memorandum of September 5, 1946, said that reexamination of the files had failed to disclose any account books relating to the organization's sources of support or manner of expenditure. The bank records also contained no reference to the source of funds. "Adequate exploration of the correspondence files and perusal of the publication files of the IKPK would require the full time services of one person for several weeks," the memorandum added.

The obviously busy Authority decided to cut corners. Instead of investigating further itself, it wrote to Secretary General Ducloux on September 10, 1946, and asked him about the origin of the funds, why they were located in a Berlin bank, and what countries were members of the I.C.P.C. when the funds were collected.

Decloux wrote back on September 20 that "the funds deposited in Berlin came from the subscriptions paid annually, previous to 1939, by each nation which was a member of the organization."[6] He said that nations represented in the International Commission at the time when the funds were deposited totaled thirty-three, including Great Britain, the United States, and Ireland.

The Allied Control Authority did not investigate further, and on November 14, 1946, it approved collection of the 25,000 marks by a representative of Interpol.

If, as we know, Interpol continued to exist during the war, it seemed unlikely that the beleagured German treasury would take kindly to the sole support of an organization with a staff of fifteen or twenty and international ties. Nor did it seem likely that the avaricious Reich would let funds sit in a Berlin bank for more than five years, not when it could put it to good use.

New research shows that between 1939 and 1943, twenty-three countries paid membership dues to Interpol: Belgium, Bohemia, Bulgaria, Croatia, Finland, Holland, Hungary, Iran, Ireland, Italy, Latvia, Luxembourg, Lithuania, Norway, Poland, Portugal, Slovakia, Switzerland, Spain, Sweden, Turkey, Yugoslavia, and, of course, Germany.

Both Decloux and Louwage had lied to the Allied Control Authority. The money used to start Interpol again after the war came from the coffers of Nazi Germany, its allies, puppets, and "neutral" nations—not, as claimed, from members before the war.

The German surrender of Paris on August 25, 1944, initiated a general scramble for the files at the Sûreté Generale, rue des Saussaies, where the SS and Gestapo representatives had had their seats. The Resistance went after the files of Nazi collaborators, as did the collaborators. In the free-for-all that ensued, both sides had limited successes.

The April-May, 1973, *International Police Review*, as Interpol's official organ is now called, claimed that "When the general secretariat moved to France, in June, 1946, the records that had been built up over more than twenty years by the I.C.P.C. in Vienna no longer existed—they had been destroyed during the Second World War." The January, 1958, Interpol magazine had presented a similar story, although it had placed the files in a different location: "The I.C.P.C. files, and, indeed, the organization as a whole, disappeared during the fall of Berlin a few years later." Perhaps, by claiming that the files had been in Vienna, the Interpol of 1973 was attempting to deny, once again, that Interpol had been taken over by the Nazis and that the whole organization had been incorporated into the Nazi police network in Berlin.

Harry Soderman, one of the prime movers in the reorganization of Interpol after the war, has a different tale. According to an account in *Policeman's Lot*, Carlos Zindel, a man he describes as "gay and cultivated" and a "very mild" Nazi, headed up the German criminal investigation department and later became a lieutenant colonel in the SS (an organization that did not tolerate "mild" Nazis, but then Soderman used the same word to describe Artur Nebe).

According to Soderman, "Carlos Zindel left Berlin just before the collapse of the Third Reich and headed for the south in his car, which was filled to the brim with the documents of the Commission. When he reported to French headquarters in Stuttgart to give himself up, he was badly treated, kicked out and told to return in the afternoon. His dignity mortally injured, he went to a park and swallowed a capsule of potassium cyanide."*

On March 4, 1946, Louwage, then calling himself the Permanent Recorder of the I.C.P.C. (by March the Commission had not yet been "reconstituted," and Louwage was giving himself the title of the post he had attained in the Nazi Interpol), wrote a letter to the members of the Public Safety Committee of the Allied Control Authority in Berlin. In it he said that he had learned that the documents of the Commission were being held in the Berlin Document Center and requested that they be turned over to him in Brussels.

A memo written by the U.S. member of the Allied Control Authority said the files were located at number 16 am Kleinen, Berlin-Wannsee, and had "escaped the hazards of war and occupation, stripping of the house of furniture and use of the premises by troops . . ." The undated memo listed the contents of the files:

(1) Alphabetic card index, including every subject whose record was referred to the IKPK since its inception. This contains approximately 10,000 cards. The register to which the index refers has disappeared.

(2) Alphabetic index of subjects circularized in "IKP" (International Criminal Police). Consists of cards with the German language insertion pasted upon them.

(3) Index cards from (2) upon which there had been

*Soderman's story raises more questions than it presents answers. First, Stuttgart is about four hundred miles south of Berlin. In the closing days of the war it could by no means have been called a Sunday drive. Denmark was closer, the Allies were closer, Holland was closer. Second, one wonders what the files contained that made them valuable enough for Zindel to take the trouble to fill his car with them while, presumably, escaping for his life. Third, it is hard to imagine a high-ranking SS officer surrendering to the French and being told to "return in the afternoon." Military intelligence would have been only too pleased to have Zindel in their hands.

Stuttgart is just across the border from Switzerland, a refuge innumerable top Nazis found exceedingly attractive toward the end of the war. It is more logical to assume that Zindel was attempting to escape to neutral Switzerland with the files and that, when apprehended, he killed himself.

published cancellations. The printed cancellations are added. Index (2) and (3) together contain about 7,500 subjects.

(4) Index cards relating to counterfeit currencies. About 500 cards.

(5) Index cards relating to stolen jewelry, works of art, etc. (six). About 500 cards.

(6) Index cards relating to subjects whose description slips, fingerprints and photograph had been circulated. The guides used were those of the classification used in Amt V of the Reichskriminalpolizei, followed by the name cards in alphabetic order. Metal tabs, with both the position and color indication, were used to show the country of birth of subject. According to the arranger, this index is far from complete. (These files were arranged by a former German I.C.P.C. employee.) One large omission was noted, estimated at about 1/3 of those classified as pickpockets.

(7) Numerical files of envelopes containing copies of the circular slips, photographs and fingerprints of persons circularized outside of the magazine. This file appears to be complete for the period from 1929 to about 1939. The drawers for the later circulars are missing.

(8) Two drawers of old alphabetic indexes brought from Vienna. These do not appear to be in usable condition as they do not refer to currently existing records.

Hoover also became involved with the Interpol files. Apparently, he saw a newspaper story announcing the discovery of the files and on August 10, 1945, he wrote to Frederick Ayer, Jr., one of his agents in Frankfurt, quoting the story in full.[7] "It is known that the Gestapo frequently employed criminals as agents and the files with fingerprints and front and side photographs could be useful in ferreting them out," the story said, mentioning also that Interpol's office was a "four-story house in the suburban district of Wannsee. The Nazis also used it as a jail after the attempt of July 20 last year on Hitler's life, and two German generals were imprisoned there. It was also used as quarters for visiting foreign police dignitaries."

In his letter to Ayer, Hoover wrote, "You can appreciate that the location and present status of those files are of considerable interest to the Bureau. You should make enquiries among Army officials to determine what disposition is planned for them."

Ayer replied that prior to receiving Hoover's request he had already sent Special Agent John I. Condon to inspect the files which were at that time being kept in a small garage, as the main building was being used as billets for American troops.[8] "It is the personal opinion of Special Agent Condon that these records could prove of little value to the Bureau, and that it would be impractical to attempt to ship them to Washington," Ayer concluded.

On October 9, 1945, the FBI's Executive Conference met to consider the matter of the files. They told Hoover they were "unanimously of the opinion that the records would serve no useful purpose to the Bureau, and if you agree Special Agent Condon will be so advised."[9] Hoover agreed, and the FBI lost its interest in the files.

On November 14, 1946, the same day that the Allied authorities approved Interpol's collection of the funds in the Berlin bank, the Allied Control Authority wrote Louwage and gave him permission to come to Berlin and collect the Interpol files.

That makes three versions of the missing files: (a) Interpol's "Official" claim that they were destroyed; (b) Soderman's story of Zindel's flight; and (c) the documented account of Louwage's collection of files, which had large segments missing.

On October 17, 1949, the London *Daily Express* gave a fourth version. Reporting on the annual Interpol meeting, held that year in Berne, Switzerland, the paper said that delegates were told that the records and fingerprints of 2,000 criminals had been found in Berlin. The records, the paper said, were recovered from the bombed wreckage of a former Gestapo depot.

Yet another version of the mysterious files story appeared in the Swedish newspaper *Børsen* on October 25, 1973. *Børsen* spent one week at Interpol's French headquarters interviewing officials. It reported that in 1944 the Berlin Interpol headquarters were destroyed by fire, "but according to rumors, the Russians managed to get a minor part of the archives home to Moscow."

A slightly altered version of Soderman's story can be found in *The Story of Scotland Yard*, by Sir Ronald Howe, who said, "Most of the documents were lost or destroyed in the blitz, but some were extricated from the ruins by Carlos Zindel who had been a delegate of Interpol before the war. Zindel took the rescued files to the French Army headquarters in Stuttgart."

With the exception of Interpol's denial of the existence of the files, the other stories do not necessarily conflict. However, we are now back in the realm of speculation. Zindel *may* have been carrying the files the Allied Control Authority noted as missing. On the other hand, he may have been carrying files whose existence they were not even aware of. The files found later in 1949 may have consisted of the missing pickpocket records. Perhaps the files Zindel was carrying could have fully documented Interpol's involvement with the Nazi terror during the war. The Nazi penchant for files is well known. Commando units moving into captured cities would be followed by Heydrich's men, who would gather up police files and use them to extort, blackmail, and find political dissenters and "trouble-makers." In view of Nazi plans as early as 1936 to use the European police for counterintelligence, one could also come up with some interesting guesses as to the significance of the files Zindel carried on his frantic flight.

Whatever the story, Soderman states that Zindel's files fell into French hands. And considering the fact that France had supported Interpol since the war, it is safe to assume that Interpol now has the Zindel files. Member police forces also supplied Interpol with material for the "new" files. Possibly Interpol drew from other countries to rebuild their files, under the pretext that the "old" files had been destroyed.

Philip Marabuto wrote in the Interpol journal of April, 1950, that

Crime is also suggestive when examined from the angle of religious creed: Jews and Catholics do not differ so much in the extent as in the form of their offenses. Jews hardly participate in offenses which require a man to drift away from society and adopt a purely passive attitude. On the other hand, they seem to be more inclined to offenses with a materialistic purpose to them. But what, above all, appears from statistical comparisons, is the preference which Jewish offenders have for offenses which require the use of craftiness and, similarly, their hatred for violence. This statistical fact is in contradiction with the assertions of pre-war German propagandists; it explains, on the other hand, why the I.C.P.C., which is particularly concerned with eliminating swindling, monetary or otherwise, has so many Jewish names in its files.

A more credible explanation seems to be that much of Interpol's present "criminal" file collection owes its existence to the years of Nazi barbarism.

The truth is that the Justice Department doesn't want anyone else in this government involved in law enforcement.

——TREASURY OFFICIAL

Chapter Five

THE TUG-OF-WAR BETWEEN TREASURY AND JUSTICE

Hoover's FBI enjoyed a number of domestic successes during World War II, and its reputation as a counterintelligence organization emerged intact. Although lacking the glamour of Major General William J. Donovan's OSS, Hoover's Special Intelligence Service (SIS), which had concentrated most of its activities in Latin America, had achieved a number of unpublicized but nevertheless important victories. After the war, Hoover attempted to expand his Western Hemisphere intelligence system worldwide, but President Harry S Truman did not agree with Hoover's proposal and gave the newly formed CIA a fairly clear-cut title to foreign operations.

In 1946, when Louwage sent invitations through the Belgian Embassy for a reconvening of Interpol's membership, Dean Acheson, then Under Secretary of State, sent a confidential telegram to the American Embassy in Brussels, saying that an invitation had been received but that the decision to attend was in abeyance pending advice from the Justice Department. "We assume," he said, "this is same organization founded Vienna 1923 [and] taken under Nazi domination 1938 and headquarters removed Berlin at which time U.S. ceased relationship. Can you supply briefly information, subsequent history and background of present Belgian sponsorship . . ."[1]

Hoover was way ahead. As soon as he heard of the plan to reconstitute the Commission, he sent Horton R. Telford, an agent from his Paris office, to confer with Louwage in Brussels. Acheson's man in Brussels, "Kirk," informed Acheson, two days after he had sent his telegram to the Embassy, that the agent Telford "is believed to have reported fully results of his conversation to FBI Washington." Acheson was also told that it was the same Commission that had been founded in Vienna, but it was stressed that Belgium was not sponsoring it. They had "merely consented to transmit invitations at request of Belgian and other interested police officials."[2]

Acheson sent the Belgian invitation to Attorney General Tom Clark to ask his advice on the matter. Clark replied on May 21, writing that "It would appear that as a result of the war the majority of the European Police Departments have not yet been sufficiently reestablished or activated to permit the undertaking of efficient police programs . . . I do not believe that any affirmative progress will be made by such a conference at this time." Clark added that the selection of governments invited to attend the conference "has been made upon rather an arbitrary basis and undoubtedly there will be protests on the part of a number of governments because they were not invited to participate." He did not expand further, although it is known that Germany was not allowed to attend. Acheson duly informed the Belgian Ambassador that the United States would not attend because the European police had not been sufficiently reestablished.

Meanwhile, and apparently unknown to the State Department, the FBI was quite busy in Brussels. Acheson didn't find out about it until 1947, when the State Department was invited to the second postwar conference, which was to be held in Paris. In a note accompanying the invitation forwarded by the French Embassy, Interpol officials stated that "The Department of State will recall that the American delegate to the Brussels Conference in 1946 was Mr. Y. E. Hoover (sic), Chief

92

of the Federal Bureau of Investigation in Washington." One can only imagine State's surprise to learn that Hoover was possibly in attendance at a foreign conference that Attorney General Clark had found to be undesirable, but as General Harry Vaughan explained in an interview in 1972, "Theoretically, the Attorney General is over the FBI, but in practice the FBI is an independent agency. The reason was that Hoover was such a dynamic personality. By 1945 Hoover had already established his position in terms of power and importance. I don't think there was any doubt about it."[3]

Efrem Zimbalist, Jr., clarified Hoover's position further: "He didn't want to build an empire. My personal opinion is that his attitude toward attorneys general—he was criticized for being uncavalier to an official who was over him—I think his attitude was that the FBI was a continuing body, and an attorney general was a political appointee. He wasn't about to put the Bureau's destiny under somebody who was appointed because he helped somebody get elected. He saw that very clearly, I think, from the very beginning."[4]

The liberties Hoover took with Attorney General Clark may be explained in part by the fact that in 1943, Clark was the head of the Justice Department's criminal division, and, as Clark said in a 1972 interview, ". . . the Criminal Division, I suppose, is closer to Mr. Hoover than any other division, and I was head of it until I became Attorney General in 1945."[5] Clark further explained Hoover's independent authority by saying that Hoover "was told by Mr. Stone in 1924 that he would have free wheeling, and I think it would be fair to say he had free wheeling for the rest of his life. He was pretty powerful in 1937 when I came in. He occupied a high position with government people and I think he had all the federal backing then that he had later."

Obviously, Hoover and Clark had an extremely loose relationship, and Hoover could do almost anything he wanted to.

As it turns out, Interpol had its information wrong. Hoover did not attend the 1946 conference, but the surprises had not ended. Nearly two months after the Belgian invitation had been issued, Assistant Secretary of State Acheson forwarded it to Attorney General Clark. "It now appears," Acheson wrote tactfully, "that the International Criminal Police Commission has been reconstituted. . . . If, in your opinion, it is deemed advisable for the United States to be represented at this meeting, the Department of State will wish to consult with you regarding the selection of a delegate and the policy which such delegate should follow at the meeting."[6]

Clark replied that in his view the United States should be represented at the conference, adding that "at the annual meeting of the International Criminal Police Commission in Brussels, Belgium, in 1946, Mr. J. Edgar Hoover, Director of the Federal Bureau of Investigation was elected Vice President. Upon his acceptance of this elective post, steps were taken to make the Federal Bureau of Investigation an official member of the Commission."[7] Clark told Acheson that Hoover had been invited to attend the forthcoming meeting in Paris, but because of prior commitments he had been unable to accept and had appointed Horton R. Telford as the Bureau's representative.

In 1948, the chief of the U.S. Secret Service, James J. Maloney, received an invitation to attend the Interpol conference in Prague that year. Noting that Interpol had paid considerable attention to the subject of counterfeits and forgeries at its 1947 conference and had published a confidential illustrated booklet on the subject, Maloney expressed interest in attending. "It seems to me that active participation in the Commission's activities might be beneficial not only to the Secret Service, but also to the other Treasury Department law-enforcement agencies," he wrote in an interoffice memorandum on January 13.

The Secret Service was already in contact with the Commission at this time, to the extent that it was sending Interpol descriptions of counterfeit U.S. paper money of foreign origin. Much of the criminal traffic was between Europe and the United States, and it seemed logical for the Treasury Department to utilize an organization that would enable its agents to cooperate more closely with European police officials. A dramatic increase in crimes directly affected Treasury enforcement agencies, and with counterfeiting, narcotics, and the smuggling of gold and diamonds, the Bureau of Customs and the then Bureau of Narcotics had their hands full.

The Bureau of Narcotics, created in 1930, together with the Bureau of Customs formed the main line of law enforcement defense against the increasing drug traffic. The Bureau of Narcotics' program of sending its officers overseas was intended to cut off illicit narcotics as close to their source as possible, before they became a major problem in the United States, but once overseas the agents ran into problems with local governments and law enforcement agencies: they had no powers of arrest and depended entirely upon the beneficence of the officials with whom they were dealing, and they actually lacked any legal basis with which to operate.

Maloney later discussed the matter with the General Counsel's office and other Treasury agencies. He began to formulate a program for Treasury cooperation with the Commission, but his plans to attend the Interpol Prague conference were thwarted when the news reached Hoover. The FBI called the Secret Service's plans for participation "most provocative," since Hoover had decided not to send a representative to Prague, "as it felt that in light of all the circumstances, it would be presenting the Russians with a chance to embarrass this Government."[8]

Hoover, however, had become a staunch supporter of Interpol, even contributing tales of the Bureau's exploits to Interpol's magazine, but it had not taken long for mutual suspicion to develop between FBI and European police officials.

Hoover worried that some nations, especially the communist-controlled ones that became Interpol members, would not abide by its charter's exclusion "of all matters having a political, religious or racial character"; the Europeans, for their own part, were skeptical of the Bureau's renewed postwar preoccupation with the Red Menace and other antisubversive work, which in their view was "political." What is more, some American officials regarded the French civil service, which was filling many of the administrative posts at Interpol headquarters, as corrupt, and they were concerned that the integrity of confidential information transmitted from Bureau files might be compromised in the Interpol network.[9]

In 1950, Hoover's fears were proved to be justified. That year Czechoslovakia used the Interpol network in an attempt to track down a group of ten Czechoslovakian refugees who had fled to West Germany for political reasons.* When Hoover learned of the incident, he was furious and immediately withdrew the FBI's membership from Interpol. The reason for the resignation was never made public.† Interpol announced that Hoover's decision was "based on special reasons" and was quite content to leave it at that. The FBI, never one to wash its dirty linen in public view, had no comment, and the Treasury Department, eager to begin a relationship with the Commission, adopted the later Interpol line that the FBI withdrew because the nature of its own activities permitted it to take advantage of very few of the advantages Interpol offered.

A memorandum from Hoover to Attorney General Robert F. Kennedy, dated November 22, 1961, left no doubt about his real feelings. He stated that the FBI withdrew "as a direct result of the circulation by Interpol of wanted notices for political refugees from Czechoslovakia." In addition, he said, "our observation of the internal mechanism of Interpol convinced us

*This story was first related by a British crime reporter, Tom Tullett, in his book *Inside Interpol*. Michael Fooner, a strong supporter and a writer who has made a career out of promoting the organization, disagreed in *Interpol*. The facts, however, support Tullett. They were overlooked by Fooner, who, like Interpol, insists that the organization ceased to exist during World War II.

†The first public admission by any U.S. official of the Czech incident was made by Secretary of the Treasury William E. Simon at the May 6, 1975, Montoya Senate hearings on Interpol, following testimony by Vaughn Young two weeks before.

that it was being utilized by certain police officials for the furtherance of their personal ambitions with little regard to law enforcement problems.*

Interpol's President Florent Louwage made a special trip to Washington to plead his case before Hoover. He "vainly urged Mr. Hoover to reconsider his decision," but Hoover was adamant. His decision, he said, was irrevocable, and he resigned from his position as Vice-President of the group.†

After Hoover pulled out, Treasury quickly sent an unofficial observer to Interpol's 1951 meeting in The Hague, thus beginning a relationship that exists to this day. In a sense, Treasury's initial relationship with Interpol was illicit, since Congress had given the membership to Hoover, and despite the fact that he had stopped cooperating with the organization, the bill had never been amended or canceled in any way.

Treasury's use of "unofficial observers" did not seem to make any difference to Interpol, which was only too pleased to welcome any kind of U.S. participation. Its claim of being a truly

*Interpol's structure has remained virtually unchanged since 1924. The original 1924 constitution was slightly altered in 1946, but underwent its most radical overhaul in 1956, when a rewritten constitution was voted in. Although the previous constitution had forbidden political involvement, the now famous Article 3 was formulated and accepted in 1956, after bitter criticism and the resignation of the United States, Bulgaria, and Czechoslovakia, who all pulled out because of political matters, threatened the existence of the organization. Article 3 reads, "It is strictly forbidden for the Organization to undertake any intervention or activities of a political, military, religious or racial character."

†During the war, Hoover had built up a network of agents and stationed them in American embassies in South America, Europe, and Asia. They operated under the cover title of "legal attaché," and when Hoover lost his bid to conduct U.S. foreign intelligence after the war, he kept many of his "legats," as they became known, on their posts and also increased their numbers. After withdrawing FBI membership from Interpol, Hoover bolstered up this legat system, and to this day the legats are engaged in liaison relationships with foreign police and perform many of the functions that would have been accomplished by an Interpol NCB. Since 1960, legats have on occasion attended Interpol meetings as observers, although, apart from ordinary criminal data, their main interest is counterintelligence and internal security matters and, albeit unofficially, intelligence.[10]

international organization was considerably weakened by the fact that the most powerful nation in the West was not represented.

Ostensibly, an unofficial observer is permitted merely to observe and cannot commit his parent agency to any agreements, but in 1951 Malachi L. Harney, Assistant Commissioner of the Bureau of Narcotics, attended Interpol's annual meeting in Lisbon as an "unofficial observer" and sat as a member of a subcommittee on drugs. Earlier that year, two inspectors of the Washington Narcotics Bureau had visited Europe and contacted Interpol to smooth the way. Harney urged an exchange of information about illegal narcotics traffic between the Commission and the United States, and an agreement was made to that effect.[11] The American Ambassador in Lisbon, Lincoln McVeagh, reported to the Justice Department that, aside from the two American observers who had attended the 1951 General Assembly meeting in Lisbon, representatives from Pan American and Trans World Airlines were also in attendance. The Ambassador said that the nonpolitical character of Interpol had been discussed in the meeting and that the principle "has been violated from time to time by members who have attempted to use Interpol in the apprehension of political fugitives." He said he did not know if politics were "discussed informally 'outside the classroom.' "[12]

The June 1952 Interpol General Assembly was held in Stockholm, and the United States was listed as a member with A. A. Christides, Treasury representative from the Paris Embassy, and Charles Siragusa,* district supervisor of the Narcotics Bureau in Rome, listed as the official U.S delegates.

Christides joined a consultative committee to produce an In-

---

*Siragusa has an interesting background, much of it in intelligence. In 1939, he joined the Bureau of Narcotics as a stenographer. During the war, Siragusa joined the OSS and was stationed in Italy with the cover of "naval officer." His chief function was to break up espionage networks, and his best-known case involved the arrest of the glamorous Baroness Annabella, who was the head of a fascist network. According to Harry Anslinger in *The Protectors*, "Siragusa's coup vexed American military police and intelligence agencies and their Allied counterparts."

terpol film on counterfeiting and was also elected a reporter to a subcommittee on drugs and another on police science and technique. Siragusa told the Assembly about his Narcotics Bureau in Rome.

During his progress report to the Assembly, Secretary General Marcel Sicot mentioned how pleased he was that the U.S. Treasury Department had joined the I.C.P.C. "In October last [1951]," he said, "Mr. Graham, Assistant Secretary of the American Treasury Department, honored the General Secretariat with a visit and, after an interesting talk, informed us that he would like the Treasury Department to join our organization."[13]

He mentioned that the I.C.P.C. had been cooperating for some time with Harry Anslinger, Commissioner of Narcotics, and U. E. Baughman, chief of the Secret Service, but, Sicot continued, "since April 15, 1952, this collaboration has become official."[14]

Treasury had no authority, Congressional or otherwise, to join Interpol, and since the relationship was technically illegal it was quickly nulled, and Treasury returned to its "informal" relationship. But illicitly or not, Interpol was happy to cooperate with the United States.

In 1975, Treasury official and U.S. Interpol NCB chief Myles J. Ambrose said that Interpol never considered that the United States had left.* It "ignored the irregularities" of no dues money paid and still allowed U.S. representatives to attend.[15] Ambrose was not quite correct regarding "no dues being paid," since the Treasury Department made illegal financial contributions to Interpol from 1952 onward. In 1954, the State Department found out about the contributions, and on May 7 the Assistant Secretary David McK. Key wrote to the Secretary of

*In 1957 Myles Ambrose was Assistant to the Secretary for Law Enforcement. Ambrose left Treasury in 1960 to become director of the Waterfront Commission in New York. In 1969, he came back and headed up U.S. Customs. In 1972, he once again became an Interpol delegate. In 1973, he was appointed the first head of the scandal-ridden Drug Enforcement Administration (DEA) by President Richard M. Nixon. Again he worked closely with Interpol.

the Treasury querying the fact that the Bureau of Customs had made financial contributions of $3,000 each year from fiscal 1952 and 1953 funds. He quoted the law: "All financial contributions by the United States to international organizations in which the United States participates as a member shall be made by or with the consent of the Department of State regardless of the appropriation from which any such contribution is made. The Secretary of State shall report annually to the Congress on the extent and disposition of such contributions."[16] McK. Key went on to say: "There would appear to be no record that this provision of law was complied with when the Department of the Treasury decided to make financial contributions to the International Criminal Police Commission."[17]

In a letter dated June 1, 1954, H. Chapman Rose, the Assistant Secretary of the Treasury, replied that the Bureaus of Customs and Narcotics and the U.S. Secret Service had been receiving extremely valuable information from Interpol since the FBI withdrawal in 1950, and that "to obtain and assure access to information in Interpol files and papers and the best flow of information from European police officials and an extra degree of collaboration and assistance by them to American Treasury agents carrying on Treasury business in Europe, it has been considered advisable to make certain payments to Interpol at a stipulated rate."[18]

The reason it did not violate the law, Rose said, was because, "In its connections with Interpol, the Treasury Department did not assume the connections normally implied by a membership." He went on to assure the State Department that, "The instructions to our Treasury people here and abroad were that ours was a special and limited participation. United States observers to Interpol meetings were formally instructed that they should 'tactfully avoid being selected for membership on any of the permanent committees or from being involved in the structural set-up of Interpol.' "[19]

Rose neglected to mention that (a) Treasury "officially" joined Interpol in 1952; (b) since 1951 Treasury officials had served on Interpol committees; (c) the "limited participation" gave Treasury all the benefits of membership; and (d) almost two months before, Treasury had known that Interpol had "upped the membership ante to $6,000."[20]

The State Department apparently accepted the explanation and let the matter drop, because Treasury continued as if nothing had happened. Four months later, at Interpol's Twenty-third General Assembly in Rome, Siragusa was still a member of the committee on drugs, Christides was appointed a member of the subcommittee on gold, and both were sponsoring resolutions.[21]

There is no doubt that, albeit illegally, the United States Treasury Department was a member of Interpol, and a powerful member at that. This was no "limited participation."

At the 1955 Interpol meeting in Istanbul, Charles Siragusa even set policy for the organization. In a memo he wrote dated September 12, 1955, to Harry Anslinger, then Commissioner of Narcotics, Siragusa reported on the Twenty-fourth General Assembly just conducted, giving a few examples of the powerful influence the United States exerted on Interpol: "Following is quoted a draft resolution which I prepared and had mimeographed . . ." (This was a series of recommendations on illegal narcotics traffic.) "Several weeks ago when Agent Knight was in Paris, Assistant Secretary General Nepote asked for a special favor. Nepote wanted me at this Istanbul meeting to introduce a resolution in order that narcotic specialists be included in future delegations and to have these specialists get together during the year." Siragusa drew up the resolution. "Some weeks ago I furnished the Bureau a mimeographed booklet prepared by the Interpol General Secretariat on the 'Proposed Reform of the Statutes.' At that time I thought we could try to have another paragraph added to Article 5 so that large American police departments could qualify for Associate Membership . . ." Mr. Emerick of the U.S. Treasury delegation made a statement before a Plenary Session generally supporting proposed reform of the statutes "as a special favor" to Nepote.

In 1975, Myles Ambrose said that, "Operational agents from the Bureau of Narcotics abroad could claim and did claim to be

Interpol agents to give their work a veneer of legitimacy. We didn't give a goddamn about Interpol early on. We wanted Interpol to legitimize our police operations overseas as we were the only country in the world that sends cops abroad operationally." Ambrose also revealed that U. E. Baughman, the chief of the Secret Service, was elected a vice-president of Interpol but was quickly "unelected," and the matter has never appeared on any Interpol records.[22] He did not explain further, but it is believed that this occurred at the Vienna conference in 1956.

Another indication of the extent of Treasury's "informal" relationship to Interpol appears in an October 28, 1957, memo, in which Assistant Secretary of the Treasury Rose tells the Deputy Attorney General, Bill Rogers, who became Attorney General in 1958, that the "informal" work "over the past few years has meant a good deal to Siragusa's operations in Europe and the Middle East generally."*

By 1957, both Treasury and Interpol wanted the prestige of legal Treasury membership. Myles Ambrose, then Assistant to the Secretary for Law Enforcement, approached Hoover to convince him to relinquish the Justice Department's membership, since technically it had ended. Using what he called in an interview his "Irish charm,"[23] Ambrose held a series of meetings with Hoover and his staff and persuaded the FBI to allow the change. Treasury also held meetings with the State Department on the subject of official membership.

The next problem was the exact form of legalization. The Attorney General technically held the membership as per the earlier bill, and the membership fees were limited to $1,500, although by 1957 the dues had increased to $11,000. It was decided to amend the current statute. On December 16, 1957, Siragusa, district supervisor of the Narcotics Bureau in Rome,

---

*In view of Ambrose's statement about Treasury's initial attitude toward Interpol and of Siragusa's OSS background, it is possible that the Treasury-Interpol liaison involved matters that went beyond purely criminal cases of narcotics traffic, smuggling, and counterfeiting.

and Robert Bouck of the Secret Service met with Interpol Secretary General Sicot and his assistant, Jean Nepote, in Paris. Sicot mentioned that he hoped the matter would be cleared up before the General Assembly meeting in London in September, 1958, and Siragusa and Bouck indicated that the amendment would change the authorization for membership fees from $1,500 to $11,000 per year. In a memo to Anslinger, the Commissioner of Narcotics, on December 23, 1957, Siragusa said, "Mr. Sicot thought it advisable not to specify that particular amount since in future years the membership fee might be increased just as it might be decreased. Instead, he suggested that the wording of that particular sentence of the amendment be 'not to exceed an annual fee of $20,000.' "

Negotiations continued. On February 11, 1958, Myles Ambrose wrote a reassuring letter to Hoover saying that Treasury's membership in Interpol, if approved, "will in no way interfere with the direct liaison relationships which now exist between your Bureau and various foreign police agencies." The wording of other particulars of the proposed amendment was also the source of much discussion between Treasury and Justice. Treasury had two versions: A, in which the Attorney General or *the head of any Department or agency designated by him* held membership, and B, in which the Secretary of the Treasury held membership. On one hand it was felt "inappropriate" for the Attorney General to have to pass upon membership for another governmental agency,[24] but on the other hand, alternative B would "apparently preclude the Department of Justice from membership without a subsequent statutory amendment," if Justice wanted to join Interpol again in the future.[25] On February 26, 1958, Justice informed Treasury that alternative A was preferable.[26] Officially, control would remain in the hands of the Attorney General.

Meanwhile, Interpol grew impatient. On April 19, Sicot wrote to Siragusa and confirmed an agreement they had reached during a telephone conversation two weeks before, in which Siragusa had persuaded Sicot to agree that the $3,000

should be paid "in the same way as during previous years
. . ." Sicot told Siragusa, "I must stress the fact that the
present situation is an exceptional one and cannot last indefi-
nitely; I know that you understand.

"For this main reason, and for many others, it is essential
that our cooperation with the Treasury Department should be
placed on an official legal footing."

Sicot again requested that the matter be cleared up before
the September General Assembly meeting in London.[27]

On August 27, 1958, Congress passed an amendment to the
1938 act that would permit the Attorney General "to designate
any departments and agencies which may participate" with Interpol and to permit the dues allowance to be raised from
$1,500 to $25,000.

The Senate report (No. 2403, August 15, 1958) that accompanied the bill and was entered into the Congressional Record
the day the amendment was passed presented Treasury's reasons for requesting membership and reiterated Treasury's profile of Interpol in glowing terms:

. . . The Department of the Treasury desires to reactivate
membership in Interpol by reason of the responsibility of
that Department relating to the suppression of narcotics
traffic, counterfeiting, and smuggling. Representatives of
the Department and its constituent agencies engage in
criminal investigations overseas in these fields and they
must necessarily rely on local police for permission to
operate and for assistance in operation. The Department,
in its memorandum observed: The excellent result of the
work of our agents overseas is far out of proportion to their
number, and is in great part attributable to the splendid
cooperation rendered by Interpol and its member police
agencies . . . The work of our agents overseas has also
resulted in better understanding of our enforcement problems by foreign police agencies who are members of Interpol. The effect has been greater attention to criminal

activities originating overseas which would culminate in the United States . . . the relationships of its representatives and agents with the International Criminal Police Organization have been seriously prejudiced by the lack of formal United States membership in that organization . . . It is readily apparent that effective enforcement of Federal laws by authorities rests in many respects on the information and intelligence available to these authorities . . . participation by the Department in Interpol is of the utmost importance to that agency in carrying out its heavy law-enforcement responsibilities.

On September 4, the Attorney General designated the membership to Treasury, just in time for that agency to send the first official delegation to the General Assembly meeting in London.*

It is significant that the House report (No. 2577) that accompanied the House bill, the first postwar report on Interpol given to Congress, contained a number of inaccuracies, namely that Interpol's activities were disbanded during World War II and that the United States was a participant in the reactivation of Interpol in 1946. The United States had not attended that meeting, although Hoover was elected a vice-president. Also worth noting is the fact that although Interpol is fond of stating that such-and-such a country is a member, in fact its members are the police forces of various countries. Perhaps it is inconsequential, more a matter of semantics than anything else, but it does give Interpol the persona of an intergovernmental organization, which strictly speaking it is not. The FBI, not the United States, had joined Interpol in 1946.†

---

*The Department of Justice did not send a representative to the 1958 London meeting. The Department of Defense sent unofficial representatives.[28]

†The Interpol name and symbol were registered as a trademark with the U.S. Patent Office August 16, 1966, sandwiched between an "Interpol textile fabrics" and a trademark for a resinous substance used to produce a plastic coating. The action stemmed from a General Assembly resolution of 1958.

In 1959, a group of Congressmen, members of the Committee on the Judiciary, toured Europe and visited the Interpol offices between February 3–17.*

Their report reads, in part: "The International Criminal Police Organization was formally organized in 1923 and had headquarters in Vienna, Austria, until World War II, when its activities were disbanded. . . ," which was similar to the information given Congress in 1958. The report reads further that "in 1950, the FBI withdrew its membership, because the nature of its own activities permitted it to take advantage of very few of the benefits offered by Interpol." Considering that the Congressmen spoke with one of Hoover's right-hand men, "Deke" De Loach, upon their return, possibly they heard the real reason but decided to cover it up. The incident that prompted Hoover to pull out in 1950 appears in their report in guarded terms. "One of the chief concerns of the subcommittee," the report said, "was whether the organization (Interpol) is susceptible of being used in any way by other countries for political activities. It is conceivable, for example, that a person, having fled from political persecution, could be apprehended with the assistance of the facilities of Interpol in another country and arrested under the guise of robbery or smuggling in order to secure his return to the demanding country for prosecution as a political criminal." Interpol officials were evidently most reassuring that such a case would be impossible, since the Congressmen reported flatly that "such practices do not exist" and that, "in the nature of things Interpol could not tolerate anything which carries any suggestion of political activity and retain the good faith and membership of the participating countries." To convince them further, Interpol officials showed the Congressmen the Interpol constitution, which prohibits such activity.

Finally, the Interpol officials gave the Congressmen the "of-

*The Representatives were Frank Chelf (Ky.), Basil L. Whitener (N.C.), William E. Miller (N.Y.), and George Meader (Mich.). The report was of "A Special Subcommittee on the International Court of Justice and the International Criminal Police Organization" (April, 1959).

ficial line" about the files. "When Interpol was located in Vienna," the Congressmen reported, "all of its files, because of the imminence of World War II, were destroyed and were thus lost for future use." The subcommittee accepted the story and recommended that the United States offer to keep copies of Interpol's files for them in the future.

It wasn't until Robert Kennedy became Attorney General in 1961 that Justice began to renew its interest in Interpol. Kennedy's much-promoted war on organized crime and racketeering, and the Criminal Division's new responsibilities in that area, led certain Justice Department officials to believe that, despite the FBI's still adamant views regarding Interpol, some liaison with the organization might be beneficial.

Before Kennedy's term as Attorney General, the FBI had not concerned itself with organized crime to any significant degree. William Hundley, who worked for the Department of Justice's Internal Security Division, "the hottest section" in 1951, became chief of the organized crime section in 1958. "There was absolutely nothing going on in the Justice Department," Hundley said.

Apparently the Internal Revenue Service had done something back in the Kefauver days, and Immigration, and they all got hit on the head, so nobody was doing anything. The Bureau certainly wasn't doing anything . . . Everybody had different theories as to why the FBI really had to be brought into organized crime kicking and screaming. Some of the ex-agents felt that Hoover didn't, first of all, want to get into it because his statistics would go down. You know, the cases would be harder to make. Some of them said he didn't want to put his agents into a position where they could be corrupted, have them dealing with gamblers and hoods. Others said that he got himself locked in because he got in a big pissing match with Harry Anslinger over at Narcotics, who he didn't like, and Anslinger had the Mafia coming up out of the sewers the same way Hoover had the Communists coming up out of the sewers. So Hoover got himself locked in saying there was no Mafia. It was probably a combination of every-thing, but he just wasn't in it. There isn't any doubt, no matter what he said, he wasn't in it. He had no in-telligence, he didn't know what the hell was going on . . . When he found out that Bob Kennedy was coming in and that he was kind of hot on this, he knew he had to do something.[29]

In May, 1961, an official from the Justice Department's Criminal Division asked an official from the State Department to keep Justice fully informed of the "activities of Interpol as they affect organized crime and racketeering."[30] Then, in June, 1961, Kennedy wrote to Secretary of the Treasury Douglas Dillon, requesting the same information. Kennedy explained to Dillon that Justice would not be able to send a representative to the September General Assembly meeting in Copenhagen, to which Dillon replied, in July, that Treasury would be sure to keep Justice informed and that Arnold Saga-lyn, Treasury's Interpol representative, would send Justice his reports on the meeting. The State Department had meanwhile queried Hoover, noting that the FBI did not wish to attend the Copenhagen conference, and asking for Hoover's confirmation of the FBI position. Kennedy subsequently learned that organized crime was on the agenda for the Interpol meeting, and he wrote Dillon to ". . . request that the Department of Justice be permitted an observer to attend the meeting." Kennedy told Dillon that "It would be possible for Mr. Norman Philcox, of the Federal Bureau of Investigation, who is now located in Paris, to perform this function on my behalf."[31]

Kennedy and Hoover didn't get along. Hoover knew that Kennedy wanted him out, but he complied with Kennedy's fight against organized crime by putting in unauthorized bugs—which he later tried to blame Kennedy for when there was a leak and all the bugs were uncovered.[32] Hoover was still anti-Interpol when Kennedy came in, and it might be said that Kennedy's trying to steal some of Hoover's fire cemented Hoover's attitude. It is also possible that Interpol created their interest in organized crime for Kennedy's benefit and to win back the confidence of the Department of Justice. There is nothing to confirm this possibility except the fact that, as we shall see, organized crime was indeed familiar with the inner workings of Interpol and their activities were even aided by Interpol's turning its eyes and ears away and, in some cases, contributing to the successes of the syndicates.

In 1963, U.S. Attorney Joseph D. Tydings (later a U.S. Senator and still later to become involved in a financial scandal) went to Helsinki, Finland, and addressed the Interpol General Assembly on behalf of Robert Kennedy. Tydings came back enthused, and he recommended closer cooperation between the Justice Department and Interpol. In his opinion, "The principal benefit of the Interpol Organization insofar as it pertains to the Department of Justice in my judgment is the personal contact which can be made with important police officials over the world at the annual conferences."[33] He suggested that the Assistant Attorney General in charge of the Criminal Division attend the Interpol General Assembly during his first year in office and then send a permanent career officer to subsequent meetings. "I think it important," he said, "that the moral support of the Department of Justice be behind Interpol and that the other countries feel that this is true."[34]

Tydings's suggestions were not wholeheartedly accepted, however, and though Justice continued to send observers to Interpol's meetings, it made no move to deepen the relationship.

In 1965, Treasury put out feelers to see how Justice would react to the suggestion that Interpol be completely turned over to the Secretary of the Treasury.

Fred M. Vinson, Jr., Assistant Attorney General in the Criminal Division, did not react favorably and said in a memo to Deputy Attorney General Ramsey Clark that

The Attorney General, besides his responsibility as chief law enforcement officer in the United States, is currently

Chairman of the National Crime Commission, and has additional responsibilities in the area of criminal law under the Law Enforcement Assistance Act and the Criminal Justice Act. Further, the responsibilities of coordination of all Federal investigative agencies in the area of organized crime is placed in the Criminal Division. Therefore, because of the Attorney General's broad responsibilities in the area of criminal law enforcement, it would seem more appropriate and advisable that the Attorney General appoint a representative from the Department of Justice as his representative to Interpol.[35]

Vinson's proposal to take Interpol back was also in reaction to a Treasury Department proposal that the Interpol Enabling Act of 1958 be amended to increase the authorized amount of dues from $25,000 per year to $75,000. The U.S. dues for 1966 were to increase to $28,000, but Treasury wanted the act to increase dues to $75,000 to avoid the need to go to Congress with its hands out every time Interpol raised the amount.

Vinson's proposal met with mixed reviews within the Department. His Criminal Division found itself pretty much alone as a champion of Interpol, and Justice's Immigration and Naturalization Service felt that Treasury should keep the membership, as it had primary interest in Interpol.

Hoover let it be known in his usual blunt manner that he still held a dim view of Interpol and, regarding the dues increase, questioned whether the benefits received from Interpol justified additional expenditure. He also, and in no uncertain terms, opposed the transfer of membership to the Treasury Department, on the theory that it would place the Attorney General in a position of not knowing the commitments and policy discussions made by American representatives at Interpol meetings. Ramsey Clark was informed that the FBI "believes that since the Attorney General is the chief prosecutor of the United States, he should have control over policies and commitments made to foreign countries."[36] But although Hoover wanted the control over Treasury's membership to continue, he himself wanted no part of Interpol.

Vinson's proposal was not acted upon, probably on the basis of Hoover's objections, but Vinson was tenacious, and in August, 1966, he wrote to Hoover suggesting that the Bureau become the U.S. representative to Interpol on behalf of the Attorney General. This time Vinson tried a different approach, saying that "The Treasury Department has recently informally indicated a desire to be relieved as the Attorney General's designee."[37] It is uncertain whether this was true or not, but noting his awareness of the FBI's "cogent reasons for withdrawing" from Interpol, Vinson went on to assure Hoover that "the Secretariat's handling of political matters has definitely improved and that a greater awareness of law enforcement problems has been developing in Interpol."

Hoover was not impressed, and he let Vinson know that he was still opposed to FBI membership in Interpol.

Vinson next played around with the idea of designating the Immigration and Naturalization Service of the Justice Department as its official member. But once again nothing came of it and Treasury continued to hold the membership.

During this period, the Interpol NCB was located in the Treasury Department's Office of Law Enforcement Coordination, but in 1967, in an effort to reduce the office's operating functions, the NCB was transferred to the Bureau of Narcotics, under the supervision of the Commissioner of Narcotics. The transfer was somewhat schizophrenic, for even though the Interpol NCB's staff and operations services were moved to the Bureau of Narcotics, the responsibility for representation and policy remained in the enforcement section of the Office of the Special Assistant to the Secretary of the Treasury.

By 1968 the matter of Interpol jurisdiction arose again. The Bureau of Narcotics was going to be moved out of the Treasury Department and to the Department of Justice, where it would become the short-lived Bureau of Narcotics and Dangerous Drugs (BNDD). This reorganization was to take effect early in

1969, and on February 15, 1968, J. P. Hendrick, Special Assistant to the Secretary of the Treasury (for Enforcement), wrote to Vinson in Justice to suggest that either the Attorney General take Interpol over or that it be transferred back to the Enforcement office. Surprisingly, Vinson agreed with Hendrick that the NCB should be transferred back under Enforcement, and he missed a chance to gain the ends he had been promising since 1965. The transfer to Enforcement was duly made in March, 1968; but by August, Vinson had changed his mind and was writing to the new Deputy Attorney General, Warren Christopher, to suggest, once again, the transfer of Interpol to the Department of Justice, this time to either the BNDD or the Immigration and Naturalization Service (INS). The Attorney General then drafted a letter to the Secretary of the Treasury informing him that Justice would take Interpol back, but no action was taken because of the change in administration from Johnson to Nixon.

Once the new administration was in, Andrew Tartaglino, chief of the U.S. NCB, wrote to Carl Belcher, Chief of Justice's General Crime Section, and pushed for Interpol's reassignment to Justice as quickly as possible, "since the Department of the Treasury may make decisions contrary to the best interests of the Department of Justice."[38] Belcher then suggested the move to the new Assistant Attorney General, Will Wilson, and also met with the Assistant Secretary of the Treasury, Eugene T. Rossides.

Reporting on the meeting, Belcher said, "I asked Rossides for the views he would have with regard to the reassignment of Interpol and he reacted with the statement he would find such a reassignment extremely adverse to his efforts to upgrade law enforcement in Secret Service and the Bureau of Customs and would further regard such an effort as 'particularly unfriendly.' "[39] Rossides had mentioned that he was thinking of proposing legislation to transfer the statutory assignment of Interpol to Treasury. Belcher said, "Mr. Rossides did not ask and I did not volunteer any reaction to this change in statutory assignment." Belcher decided that because of Rossides's strong opposition it was "not the appropriate time to seek the reassignment . . ."

By June, Rossides had gotten the Interpol NCB transferred into his office, and Justice withdrew its efforts to take over the Interpol function, presumably to wait for the "appropriate time." Rossides appointed Kenneth Giannoules, an eleven-year Secret Service veteran as chief of the NCB. When Giannoules went in, he had a staff consisting of one secretary; when he left in 1974 he had three agents and six administrative personnel.*

Probably in 1975, the Justice Department Management Programs Staff of the Office of Management and Finance prepared an undated report entitled "Interpol: A Discussion of Its Activities and Membership." Although the report was noteworthy for its superficiality, it did say that "Under the Treasury Department, the U.S. delegation to Interpol has become too parochial, too large, too representative of Treasury, i.e., no other country sends a representative of their customs service, and too static. The U.S. delegation is not representative of criminal police activities in this country and is not professionally competent to deal with the General Assembly agenda."

Anticipating Treasury arguments that Treasury should be the U.S. representative of Interpol because of its work in the areas of counterfeiting, contraband, and presidential security, the report stated that those responsibilities "represent a small percentage of the total Interpol caseload and do not offset the vast majority of Interpol activities that impact on the Department of Justice."

In their statistical analysis of the U.S. NCB's 1973 report, the Justice staff said that, given Interpol's extensive drug activity and the mission of the DEA, which is in Justice, "U.S. rep-

---

*In an interview in 1975, Arnold Sagalyn, head of the U.S. NCB from 1960 to 1967, said that when he was with the Treasury Department, the United States had little to do with Interpol on a day-to-day basis and that since both Treasury and the FBI had people overseas, Interpol was of little use to the United States. Sagalyn said the U.S. NCB only began to grow under the Nixon Administration but that previously it had maintained a low profile. "When you develop your facilities you tend to develop the necessity of the group," he said.[40]

resentatives to Interpol should return to the Department of Justice." They reported that about one-third of the NCB's total caseload of 3,198 items were drug investigative requirements, and 1,200 were drug intelligence items. They claimed that ". . . 648 of the entire caseload involved drugs, a statistic not reflected in the NCB reports."

The report also brought up the fact that the Attorney General is considered the nation's chief law enforcement official and the Department of Justice the principal law enforcement agency. It said that state and local participation in Interpol was inadequate and that the Justice Department, because of its existing influence, was in a better position to foster coordination.

The Management Programs Staff's final recommendation was that Justice should pursue a far more active role in Interpol activities, and they suggested that Justice and Treasury conduct a joint study to assess the U.S. role in Interpol.*

In October, 1975, Justice decided to take Interpol back, and in January, 1976, they opened up an Interpol liaison office in the Justice Office of Administration headed by Andrew Tartaglino, the former chief of the NCB when the Bureau of Narcotics was still under the Treasury Department in 1967.

Treasury officials bitterly fought the impending loss but without success; finally they sought a compromise by proposing joint operation with Justice. The proposal was turned down by then Attorney General Edward H. Levi and, on June 30, 1976, the Federal Register announced that the Justice Department was withdrawing its designation of Treasury as U.S. representative to Interpol and that Justice itself was reassuming responsibility for the liaison and central operational activities.

Scripps-Howard writer Richard Starnes reported that some Treasury officials angrily denounced the move as an effort by the Justice Department to extend its international operations. Senator Joseph M. Montoya, who at the time was conducting Senate hearings into Interpol and its activities, expressed a dif-

*The FBI's high-ranking Associate Director Nicholas Callaghan attended Interpol's 1974 conference in Cannes and heard arguments for renewed FBI participation, which initiated changes in the Bureau's attitude.

ferent concern. "Could it be," he asked, "that the Department of Justice doesn't want Interpol overseen by this subcommittee and this is a way to take the oversight authority away from us?"[41]

Treasury Secretary William E. Simon fought the move all the way to the White House, and action was postponed until after the 1976 elections.

What also irritated Treasury was Andrew Tartaglino being named acting director of the Interpol liaison office. "A considerable part of the criticism of the transfer of the Interpol bureau appears to stem from Tartaglino's reputation as a bureaucratic empire builder and a hard charger who frequently runs roughshod over opposition," Starnes reported.[42] He quoted a Justice Department source as saying, "The Central Bureau is small potatoes now, but just watch it grow now that Andy has his hands on it."

Tartaglino had a reputation as a tough, incorruptible man. In 1975, when he was an official in the DEA, he charged that the agency had been slack in pursuing allegations of corruption. An FBI investigation failed to substantiate his charges, but they nevertheless resulted in the resignation of DEA Director John R. Bartels. According to *Washington Post* columnist Jack Anderson, Tartaglino's reputation as a brilliant, innovative investigator is marred by over-zealousness: "his tactics have forced the government to drop the prosecution of at least half a dozen cases."[43]

As an example, Anderson brought up an incident involving a New York police detective named Joe Nunziata. In a complex set of maneuvers, Tartaglino, at government expense, flew a former informant from Italy to the United States, supplied him with twelve grams of pure heroin, and arranged his arrest. Tartaglino told the informant to bribe the officials, one of whom was Nunziata. The first bribery attempt failed, but then the officers accepted it—to make a case against the man, they claimed. Tartaglino, Anderson said, brought intense pressure to bear against Nunziata to gain his cooperation in the investigation, even though he wasn't the target. "Tartaglino told

Nunziata his police career was finished, winding up with three options. Nunziata could cooperate, face jail or commit suicide."

Nunziata sat down and wrote a three-page letter in long-hand, protesting his innocence. Then he killed himself.

During his short involvement with the U.S. NCB, Tartaglino certainly made his presence felt. As early as January, 1977, he demanded that the NCB accept on its staff a DEA intelligence research analyst, a Ms. Philpot. For a week, she worked half-days in the NCB, but then Tartaglino backed down and pulled her out. Tartaglino next created a flap by showing up uninvited at the February 25–26 Interpol conference in Paris on "Violent Crimes by Organized Groups." Treasury officials objected to his presence and hastily informed Nepote that he was not the official U.S. representative and that only those authorized by Treasury were authorized to attend Interpol conferences. Nepote was placed in a difficult situation, but the matter was resolved by allowing Tartaglino to attend as an observer. After all, he represented the agency that was soon to take over the U.S. NCB, and he no doubt let Nepote know it. His presence was doubly irritating to Treasury officials as, while he was in Paris, the official head of the U.S. NCB, Louis B. Sims, was being forced to testify before a Senate subcommittee in Washington.

Tartaglino might have been the next chief of the Interpol NCB; but, according to one confidential source, after heavy political in-fighting within the NCB office, he left to join the staff investigating the Korean bribery scandal but went back to Justice in a matter of months.

On January 18, 1977, a "Memorandum of Understanding" was executed between Justice and Treasury officials, and on March 17, 1977, the U.S. NCB was physically moved to the Justice Department. The memorandum provided for the position of U.S. representative of Interpol and the chief of the U.S. NCB to be alternated between the Justice and Treasury Departments. According to NCB chief Sims,* however, the "most

* The head of the Washington NCB since 1974, Sims is no stranger to headlines. Sims became chief of the Secret Service technical security division in

116

important" part of the understanding was that "It seems likely that the physical movement of the U.S. Interpol office to Justice presages the eventual loss of all Treasury responsibilities in this area."[44] Another source told us in May, 1977, that "Now they [Justice] have the office in the building, they'll just make it impossible for the Treasury guys to operate and squeeze them out." Although Sims was still in charge of the operation at the time of writing, the end of Treasury participation in Interpol is in sight.

"It was a great battle," said Acting Assistant Secretary of the Treasury John H. Harper. "I don't know ever in the history of small bureaucracy has there ever been such a huge battle over about fourteen or fifteen people in a budget of a couple hundred thousand dollars."[45]

Secretary of the Treasury Simon, when asked for the ongoing reason for the proposed change of control, summed up the battle between the U.S. Government departments by responding, "In the government, it is called turfmanship."[46]

November, 1972, and was privy to the inner workings of the highly secret White House tape-system long before the revelations of Watergate. Sims testified publicly before Judge John Sirica in January, 1974, and twice appeared before the Watergate grand jury in the fall of 1973. Sims was not under investigation himself, but his testimony made headlines in Washington.

The narcotics traffic of today, which is destroying the equilibrium of our society, could never be as pervasive and open as it is unless there was connivance between authorities and criminals.

———FORMER CHIEF JUSTICE EARL WARREN

Chapter Six

THE NARCOTICS TRADE

While Interpol has been making loud noises about the "war on drugs" and "our number one problem," its host country, France, has been dominating the world heroin market since World War II—a period that roughly coincides with Interpol's domicile there.

Drug traffic began on a grand scale in 1946, in what was then called French Indochina. At that time, French intelligence and paramilitary agencies took over the opium traffic to finance their covert operations during the First Indochina War (1946–54). By 1951, the French controlled the opium trade. The program, dubbed Operation X by insiders, was sanctioned at the highest levels by the French Expeditionary Corps and the SDECE. The CIA also played a significant role in placing the Corsican syndicates into a position of power. In 1947, soon after it was formed, the CIA grew apprehensive over the gains of French Communists. According to former director of the CIA's international organizations division, Thomas W. Braden, "A takeover of the government was feared."[1]

The CIA sent agents to Marseilles to deal directly with the Corsican syndicates, offering money and weapons to them to assault Communist picket lines, meetings, and officials. In 1950, when Communist dockworkers sought to shut down shipments of supplies to Indochina, the CIA again recruited a criminal terror squad to break the strike. "In supplying the Corsican syndicates with money and support, the CIA broke the last barrier to unrestricted Corsican smuggling operations in Marseilles."[2]

It is now known that the CIA supported Laotian and Vietnamese leaders who ran the opium traffic and that it also assisted in the transportation of the drug. Marseilles' first heroin laboratory was opened in 1951, only months after the syndicates had taken control of the waterfront.

When the French finally gave up Southeast Asia, a strong Corsican community stayed behind to continue the narcotics trade, transporting morphine-base to their Marseilles laboratories, then turning it into heroin. The "clandestine opium traffic" put into power the "Corsican narcotics syndicates and corrupted French intelligence officers, who remain, even today, key figures in the international narcotics trade."[3]

French government involvement in organized crime and narcotics traffic must be viewed with an understanding of the complicated political situation in which "favors" play a large part. Just as the American CIA has been willing in the past to recruit the help of the Mafia and, in the late forties, the Corsicans, so the Gaullist government in France has used the services of its underworld.

In France, the government's ties to the underworld began during Charles de Gaulle's crusade against the right-wing Secret Army Organization (OAS). Algeria was at stake. De Gaulle's concern was that his Fifth Republic would survive, and that governments sympathetic to French economic and political programs remain in power.

From 1959 to 1964, officials from two agencies, the SDECE and the SAC (*Service d'action Civique*—the "parallel police"), were left to recruit the forces they needed to meet the demands of their president. The SDECE formed a special action group composed mostly of Corsican gangsters and Vietnamese.

This group, called the *barbouzes* (bearded ones), was hired as counterterrorist assassins. SAC's members were composed of the French underworld, former resistance fighters, and old Gaullist soldiers. These men were recruited to protect the members of de Gaulle's political party, the *Union des Democrates pour la République* (UDR).

Jacques Foccart, the secretary of the community and African affairs, was the most powerful official involved in the formation of the SDECE's *barbouzes*. To carry out his duties, Foccart was given control of the African section of the SDECE, as well as a network of spies and assassins who operated outside of the official organization. Foccart was ambitious, and later he unofficially extended his operations to South America.[4]

The *barbouzes* organization was guided by Roger Frey, who became Minister of the Interior in 1961; Alexander Sanguinetti, operational head of the French police from 1960 to 1962; and Jean Bozzi, member of the National Assembly from Corsica, and head of the national police from 1962 to 1967. Interpol, it must be remembered, is under the authority of the Interior Minister, who is also the head of France's national police.

While Frey, Sanguinetti, and Bozzi were directing the nation's police, they were also recruiting gangsters for the counterterrorist organizations from syndicates that the police were supposed to be eradicating. While Interpol was loudly declaring war on drugs, powerful French officials, who must have had strong influence over the French-based organization, were actively supporting the men who were partly responsible for the drug traffic.

The members of both the *barbouzes* and SAC in their dirty war against the OAS were required to do things that would have otherwise compromised the regular members of France's intelligence and counterterrorist agencies. In return for their loyalty to the Fifth Republic and to the cause of France, many of the Corsican gangsters, who had already started to deal in heroin before they were recruited, received protection of their businesses after the war.

Marcel Francisci, owner of an international gambling syndicate and a man identified as the top organizer of France's heroin traffic, was involved in the formation of the *barbouzes*. Francisci, a Corsican, was a Resistance fighter and was awarded four medals for his wartime work. Francisci has not concealed his friendship with Sanguinetti and Bozzi, both of whom he has supported politically. Francisci, Foccart, Sanguinetti, Charles Pasqua—a Gaullist deputy who chaired a parliamentary narcotics commission—and other SDECE officials are all old friends. Francisci has entertained them all at his table, at his club, and on his yacht.[5]

"In 1964, the editor of a large Paris newspaper, a Corsican, received a call from Francisci. He said he understood that one of the paper's reporters was checking into the home life of Achille Peretti, a UDR . . . deputy and president of the National Assembly. Francisci suggested that the story be killed. It was."[6]

A retired U.S. federal narcotics agent who served in France was quoted as saying, "Every time we mentioned the name Francisci to the French police, they froze. You could tell they didn't want to hear anything about him, much less work on him. He was a no-no. In this country [the United States] we would have gotten him on conspiracy a long time ago."[7]

One can only assume that when SDECE guarantees Corsican gangsters safe-conduct passes, all the bases are covered, including that of the French-run Interpol organization.

Jean Nepote joined Interpol in 1946, became Deputy Secretary General in 1958, and five years later took his current position as Secretary General. During his rise to power, Nepote served under and was friends with Bozzi and Sanguinetti.

Former Ajax companions Jean Nepote and Achille Peretti are today both members of the *Maison de l'Amérique Latine Club* (MAL). Nepote is on the board of directors, as are intelligence chief Jacques Foccart and his close friend, industrialist Gilbert Beaujolin. The Beaujolin industrial group is considered a main cog in the Foccart intelligence network.[8]

Beaujolin and Foccart were co-chiefs of the Allied resistance network during the war.

Alain Joubert's book, *Dossier D*, lists twenty-nine major French heroin traffickers. Of these, twenty-one are connected in some way to SDECE and/or SAC. Thirteen show connections to Foccart, Frey, and Sanguinetti, people that Interpol Secretary General Nepote is, or has been, connected to.

In 1968 Jacques Foccart was named by the CIA as a Soviet spy. The information came from a Russian defector who "blew" more than two hundred other KGB (Soviet secret service) operatives. The French held two views on the matter: (*a*) that it was an anti-French CIA plot, and (*b*) that it was a deliberate ploy by the KGB to discredit the French in American eyes. Richard Deacon, in *A History of the Russian Secret Service*, said that the KGB had an "urgent desire to discredit one of the best brains and certainly the ablest intelligence adviser in Paris, Jacques Foccart, officially the Secretary-General for Madagascar and African Affairs, but unofficially de Gaulle's number one adviser on all intelligence matters and watch-dog on counter-espionage." Only the KGB and Foccart know the truth of the matter. However, the KGB would no doubt be extremely happy to flood the United States with drugs, and if they could, they would.

In May, 1971, an alert customs agent, twenty-two-year-old Lynn Pelletier, examined a Volkswagen camper that had arrived in Port Elizabeth, New Jersey, from Le Havre, a port in northern France. After poking around in the camper for a few minutes, Ms. Pelletier unearthed ninety-six pounds of pure heroin—with a street value of about $12 million. Customs agents arrested Roger Delouette, forty-eight, when he came to pick up the vehicle.

Delouette subsequently revealed that he had smuggled the drugs into the United States for the SDECE, that he had shipped $17,000 worth of counterfeit U.S. currency into Italy, and that he had been recruited for the job by Colonel Paul Fournier. Fournier was the cover name of Paul Ferrere, the operating chief of SDECE. Fournier had worked in Indochina during Operation X. Delouette had run errands all over the world for SDECE since 1948. In the late fifties Delouette was sent to Algeria.

French government officials denied the story totally, and called Delouette a liar who was attempting to save himself by implicating SDECE. U.S. officials believed Delouette's story implicitly after he had taken two lie-detector tests, and a federal grand jury in Newark indicted Fournier-Ferrere.

By this time the affair had created diplomatic earthquakes. In the midst of it, the French government demanded that John Cusack, the European chief of the Bureau of Narcotics and Dangerous Drugs, be transferred back to the United States. Cusack, who had been interviewed by *Le Méridional*, a Marseilles paper, had apparently compared some of the top French heroin traffickers to Al Capone, saying that the men were left alone, "thanks to their bank balances, special connections and consideration shown them."[9]

Max Fernet, head of the Sûreté and chief of Interpol's French NCB, reacted by saying, "Over there [in America] organized crime really exists. There are big wheels with protection who are the head of it all. It is not the same thing in France. In narcotics, France plays fair and the Americans are aware of all our investigations."[10] Fernet had also been associated closely with Interpol in 1956–60, 1962–65, and from 1967 to 1971 as a delegate to Interpol's General Assembly.

French authorities refused to admit that Fournier-Ferrere even existed until they were embarrassed into it when a member of a rival French intelligence department said publicly that not only did Fournier-Ferrere exist, but he knew for a fact that Delouette had been working for Fournier-Ferrere. U.S. Attorney Herbert J. Stern sent evidence of Fournier-Ferrere's complicity to Sûreté and Interpol NCB chief Max Fernet. Fernet refused to take any action, presumably on orders from above.

A few of the other Frenchmen with both SDECE and heroin connections are Michael Victor Mertz, who headed a ring that annually smuggled about a third of a ton of pure heroin into the United States for about eight years, and who had worked with French intelligence since the end of World War II and for SDECE in Algeria. Mertz was convicted and sentenced to five years in jail in 1971, but he was apparently released after serving eight months of his sentence.[11]

Christian David was employed by SDECE as an assassin. He was arrested in Brazil in 1972 for smuggling heroin to the United States and is now in jail here.

Ange Simonpieri joined the SDECE *barbouzes* in 1960 and worked for a special counterterrorist SDECE group in 1961 and 1962. In 1963 he won a seat in the National Assembly. Simonpieri trafficked in heroin while serving in the organization and afterward. Following the publicity the Delouette case received, he was finally sentenced to a five-year prison term in 1971.

Andre LaBay started working in SDECE in 1960. In 1971 he was arrested with 106 kilos of heroin by French police after a tip from the U.S. Bureau of Narcotics and Dangerous Drugs. If the tip had not come from the United States, he might never have been arrested. International pressure forced the French to convict many known traffickers who would have otherwise remained free to run their trade.

Joe Attia, an assassin for SDECE, was a powerful heroin financier. He died in 1972.

Large wall-maps at the Interpol Saint-Cloud headquarters show the major routes taken by international drug-traffickers. The heroin laboratories of Marseilles are clearly shown. These routes have been "under investigation" by Interpol for almost twenty-five years, but before French government involvement was brought under harsh public scrutiny, French action toward drug traffic was at best token. After the Delouette case in 1971, a number of top traffickers were arrested, but the effort seems feeble when one considers the short terms served by those such as Mertz.

Around 1970, France began to develop a drug problem of her own. The official position of the French police prior to that, explained Gilbert Raguideau, a high-ranking official of the French national police force, was: "In the past, narcotics enforcement in France had been an American priority, not a French priority. We had other, more pressing problems facing our police. First, we had the problem of rebuilding the police after World War II. Then, in the late fifties and early sixties, we had to cope with the Secret Army Organization terrorists. And after that, we had the student revolution of the left. These priorities involved the survival of the state. It is only recently that we have been able to concentrate on narcotics."[12] Perhaps the involvement in the traffic of government officials helps explain that attitude.

Our research has raised more questions than answers, particularly where Interpol's true involvement in international drug traffic lies. It does tend to substantiate Alfred W. McCoy's opinion, however. In his authoritative and incomparable overview of the evolution of France's role in heroin traffic, McCoy says as a final note that "The Corsican syndicates in France are protected by the highest echelons of government . . ." McCoy also says that informed observers are convinced that some of SDECE's top intelligence officers have been organizing shipments of heroin to the U.S. to finance SAC operations and that U.S. narcotics agents working undercover are afraid of being unmasked by SDECE.[13]

Drugs and politics are inextricably entwined. The CIA ignored drug smuggling in Southeast Asia because it was politically expedient to do so. Of the many Cubans trained by the CIA for the Bay of Pigs operation, about 8 percent are now dealing in drugs.[14] Whether or not this is condoned by the CIA is uncertain, but no doubt favors are owed. In Turkey, not only can the Turks not afford not to grow opium, "but many of the top narcotics businessmen—as well as legal opium growers—have cultivated social, business, or political ties with the country's political leaders. A high ranking American official [said] that most of the 112 deputies—in the 450 member National Assembly—who recently signed a petition for the repeal of the poppy ban were under strong pressure from both poppy growers and major narcotics businessmen."[15] One Turkish businessman explained that "drug smugglers from small regions register with the party that runs the government. They spend more during election time."[16] The Corsicans do the same.

In Bulgaria, a government agency called KINTEX, which is supposed to promote imports and exports, actually ensures the safe smuggling of drugs from Turkey into Bulgaria and thence into Western Europe, in return for countersmuggling of alcohol, cigarettes, and arms for Turkish revolutionaries in Turkey.[17] In many South American countries, corrupt police, including Interpol officials, are connected to corrupt politicians. In France, SDECE's use of drug-smuggling revenues to finance its operations, its involvement with criminal syndicates, and the complicity of top government officials and law enforcement officers, casts a pall of doubt over protestations of attempted efficiency in the battle against drugs. Only partially with tongue in cheek can it be suggested that perhaps Interpol's ineffectiveness against drug traffic is due to its Article 3, which forbids it to meddle in "political" matters.

Any attempt to analyze fairly Interpol's efficiency as an organization is made difficult by the very nature of its functions. Drug traffic, for instance, has been one of Interpol's major targets for years, yet it is the fastest growing form of crime and shows no signs of abating. The obvious conclusion that Interpol is therefore inefficient is difficult to prove, for on the face of it, drug enforcement is the responsibility of individual police forces.

By declaring drugs its number one problem, Interpol has made the issue its raison d'être. In the United States we have seen how the intelligence community exaggerated the Communist spy scare in order to appropriate funds to investigate that scare. Hoover was an old hand at those tactics. It is possible that Interpol is operating under the same type of system.

The earliest significant figures pertaining to Interpol's handling of drug-related cases appeared in 1953, when the organization had only twenty-seven members. That year, 319 drug cases were recorded by the General Secretariat, and out of these, only thirty-three international notices went out on traffickers. A list of twenty-nine ships known to be used for drug transportation was also circulated. In 1954 the U.N. Narcotics Commission warned of increased drug traffic and urged governments to cooperate in stopping the flow. By 1969 drug-trafficking was Interpol's number-one problem. That year Interpol handled 3,272 cases involving narcotics, approximately one-third of its total case-load for the period June 1, 1969, to June 1, 1970. In 1971 Interpol received more than 20,000 messages related to drug seizures, requests for information, and so on. In return, it sent out 1,208 messages. The result of all this activity at the General Secretariat was a total of thirty-seven international notices—four more than in 1953. By 1972 their international notices had increased to a total of 118. In 1973 only forty-three traffickers were the subjects of international notices. In 1974 the General Secretariat handled 25,679 cases, but in the fiscal year of June, 1973, to June, 1974, only 1,481 individuals were arrested as a result of wanted notices published by the General Secretariat and of other intervention.[18] That year only 437 international notices were issued; of these, only fifty-nine pertained to international drug-traffickers. Considering that Interpol had 117 member police agencies at the time, this would average out to 12.65 arrests per member force for the year. A London bobby probably does better in a week. Looked at another way, only 5.7 percent of the total cases handled by the Secretariat resulted in arrest.

The United States reported in 1962 that there were 45,000 drug addicts in the country, "a considerable decrease over eighty years ago when there had been 500,000 opium consumers alone."[19] In 1964, Harry Anslinger, former Commissioner of the Bureau of Narcotics, estimated that there were 20,000 known heroin addicts in New York City and another 20,000 to 35,000 elsewhere in the country, a total estimate ranging between 40,000 and 50,000.[20] By 1965, federal narcotics officials reported that there were 57,000 known drug addicts in the entire country,[21] but by 1969 it was estimated that there were 315,000 addicts in the United States. In 1971, the total had almost doubled to an estimated 560,000 addicts.[22]

The 1976 General Accounting Office (GAO) investigation of the U.S. involvement in Interpol found, after a random sampling of cases handled by the U.S. NCB, that most cases involved individuals with no prior criminal record. "Requests made to the U.S. Bureau generally did not involve established international criminals or large crime syndicates," the GAO said. The report pointed out that most narcotics cases (the largest category of requests handled by the U.S. NCB) involved young Americans or U.S. servicemen arrested overseas with small quantities of such drugs as marijuana.

Examples of Interpol's arrests in recent years serve to illustrate the futility police must experience much of the time. By far the majority of arrests are of couriers—hippies, seamen, tourists, diplomats, airline employees, many of whom are not habitual criminals but merely losers attracted to a fast buck. Very few cases involve the arrests of the heads of large international organizations who actually control the traffic. Couriers are plentiful, in South America particularly. Colombia cocaine, for instance, comes to the United States through couriers who earn from $500 to $1,000 a kilo, plus expenses, an attractive inducement. Mexican heroin traffic works the same way. Unlike the French, who usually send in large consignments, the Mexicans use their abundant labor force in a shotgun approach, with waves of couriers carrying small amounts. The occasional arrest of an expendable "mule" does not appreciably hurt the big heroin organizations.

At a London press conference on March 16, 1977, Secretary General Nepote refused to answer questions about the GAO's criticisms, taking "the view that the criticisms of Interpol's operations in individual countries should be answered by the national governments concerned."[23]

In 1971, when the world was in the throes of the drug epidemic, Interpol conducted a belated survey for which only thirty-two member countries bothered to provide statistics.

Twenty-three others, including the United States and the United Kingdom, provided incomplete statistics or none at all. The thirty-two reporting countries said that 8,805 young drug-users were arrested in 1968, and 13,469 were arrested in 1969—an increase of 53 percent. Strangely, the survey was interested only in drug-users and asked for no information on drug-dealers.

The Delouette case took place in 1971, and by that time, French-processed heroin was flooding the United States at a rate of ten tons a year.[24] Interpol figures for 1971 show that world-wide there were only 135 heroin seizures, which altogether totaled 353,962 grams of the drug.[25]

In 1973 Interpol reported that the previous year police around the world had seized 481,504 grams of cocaine, more than half of which was in the United States and Colombia.[26] In 1972, the General Secretariat of Interpol claimed it was "taking a very active part in the fight against illicit drug traffic."[27] In its 1974 progress report, the General Secretariat said that "the fight against international crime is never-ending; it is the Organization's raison d'être and the permanent concern of the National Central Bureaus and the General Secretariat."

Occasionally Interpol sets up liaison offices for illegal drug traffic. In 1975 there were five in Europe, one in Southeast Asia, and one in Latin America.* David R. Macdonald, Assistant Secretary of the Treasury for Enforcement, Operations and Tariff Affairs,† said that in 1975 the European offices had

---

* Interpol's Annual Report for fiscal year 1975 states that "During this fiscal year, the U.S. made a one-time non-recurring, voluntary contribution of $135,000 from Foreign Assistance Funds for International Narcotics Control administered by the Department of State. In accordance with normal practices in the case of Foreign Assistance Funds, appropriate members of the Senate and House Appropriations Committees concurred with this contribution. The U.S. contribution is being used to support Interpol liaison officers for drug enforcement, one assigned to Southeast Asia and one to Latin America."

† According to the Interpol Annual Report for fiscal year 1975, "ten full-time positions were assigned to the U.S. participation in Interpol. One of these positions is presently located in the General Secretariat of Interpol in France,

been increased from three to five because they had "been so successful in combatting drug traffic."[29] Yet by 1975 the Herrera organization in Colombia—one of the biggest cocaine gangs—was still sending out a monthly average of forty kilograms of cocaine to New York and Miami, or $14 million a year at wholesale prices.[30]

New York Times writer Nicholas Gage also noted that it was "unlikely that an organization as large as the Herreras could function without police and political protection . . . the organization's protectors include not only officials in the police, customs and the judiciary, but also several leading members of Colombia society who have invested in the lucrative cocaine trade."[31]

The Colombian situation serves to underscore the problems faced by law enforcement officials around the world: international drug traffic is analogous to a sieve—plug one hole, and it just flows faster through the others. In spite of the fact that narcotics enforcement has become almost as big a business as narcotics-trafficking, even the most impressive seizures as far as quantity is concerned have done little to stop the flow.

Since 1971 U.S. agencies have provided an annual average of $22 million to Latin American drug-control training and assistance programs. In 1974 Mexico alone received $12 million. In fiscal year 1976 the DEA's budget was almost $10 million, or $4,300 of working capital for each of its 2,300 agents.

According to Secretary General Nepote, drug traffic is Interpol's number-one problem.[32] During the latter half of fiscal

---

and the remaining nine are located in the U.S. NCB in Washington, D.C. These positions are funded as follows: two by the Drug Enforcement Administration, Department of Justice; two by the U.S. Secret Service; three by the U.S. Customs Service; one by the Bureau of Alcohol, Tobacco, and Firearms; two by the Office of the Secretary, Department of the Treasury."

By 1976 the United States had twelve full-time positions assigned to Interpol. Three were funded by the Department of Justice; two by the Office of the Secretary, U.S. Treasury Department; two by the U.S. Secret Service; three by the U.S. Customs Service; and two by the Bureau of Alcohol, Tobacco, and Firearms.[28]

year 1975, of the cases entered into the computerized Treasury Enforcement Communications System (TECS) by the U.S. NCB, almost 34 percent were related to drugs.

Drug-traffic patterns have been through what some authorities on the subject like to term "significant" changes in the past decade, but the only really significant factor is that the flow of hard drugs into both the United States and Europe has increased. When the French started to convict major traffickers and to close down laboratories in 1971—at the same time U.S. officials were arresting some members of a powerful group of French-Corsican traffickers who were channeling French heroin through their base in South America—the French-Corsican network was disrupted and a Mexican system jumped in to fill the temporary gap. In the last five years the Mexican share of the U.S. heroin market has increased from 20 to 60 percent.[33]

French traffickers were also hit when Turkey announced a ban on poppy cultivation in 1972, but by 1974 Turkey began to resume poppy cultivation on a "limited" scale, and the French traffickers began to reorganize. By April, 1975, John Fallon, the DEA regional director in New York, admitted that "It's a buyer's market again" for French heroin.[34]

Cocaine, on the other hand, comes almost exclusively from South America. It is grown mainly in Bolivia and Peru and is processed in Brazil, Uruguay, Argentina, Paraguay, and Colombia. Attempts at international cooperation to squelch drug traffic stumble on the fact that police in South America are poorly paid, with salaries that range from $60 a month in Bolivia to $250 a month in Argentina. Corruption has become a way of survival.

In April, 1970, two members of the U.S. State Department's Agency for International Development (AID) investigated the state of drug law enforcement in Bolivia and reported that two former Interpol chiefs had been dismissed for corruption. "Because of the corruption and graft that has prevailed in the past in dealing with cocaine, 'Interpol' (and the rest of DNIC, the National Directorate of Criminal Investigations) has been the target of criticism by the public. However, there have been many changes and arrests made in an effort to improve this situation," they said.[35]

At that time the DNIC had an eleven-man Interpol unit that was "responsible for drug law enforcement." This Interpol unit had been affiliated with Interpol, France, since 1963, the AID officials reported, and its sole purpose and responsibility was "to enforce existing narcotics laws."

This was no post office that passed along messages. This Bolivian Interpol office investigated information and made arrests. And it "reports regularly to Interpol, France through Argentina."

Noting that the two previous Interpol chiefs had been arrested for trafficking in cocaine and that the personnel "had absolutely no training of any kind," the U.S. AID officials suggested that "The 'Interpol' unit should be renovated and remain in the DNIC organization, but kept under close scrutiny by the Ministry of Government." It also recommended that the U.S. Government should provide the unit with funds for "a system of rewards . . ." because "Although sufficient pay to overcome temptation cannot be offered at present salary scales, a system of rewards, possibly provided by the United States, could fill the gap."

Typical of the situation is the case of Luis Rivadeneira of Ecuador, who was arrested there in December, 1974, with two kilos of cocaine paste in his possession. *The New York Times* reported that soon after his arrest, Admiral Alfredo Poveda Burbano, Ecuador's Minister of Government, who directs all law enforcement agencies in the country, including the Interpol NCB, called the police and ordered them to change the evidence so that the charges against Rivadeneira would have to be dropped. Apparently the arrested man was a close friend of one of the admiral's relatives, and the police did as they were told.[36]

In January, 1976, Admiral Poveda became chief of the military junta that took power in Ecuador. A United Press International (UPI) correspondent, Pieter van Bennekom, was ordered to leave the country on January 14 for asking Poveda about the drug incident at a press conference.[37]

Interpol also works closely with the U.S. Drug Enforcement Administration, and there is at least one DEA official permanently stationed at the Saint-Cloud headquarters.

Writer Frank Browning said, "The real character of the DEA was best expressed to a doctor who had dared criticize Nixon's scheme for creating a super-agency called DEA by White House aide Egil (Bud) Krogh, Jr.: 'Anyone who opposes us we'll destroy. As a matter of fact, anyone who doesn't support us we'll destroy.' "[38]

The agency out of which the DEA grew, the U.S. Bureau of Narcotics, wasn't much better either. In 1968 thirty-two agents were forced to resign after a Justice Department investigation showed that they were selling confiscated heroin and accepting bribes from known traffickers.

The first head of the DEA in 1973 was Myles Ambrose, the man who persuaded J. Edgar Hoover to give Treasury the Interpol membership in 1957. Ambrose led a number of U.S. Interpol delegations over the years and remained a fervent supporter of the organization. Ambrose's government career ended after it was revealed he had gone on a pleasure trip to the ranch of a Texan who was under indictment for narcotics and gun-smuggling. Today, Ambrose has a private law practice in Washington, D.C.

In 1974 a team of DEA intelligence specialists came up with enough material to take before a grand jury and disclose a major narcotics operation between New York, Chicago, Las Vegas, San Diego, and Tijuana, involving "very prominent criminals," including known Mafia figures. The agent in charge ordered the project dropped. One agent was quoted by Browning as saying, "He informed us that he didn't want us wasting our time on organized crime probes, that the real problem was the Mexicans and we were to drop this. We were to work with Mexican violators and their extensions abroad. Can you believe it? Fucking wetbacks!"[39] That was the end of the DEA investigation of interstate Mafia narcotics traffic.

New York Post columnist Jack Anderson said in 1975 that "The CIA has had an undercover relationship with both narcotics and customs agents. This raises the question of whether the CIA has hidden its illegal domestic operations behind other federal agencies."[40] Anderson also divulged elsewhere that federal narcotics agents had maintained secret, bugged apartments for the CIA in San Francisco and New York in the early sixties, and that it had used the apartments as sex traps to blackmail foreign diplomats (recalling Arthur Nebe's "Kitty Salon" during World War II).[41]

Several years ago, the CIA trained thirteen narcotics agents at its counterespionage school, and most of the agents still work for the Drug Enforcement Agency. In July, 1975, the National Commission on Law Enforcement and Social Justice (NCLE) obtained a reliable list of fifty-eight former CIA employees who were at that time employed by the DEA—half of them in the intelligence unit. In presenting the list to Congressional investigators, the NCLE charged that according to its sources many, if not all, of the individuals named still continued to work for the CIA.

Thirty-three of the agents were stationed in Washington, D.C., with thirteen others located in nine other U.S. cities.* The remaining twelve agents were stationed in Thailand, Malaysia, Mexico, Colombia, Spain, Italy, and France. The DEA works extremely closely with Interpol in Paris and even has one of its own men permanently stationed in the Washington NCB. We do know that one of the men mentioned on the list was stationed in Paris and has been an influential figure at Interpol's headquarters since at least 1955.

One of the men on the list was Lieutenant Colonel Lucien Conein, an acting director of the Special Operations and Field

* The cities were Miami, San Diego, Dallas, Baltimore, New York, Albuquerque, Norfolk, Wilmington, Delaware, and Deming, New Mexico.

Support Section of the DEA's international intelligence division. Conein was the senior operative for the CIA in Saigon in 1963 and served as the liaison between U.S. forces and the Viet forces that overthrew the Diem regime. He worked with the French Resistance during World War II and spent much of his time with Saigon's Corsican gangsters during his Vietnam tour. When Conein left, the Corsicans presented him with a medallion engraved *Per Tu Amicu Conein* ("For your friendship, Conein"). Conein explained that the medallion is worn by Corsican leaders around the world and serves as an indentification badge for meetings, narcotics drops, and so on.[42] The Corsicans, of course, controlled the opium traffic in Saigon.

In 1975 Pat Saunders, a former federal narcotics and intelligence officer, claimed that growing public distrust of the CIA had forced the agency to infiltrate the DEA in order to provide a cover for illegal domestic surveillance. "These agents are still doing the same illegal and unethical things," he said, "but now they're hiding behind the shield of saying it's a narcotics investigation." Saunders, who worked from 1969 to 1973 with the Bureau of Narcotics and Dangerous Drugs (BNDD), now the DEA, said, "I really believed that drug enforcement was a good thing and that the police and the agents were doing an honest job in stopping drug traffic. I was shocked and dismayed when I found out how wrong I was."[43]

Further evidence of CIA involvement with Interpol comes from a Marine security guard who was stationed at a U.S. Embassy in a South American country. He testified in a sworn affidavit, under penalty of perjury, that he had seen a CIA agent hand over a large sum of money to an Interpol official.*

On one occasion in 1970, our informant was ordered to dress in plain civilian clothes, carry his .38 caliber revolver, and go to the office of an Embassy official. Although he was not supposed to engage in any activities other than security activities within

---

*Although he is willing to testify before an appropriate government agency, for the purposes of publication we have changed or deleted, at his request, the names of people and places so that his identity will remain unknown until he can present the matter to interested authorities.

the Embassy, our informant did as he was told. The Embassy official told him that there was a CIA agent in the Embassy, but not to mention it to anybody. He took him to an adjacent office to meet the agent.

He introduced the CIA agent to me as Bill. He was about six feet, one inch tall, with brown eyes, dirty blond hair, muscular build. He looked about thirty-two years old and weighed about 190 pounds. Mr. ———— told me to accompany the agent and to "help Bill on anything he needed." It was all verbal orders—nothing was given to me in writing. Bill and I then left the office and walked near the ———— on the first floor of the U.S. Embassy where we met a Lt. Q from the ———— Police Force who was waiting there. We left the Embassy and drove off in a green carryall van that is used by the military group in the Embassy.

Lt. Q, Bill and I took the van and drove. At this point, Bill mentioned to us that we were going to meet someone at the ———— Hotel. We entered the hotel about midday and went directly to the cafeteria and ordered coffee. While we waited, Bill was talking to Lt. Q about a guy named Z, whom Bill had been chasing around for four months. He mentioned Z was "a slippery fucker" and "all I want to do is make a deal with him." Lt. Q said, "Yes, we know who he is. He has been trafficking drugs from ———— to ———— and from there to Florida and Mexico. He's a big one." Bill said, "His game is heroin." I asked Bill if he was out to catch this guy, Z, and he said, "No, I'm supposed to make a deal with him. Part of it will be handled by the person we're going to meet here." Then Lt. Q asked Bill who we were going to meet. Bill said, "Inspector X." Lt. Q said, "I know him. Inspector X from Interpol." Bill asked how long he had known him and he said he knew him from the police academy where they had played soccer together.

Then a Spanish-speaking man came up to us at the table and Lt. Q shook his hand in a very friendly manner saying [in Spanish], "How are you doing, brother? How have things been with you?" Bill then shook his hand, saying in English, "How are you, Inspector X? We've been waiting a long time," which the Lt. translated . . . [The entire conversation was translated by Lt. Q.] I was introduced to X. He was about 5 feet, eight inches tall, very thin, dark brown hair, dark brown complexion, wore a mustache, in his mid-thirties, and was wearing a gun underneath his jacket. We sat down and X asked Bill how his trip to ——— was and Bill said, "It was very good; it's very nice to be back here. I don't have much time, so I'd like to get down to business." Then X said, "OK, what do you want to know?" Bill said, "I want to know how I can locate Z." X said, "I know about that, the main office telexed me about it. Do you have what was asked for from your agency?" Bill said, "Yes, I have the agreed upon sum. Do you have all the information on you?" X said, "You'll find everything in this envelope," and he took out a large manila envelope fools-cap size, about half an inch thick and passed it to Bill. Bill passed an 8-½" by 11" envelope folded in half over to X.

Bill then pulled out the papers from inside the envelope. It contained half an inch of typed material stamped secret and on top a picture of whom I assumed was Z. The guy in the picture had long hair, shoulder length. He had a mustache, he was well dressed. Caucasian, about twenty-nine years old.

Then X opened up his envelope and pulled out two half-inch packs of paper-banded U.S. currency, leaving two more in the envelope. One stack was of hundred dollar bills. The other was fifties; all new currency. X put the money back in the envelope and stuck it in his inside coat pocket, finished his coffee, and left.

Even though the facts of our informant's story speak for themselves, their full significance is open to interpretation. Although we were unable to find out any more about the incident, one inescapable fact is that in spite of its denials, Interpol does have dealings with the CIA.

We can only speculate as to the extent of Interpol's role in the war on drugs. It cannot be denied that there have been specific cases of corruption within Interpol and within the agencies affiliated with it. That there are connections (possibly innocent) to those who control drug traffic cannot be denied. That Interpol has proved to be woefully inactive in attempts to halt drug traffic, particularly in its own backyard, is obvious. The questions raised by these situations certainly merit serious investigation by the citizens of the governments concerned.

We're particularly interested in seeing if the [Inter-pol] office in Washington was used for political pur-poses.

——SENATOR JOSEPH M. MONTOYA,
Chairman of the Senate Committee on Appropriations

SS Untersturmführer Paul
Dickopf (SS #337259) in
training for the
Sicherheitsdienst (SD),
1939. Dickopf was later to
serve as President of
Interpol, 1968–72. [BERLIN
DOCUMENT CENTER.]

Internationale Kriminalpolizei

Einziges offizielles Publikationsorgan der

Internationalen Kriminalpolizeilichen Kommission

Deutsche Ausgabe

(Französische Ausgabe „Police Criminelle Internationale"; englische Ausgabe „International Criminal Police", italienische Ausgabe „Polizia Criminale Internazionale")

Polizeipräsident Otto Steinhäusl †

Gestapo Colonel Otto Steinhäusl, President of Interpol 1938–40, pictured on the cover of the commemorative issue of the Interpol magazine, July 10, 1940. [U.S. NATIONAL ARCHIVES.]

SS Gruppenführer Reinhard Heydrich, chief of the German security police and President of Interpol from 1940 until his assassination in 1942. [U.S. NATIONAL ARCHIVES.]

Ernst Kaltenbrunner, who succeeded Heydrich as both head of the German security police and President of Interpol. He was executed in Nuremberg on October 16, 1946. [U.S. NATIONAL ARCHIVES.]

Streng vertraulich, nur für Behörden.

Jahrgang VII   Berlin, 29. Februar 1944

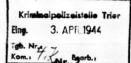

Internationale Kriminalpolizei

Einziges offizielles Publikationsorgan der

Internationalen Kriminalpolizeilichen Kommission

Deutsche Ausgabe

(Französische Ausgabe: „Police Criminelle Internationale"; englische Ausgabe: „International Criminal Police";
italienische Ausgabe: „Polizia Criminale Internazionale")

Eigentümer, Herausgeber und Verleger:

Die Internationale Kriminalpolizeiliche Kommission, vertreten durch ihren Generalsekretär, Hauptschriftleiter
Wirkl. Hofrat, Regierungsdirektor Dr. Oskar Dreßler, Berlin-Wannsee, Am Kleinen Wannsee 16
Bankverbindung: Deutsche Bank Depositenkasse H 2, Berlin-Zehlendorf, Teltower Damm 5
Creditanstalt-Bankverein, Wien I-1, Schottengasse 6
Fernsprecher: Berlin 80 62 14   Telegramm-Adresse: „Point Berlin"

Redaktionskomitee:

Hauptschriftleiter und nach dem Preßgesetz verantwortlich:

Dr. Oskar Dreßler, Wirkl. Hofrat, Regierungsdirektor, Generalsekretär der Internationalen Kriminalpolizeilichen Kommission, Berlin

Mitglieder des Redaktionskomitees:

Dr. Eugen Bianu, Vizegeneraldirektor der öffentlichen Sicherheit, Bucuresti

Jean Félix Buffet, Directeur des Services de la Police de Sûreté, Vichy (Etat français)

M. C. van Houten, Kolonel der Kon. Marechaussee b. d., Commissaris van Rijkspolitie, Leiden (Holland)

F. E. Louwage, Inspecteur general, Bruxelles

Werner Müller, Oberst, Chef der Sicherheitspolizei und Kriminalpolizei der Stadt Bern.

Arthur Nebe, Generalleutnant der Polizei, Direktor des Internationalen Büros, Berlin Reichskriminalpolizeiamt

Dr. Hans Palitzsch, Kriminalpolizei-Präsident a. D., Dresden

Dr. Antonino Pizzuto, Commissario-Capo di Polizia, Ministero dell'Interno, Roma

Dr. Bruno Schultz, Polizeivizepräsident a. D., Wien

unter Mitarbeit anderer Mitglieder der Internationalen Kriminalpolizeilichen Kommission sowie hervorragender Mitglieder der Polizeibehörden
verschiedener Staaten

Die Zusammenkunft von Mitgliedern der IKPK. in Wien (22.—24. November 1943).

Im Verlaufe der ersten Sitzung hatte der Generalsekretär der IKPK folgenden Rechenschaftsbericht erstattet:

A) Rechenschaftsbericht über die Geldgebarung.

Vom 1. Januar 1943 bis 31. Oktober 1943 sind im Sinne des Beschlusses VIII der Berner Tagung — 1928 — folgende Beiträge eingelangt:

Dänemark	RM	223.58
Bulgarien	RM	1.790.19
Spanien	RM	1.382.20
Finnland	RM	208.56
Ungarn	RM	1.048.10
Italien 4.500 sfr.	RM	
Rumänien	RM	676.32
Schweiz	RM	180.39
Belgien	RM	1.279.06
Slowakei	RM	612.42
Schweden	RM	349.26
Deutsches Reich	RM	7.787.—
Norwegen	RM	168.64
Bulgarien	RM	357.30
	RM	**16.063.02**

Von sonstigen Einnahmen der „Internationalen Kriminalpolizeilichen Kommission" sind
als Abonnement auf die „Internationale Kriminalpolizei"   RM   536.84
eingegangen.

Von den Geldern der Kommission wurden im gleichen Zeitraum verwendet:

Insgesamt   RM   10.040.89

Der Kreditsaldo der „Internationalen Kriminalpolizeilichen Kommission" beträgt:

Tägliches Geld	RM	12.985.14
Festgeld (vierteljährlich)	RM	5.140.—
Festgeld (jährlich)	RM	31.014.50
	RM	**49.139.64**

und 4.500 sfr.

B) Bemerkenswerte Vorkommnisse seit dem Zeitpunkte der XIV. Kommissionstagung in Bukarest.

(7. bis 12. Juni 1938.)

a) Oberste Leitung der IKPK.

In der Präsidentschaft der IKPK. sind folgende Veränderungen eingetreten:

1938 Antritt der Präsidentschaft durch den neuen Polizeipräsidenten von Wien Otto Steinhäusl.

1940 Steinhäusl gestorben am 20. Juni 1940. (Nr. 7/40 IKP.)

Nach dem Tode Steinhäusls wurde von den IKPK.-Mitgliedern einstimmig der Chef der Deutschen Sicherheitspolizei und des SD. in Berlin, SS-Gruppenführer

The February 29, 1944, cover of the International Criminal Police Commission's magazine. It lists the commission's permanent officials as well as the countries that had contributed in 1943. The issue featured a November 1943 Interpol meeting. On page 2, the FBI was listed as one of the representatives from countries that had joined Interpol in 1938. [U.S. NATIONAL ARCHIVES.]

Washington: The 29th General Assembly of Interpol, October 1960. Shown at the first session (*left to right*): A. Gilmore Flufs, Assistant Secretary of the Treasury and head of the U.S. delegations; Marcel Sicot, Secretary General of Interpol; and Allan Dulles, Director of the CIA. [UPI.]

Frankfurt: September 1972. At the 41st General Assembly of Interpol a new president was elected. *Left to right:* former President Paul Dickopf, who was also former President of the German Federal Office of Investigation; the new Interpol president, William Leonhard from Canada; and Interpol's Secretary General Jean Nepote. [UPI.]

Ray Kendall of Scotland Yard,
who now manages Interpol's
drug section in Saint-Cloud.
[BERT SCHWITTERS.]

U.S. Secret Service agent
Louis B. Sims, chief of the U.S.
Interpol office in Washington.
[U.S. TREASURY DEPT.]

An Interpol official examining a
file in the criminal files section
at Interpol's Saint-Cloud
headquarters. [BERT
SCHWITTERS.]

Interpol employees at
Saint-Cloud working on a small
portion of the more than two
million individual card files
kept on citizens from more than
a hundred nations. [UPI.]

A partial view of Interpol's
communications room. In an
age of high-speed
transmissions, Interpol still
uses the Morse code system for
its radio network. [UPI.]

Interpol's General Secretariat headquarters, which overlooks
the River Seine at Saint-Cloud, France. [UPI.]

The Interpol symbol at the
organization's headquarters in
Saint-Cloud. O. I. P. C. and
I. C. P. O. are the French and
English initials for
International Criminal Police
Organization. [UPI.]

Chapter Seven

POLITICAL MEDDLING

During the early morning hours of October 28, 1976, a small, determined group of Spanish Basques crossed the railway lines behind Interpol's seven-story headquarters building in Saint-Cloud. Unseen by the security guards who were at the front of the building, they entered the garden, reached the back wall, and did what they had come to do.

A few hours later, a powerful bomb exploded, damaging several offices and shattering every pane of glass in the building. No one was injured.

A telephone caller who said he represented "a group of Spanish ex-prisoners" told the Paris daily newspaper *France-Soir*, "Interpol must pay because of the support it gives to the Spanish Government in the repression of opponents of the regime."[1] Basque separatists had often charged that Interpol agents habitually aid Spanish authorities in tracking down Basques for "political crimes."

Interpol's Article 3 states: *It is strictly forbidden for the Organization to undertake any intervention or activities of a political, military, religious, or racial character.* There are no provisions for the punishment of members who violate the In-

145

terpol constitution. The organization's by-laws do not give the group the right to expel any of its members, nor does it give it the power to penalize its members for infringements. If a member attempts to violate Article 3, all the General Secretariat in Paris can do is either to caution them verbally and/or to refuse to pass along the requested information. The judgment of what constitutes political, military, religious, or racial matters rests basically with the General Secretariat in Paris or with the chiefs of the NCB's in the various countries. In many cases, enquiries are directed solely between the NCB's in two countries and don't even go through Saint-Cloud. The Interpol headquarters gets copies of only about three-fourths of the transmissions between NCB's.

The practical application of Article 3 is somewhat different from the stated ideal. It is built upon foundations of arbitraries. During an interview on December 12, 1975, Secretary General Jean Nepote admitted that there was no clear-cut line when it came to the judgment of Article 3 matters, and that each instance had to be individually adjudicated.

In 1962 the West German magazine *Der Spiegel* published an article by its editor, C. Ahlers, which stated that the West German armed forces were entirely inadequate. The outraged West German authorities responded by raiding the magazine's offices, allegedly seizing classified documents and arresting several of the editors on charges of treason. The incident developed into a political controversy, giving rise to charges of Nazism in the government and resulting in the resignation of several government officials.

Ahlers was vacationing in Spain when the controversy erupted. Spanish authorities arrested him after German authorities requested the assistance of Interpol, but in the ensuing fuss, Interpol headquarters in France denied having transmitted the request. *Der Spiegel* published the Interpol telex from the German Federal Police and publicized this political violation of Article 3.

In 1962, when Dr. H. Krug, the West German rocket expert, was reported missing, West German police requested Interpol assistance. This was a political matter.

In 1969 Mr. R. Brown, Colonial Parliament Member, Bermuda, charged that the FBI, CIA, and Interpol were at Bermuda Airport, pointing out delegates attending a four-day international Black Power conference there. If true, this is a violation of Interpol rules on both race and politics.

In mid-1976, during one of West Germany's many spy scandals, Interpol was called in after Ministry of Foreign Affairs secretary Helge Berger was arrested for being an East German spy. West German police used Interpol to hunt for Berger's main contact man, Klaus Wöhler.[2] So much for Article 3. It's not surprising that West Germany has the largest Interpol NCB in the world. They need it.

Another violation was reported in the reputable French periodical *Le Droit de Vivre* in October, 1975. The article recounted that members of the Association Against Racism–Anti-Semitism had demonstrated in July, 1975, in front of the offices of Kurt Lischka, former chief of the Gestapo in Paris, who, although accused of war crimes, lives in liberty in France. As requested by the German authorities and Interpol, officials of the Third Brigade of the Judicial Police in France later entered the homes of the demonstrators to investigate them and obtain their fingerprints. None of the demonstrators had previous criminal records. Unless, of course, one wants to count the prison sentence of Mme. Drach in Auschwitz and Bergen-Belsen a few decades before.

The real potential for abuse in the political arena can be seen in the case of Portugal, where "terror chief" Colonel Fernando C. de Silva Pais also happened to be one of Portugal's Interpol delegates. Silva Pais controlled the hated and feared Nazi-trained political police network, the Directorate General of Security (DGS).* When the new military junta took over in April, 1974, Silva Pais, the director general of security, was at the top

---

* Also known as the PIDE (International Police for the Defense of the State).

of the wanted list. One lieutenant was quoted in the London *Evening Standard* as saying of the DGS, "Their training school should be kept as a museum like Auschwitz. When I went into their school I found an album of pictures of their victims. They kept that album for the pleasure of looking at it like other people keep family pictures. They are not men—they are beasts."[3] The DGS had a mania not only for pictures of torture victims but for pornography. "The place is full of the stuff," said one lieutenant. That the man responsible for such atrocities should be trusted to abide by Article 3 is an absurdity. It also brings up the question of the validity of the credentials of other so-called criminal investigative police from totalitarian countries who grace Interpol's membership list.

Considering that Interpol's member police forces cover the political spectrum and have been trained by Nazis, Russians, Chinese, and Americans, it would not be unjustified to suspect that just a little intelligence-exchange takes place.

The policy that makes Interpol an ideal ground for intelligence agents can be seen in the 1958 Treasury report to the House, when legislation was passed to allow Treasury's membership in Interpol. The report discusses the many law enforcement problems since 1951 requiring international cooperation, chief among them being the narcotics traffic. Treasury claimed that the most effective way to ensure action was to send American agents abroad to collaborate with foreign police.

"It is quite obvious that the matter of sending agents to foreign countries is a most delicate arrangement," the report reads. "Through Interpol membership American agents, instead of appearing as obtrusive outsiders, would be working as fellow members of a recognized organization. As a matter of course they would be entitled to such information as the Organization would gather . . ."[4]

In the interests of hypothesis, substitute any country for "America," and "intelligence agents" for "agents," and one can see an added benefit of membership in the Interpol organization.

It may be that the U.S. Government planned to use Interpol

for intelligence purposes, because in 1959 a special subcommittee of the House Judiciary Committee prophetically reported that

finally, it is conceivable, in the light of world conditions, that the forms of government existing in the participating countries, could be replaced or modified and even overthrown by ones with ideologies in conflict with our own and that they, in turn, could seek to use Interpol for their own devious means. It is therefore recommended that the Treasury Department make timely reports to the Attorney General, the Departments of State and Defense, in order that the branches of our Government charged with the Nation's security may study its work for evidence which in their opinions, could have a bearing on security matters.[5]

As with most political documents, the prose is open to interpretation, and the ambiguous final phrase could have in effect been asking Treasury to report to the CIA and the armed forces intelligence services, so that they could not only watch for Interpol's use as an intelligence conduit but use it as such themselves.

It became evident during the U.S. hearings that Interpol officials at the Washington NCB have little knowledge of what goes on at Saint-Cloud and even less of what is happening at other NCB's.

Intelligence is a multifaceted field that ranges from passing along secrets to inserting false information to discredit opponents, as practiced by the KGB with its *dezinformatsiya* (disinformation), and by the CIA with its planting of newpaper stories, infiltration of radical groups, and so on.

The General Accounting Office's 1976 report on U.S. involvement in Interpol said that, "In some countries, the alliance of foreign police systems with the *intelligence branches* certainly does not preclude the sharing of such information." During visits to foreign NCB's, GAO investigators were as-

149

sured that information provided by the United States to recipient countries was restricted to police channels, but, they said, "there is no practical way to insure this is the only use made of the information."

Interpol, as was pointed out during U.S. Congressional hearings of the Senate Subcommittee of the Committee on Appropriations in 1975–76, is ideally set up to be a para-intelligence network.[6] It would come under the category of "para-intelligence," as it supposedly does not conduct any investigations itself but acts as the middleman between police departments in various countries. To obtain information, a police department sends its investigative requirements to Interpol in France or directly asks the NCB in the country from which it seeks data. One high-ranking Interpol official in France, Jean-Jacques Marc, explained in a September, 1971, article in *World Survey* that "Asked to check whether Mr. X did indeed stay at the Beach Hotel from 5th to 9th January, the low-ranking detective in Pizagu [Chile] or the constable in Dunedin [New Zealand] is perhaps unaware that he is acting as a genuine 'Interpol Agent.'"

When we asked if Interpol had ever worked with the CIA, Secretary General Nepote emphatically replied, "Never."

"I am wondering how we could be infiltrated by the CIA," Nepote said irritably. "What does it mean? Does it mean that in this building some officers are agents from CIA? I must say that I don't know. Because if they are, they will not come in my office and say, I am an agent from CIA . . ."

During the May, 1975, Senate hearings chaired by Senator Montoya, Nepote's attitude reflected Interpol's lack of concern that intelligence operatives could be using its facilities. "We have never encountered this problem, and we have never had any reason whatsoever even to suspect any employee of being an intelligence agent. In addition, every non-police employee at the General Secretariat is required to sign a declaration that he (or she) will maintain professional secrecy concerning all matters that come to his knowledge in his daily work."[7]

No security checks are required for the police, active or retired, at Saint-Cloud.

In the same hearings, Senator Joseph Montoya, chairman of the Senate Committee on Appropriations, asked Louis B. Sims, head of the U.S. NCB, if there were any rules regarding employees at Saint-Cloud acting as agents or spies for foreign countries. Sims said he had discussed employees with Nepote, Nepote's deputy, and Nepote's number-three man, and that "in general conversation, it appeared that he was just about as aware of this as we are here, of their criminal history, of their possibility of being an agent for another country, this type thing."

Nepote's other line of defense regarding the possible infiltration by intelligence agencies is that there is no need to infiltrate because "everything we do . . . it's open to police forces which are members."

In 1975 Senator Montoya asked Sims, "Have you transmitted any information to the CIA with respect to a certain individual here in this country?"

Sims replied: "No, sir. The CIA, though, Mr. Chairman, as you know, is not a law enforcement agency. I do not believe they make any arrests to my knowledge. They are an intelligence agency. Therefore, our paths do not cross, because we are not an intelligence agency."

In 1975 the National Commission on Law Enforcement used the Freedom of Information Act to request the CIA to provide material regarding its ". . . policies toward, work with, funding of and/or cooperation with Interpol, both within the U.S. and abroad."*

*The Freedom of Information Act was first signed into law on July 4, 1966, by President Johnson and took effect one year later as Public Law 93-502 and is part of the Federal Code 5 USC 552. The purpose of the Act was to make government records, with some exceptions such as military secrets, available to the public. Uniquely, the burden of proof as to why documents should not be released falls upon the agency and no argument need be presented by any requestor why he should obtain them. Movements are growing to institute similar laws in Canada and the United Kingdom.

151

The Agency refused to release any of its documents, and early in 1976 the NCLE filed suit against the CIA. In an affidavit before the U.S. District Court in Los Angeles, Charles A. Briggs, chief of CIA's Services Staff, admitted that he had eleven documents that appeared to be responsive to the FOIA request. Briggs also admitted that the documents contained "(1) information concerning intelligence sources and methods, (2) information concerning intelligence operations and (3) information the release of which could result in significant impairment of a program or policy related to the national security."

All of the documents, Briggs said, contained information concerning deliberations regarding *means by which Interpol collects intelligence abroad and describes intelligence sources and methods* (authors' italics). They also contained the names of CIA employees.

"Release of such information," Briggs said, "would inhibit internal governmental communications and force government officials to operate in a 'fishbowl.'"

Assistant U.S. Attorney James Stotter II, in his first statement to the court, mistakenly revealed further shattering information. He said that "Since disclosure of the documents would reveal that this government had cooperated with Interpol in the collection of intelligence, the possibility of maintaining that relationship, or others like it vital to the national security would be impaired. Additionally, the other government in this case would be embarrassed, and our foreign relations with that government consequently disrupted, if it were officially acknowledged that it cooperated with the CIA. No nation makes such public disclosures."

In essence, what Stotter let slip was that Interpol was being used as an intelligence conduit between the CIA and a foreign government or intelligence agency. Apparently, the CIA realized the significant nature of his remarks as well, for Stotter later changed his statement and explained to the court that "the error was mine and only mine. My preparation was a patchwork job. I took a section from another case and placed it in this one."*

The contents of the eleven memos and letters in question, which were written between 1971 and 1973, involved the State Department, the Department of the Treasury, and the Foreign Intelligence Subcommittee of the Cabinet Committee on International Narcotics Control (CCINC). A name that featured prominently in some of the documents was that of CCINC chairman Egil Krogh, Jr., assistant to John Erlichman, Nixon's special assistant for domestic policy. Krogh was also head of the inept "plumber's unit" involved in the Watergate break-in.

In February, 1976, the subcommittee heard the story of John Carlyle Herbert Bryant, Jr. Bryant had arrived in Washington after six years of selling cars and yachts in Virginia and Florida. He was appointed an assistant to White House press secretary Ron Zeigler in 1970. Nine months later he became special assistant to Nathaniel P. Reed, assistant Interior Department Secretary. Bryant's meteoric rise was due in part to his listing among his references Charles G. (Bebe) Rebozo; the mysterious Florida businessman and banker, and President Nixon's close friend. On February 20, 1973, Bryant moved into Interpol. His title was Confidential Assistant to the Deputy Assistant Secretary for Enforcement, Tariff Affairs, and Operations. Bryant was hired by Edward L. Morgan, the Assistant Secretary of the Treasury, whose responsibilities included overseeing Interpol. That same year, Morgan was elected to a three-year term as a member of Interpol's Executive Committee, but he was unable to complete the term, since he had to spend time in prison in 1975 for conspiracy to create a fraudulent tax deduction after back-dating the deed conveying

---

* Late in 1975 a reliable source informed us that the State Department was selectively shredding files dealing with Interpol from 1969 back. We were unable to confirm or deny the information elsewhere, but our FOIA requests for documents to that agency (which has assisted in the U.S. liaison with Interpol since 1945) produced only a few dozen pages, a surprisingly low quantity, particularly when compared to the approximately 50,000 pages produced by the Justice Department.

Nixon's gift of presidential papers to the National Archives. Morgan's place on Interpol's Executive Committee was taken in 1974 by H. Stuart Knight, Director, U.S. Secret Service.

At the Senate Committee hearings, the NCB chief at the time, Kenneth Giannoules, told Montoya he did not feel Bryant was qualified for the law enforcement job. "He therefore handled the non-enforcement type work, the public service type work that the office gets involved in, such as notification of the next of kin of American citizens who have died abroad." Bryant was paid a salary of $24,247 for this clerk-type activity—the second highest salary in the NCB.

Bryant left Interpol after about eleven months. When contacted by Washington columnist Bruce DeSilva and asked to comment on Montoya's concern that Interpol could have been used for political purposes, Bryant, working in Palm Beach, Florida, on the sheriff's department's vice squad, called it "paranoia."

In the United States, the use of the Internal Revenue Service for political repression, particularly during the Nixon years, has been well-documented, so it is unnecessary to go into details here. (It could also be argued that tax-evasion is not a criminal act as such, particularly in recent years, when it has become an act of philosophical and political protest on a grassroots level.) IRS liaison with Interpol, however, has been active for years. In 1973 and 1974, the Director of the IRS Intelligence Division attended Interpol meetings. Revenue Service people have also been representing the IRS at Interpol General Assemblies for many years. When asked about the close liaison between the IRS and Interpol, Secretary General Jean Nepote became very defensive. According to Nepote, the only connection Interpol has with the IRS is an interest in organized crime. "What happened in the past," he said, "is that we organized some symposiums, or two or three, about organized crime, the Mafia, the organized crime . . . and among the U.S. delegation there were (sic) a member of the Internal Revenue Service, not to investigate about the money which is sent from the United States, but to explain to us the mechanisms of the organized crime in the United States. And they never spoke of something else than the subject of the symposium."[8]

The IRS does not view its relationship with Interpol in the same light. A 1975 memorandum on "Internal Revenue Service Liaison with Interpol," stated that "The principal benefit to the Service, through Treasury's membership in Interpol, has been the receipt of information from participating foreign countries who have identified U.S. taxpayers engaged in illegal activities in those countries involving possible tax irregularities."[9]

In 1975 an American law enforcement officer based in Europe said, "I've been involved in cases where there was good reason to believe that political information was passed through Interpol and behind the Iron Curtain."*

On October 6, 1976, the London *Daily Telegraph* reported that the "Moscow Connection," which had led to the arrest of a number of Britons, Americans, and other Westerners accused of drug smuggling, was, in fact, due to Interpol, which had tipped off the Russian agencies. By the time this was revealed, four Britons had been arrested by the Russians that year. The latest was twenty-eight-year-old Donald Perkins, a painter and decorator, who was arrested at the beginning of August at Moscow Airport. He was subsequently sentenced to three years in a labor camp for smuggling nineteen packs of marijuana. His sentence is being served in a "general regime" camp, 250 miles from Moscow. Besides these four, seventeen other foreigners, including three Americans, were arrested in Moscow for attempted drug-smuggling the previous year. The Americans, Gerald Amster, Dennis Robert Burn, and Paul Brawer, were sentenced to eight, seven, and five years respectively. They appealed their sentences unsuccessfully in court and are now serving them.

British journalist S. A. Barram said that when he approached the diplomatic correspondent of the *Daily Telegraph*, the cor-

*Robert Walters, "Does Interpol Threaten Your Privacy?" *Parade*, Nov. 9, 1975.

respondent confirmed that the Soviet police had acted on Interpol notification. Another journalistic source told Barram that the Soviet Embassy had also confirmed the story. Barram contacted the Embassy himself and was informed that the law enforcement agencies in Russia do collaborate with Interpol *and that collaboration is reciprocal.*

"At this point in time," Barram said, "there is no conclusive evidence that, in fact, the Soviet Union uses Interpol for its own political ends, but it is a matter of international concern and probably will pose constitutional problems in the United States."[10]

Russia is not a member of Interpol, and British critics claimed that the collaboration from a police organization in the West with the Soviet police, which does not differentiate between political and property crime, is incompatible with the principles of democratic police procedures and justice.

According to *Børsen,* a Swedish newspaper, Interpol officials have estimated that "the whole Communist world will be part of the organization within ten years."[11] The new direction that Interpol is taking was further reiterated at the September, 1977, General Assembly meeting at Stockholm, when Carl Persson, former head of the Swedish national police and newly elected Interpol President, said, "I would like to have more channels to the Eastern bloc because only Rumania and Yugoslavia are members."[12] While Persson stated that combating international terrorism should not really be Interpol's concern, he did stress that international tourism demanded closer relations with Communist countries, something that already seems to be occurring, according to the head of the Austrian Interpol NCB in Vienna, Dr. Robert Koch,[13] who in February, 1977, boasted of successful cooperation on a routine basis with a number of Communist countries, including Czechoslovakia, Hungary, and Bulgaria.* Dr. Koch refused to expound on the frequency and nature of Interpol's relationship with non-

* Czechoslovakia and Bulgaria both pulled out of Interpol in the 1950s because of Interpol's involvement in political matters.

member Communist countries, but a senior Viennese journalist who has been covering Austrian police affairs for many years, pointed out some of the difficulties that Koch had failed to expand upon. "I've seen forged Communist documents where they were using an ordinary criminal matter as a front for political activity," he said. The incident involved a Hungarian who had allegedly killed his wife and fled to Vienna. Documents were supplied to Interpol Vienna, complete with fingerprints and photographs of the supposed scene of the crime. The young man, however, protested his innocence and claimed that he was merely being sought for fleeing Communist Hungary. A subsequent investigation by non-Interpol officials verified his story, and the Hungarian was granted asylum. The journalist said it was not unusual for Communist countries to charge political refugees with common crimes in order to seek their return.[14]

In 1959 Interpol planned to hold the Twenty-eighth Session of its General Assembly in Lahore, capital of Pakistan. The meeting, planned for November 19–25, was to be the first General Assembly outside of Europe and the first in Asia. Invitations were sent out in July, and more Americans than ever before were expected to attend, but suddenly the prospects soured. Pakistan announced that the Israeli delegation would not be invited or permitted to attend. All attempts to mediate the situation failed, and Interpol had no choice finally but to cancel the session and move the Twenty-eighth (Extraordinary) Session of the General Assembly to Paris from December 8–10, three days instead of the seven originally planned.

Hoover, who considered his distrust in Interpol thoroughly vindicated, pointed out in a memo to the Attorney General that the Pakistani position came about at the urging of the United Arab Republic and other Arab nations who were represented on Interpol. He said it appeared to be "far from a true international criminal police organization as represented."[15] A number of the delegates apparently agreed. A stormy discus-

157

sion was held during the Paris conference, but according to one military observer,* "This very delicate situation was diplomatically put to rest by Mr. Sicot, the Executive Secretary." †[16]

The 1959 conference was also noteworthy in that former SS officer Paul Dickopf was elected to Interpol's Executive Committee. He was to be Interpol's President before ten years had passed.

At the same meeting the Cuban delegate, Dr. Jorge A. de Castroverde, proposed that a last item of "Miscellaneous Subjects" be added to the agenda. After the unsuspecting conference accepted the proposal, the Cuban delegation proposed ratification of a resolution they had originally presented at Berne in 1949, which condemned violent and inhumane police methods and condemned the activities of the "brutal Batista police."[17]

According to Myles Ambrose, "This was to pave the way to have Cuban police officers of the Batista regime declared common criminals and returned to Cuba for alleged atrocities."[18] Brigadier General Penaat said, "This resolution, if accepted, undoubtedly would have been followed with a request for extradition of many officials who fled Cuba and found asylum in other countries, including police and other political refugees."[19] After argument on the proposal, the resolution was declared out of order by a vote of 40 to 2. Venezuela was Cuba's sole supporter.

When the United States submitted its invitation for the 1960 conference to be held in Washington, D.C., on October 10 through October 14, Cuba extended its own invitation and

---

*The United States was represented at the Paris meeting by three delegates and fourteen observers from such diverse institutions as the Navy, Army, Air Force, Post Office Department, Department of State, and Department of Health, Education and Welfare. The Department of Defense sent representatives to the General Assembly meetings as observers with no voting powers. Ostensibly the military's function was purely public relations. However, it does exchange information with Treasury and has wished on occasion to take a more positive part.

† Sicot was Secretary General and not Executive Secretary.

even offered to pay all delegates' expenses except for transportation. A vote was taken and the U.S. invitation was accepted 32 to 13.

In his progress report to the Assembly, Sicot mentioned that problems had been encountered with Jordan. Twice the country had decided to withdraw from the organization, but each time the decision had been revoked. He was pleased to announce that Jordan was still a permanent member of the organization. Colombia had ceased to collaborate with Interpol the year before as a result of the "internal reorganization of its administration," but Sicot announced that cooperation had resumed. On the subject of new members he mentioned that several African nations had recently or would soon receive their independence. "This freedom will not exempt them from international crime and they could hardly find a better means of cooperation, not only with other African countries but also other continents, that (sic) by becoming a member of an organization which has long ago proved itself and which scrupulously keeps out of politics."

Sicot also called for more NCB's to contribute statistics to Interpol, saying, "These would be of much use in defending any attacks which might be made by governments or other international organizations."

After the conference, the United States immediately began to make plans for the meeting in Washington. Agencies involved in the planning included Defense, ICA,* Justice, Office of Scientific Intelligence (OSI), State, and all of the Treasury agencies, plus the U.S. Coast Guard. The Department of Defense even contributed $2,000 to help defray expenses of the conference, as Treasury was unable to secure supplementary appropriations to finance the cost because of budgetary restrictions. However, the funds were "being procured from other sources within Treasury."[20]

Hoover's anti-Interpol sentiments had grown over the years,

*The International Cooperation Administration. The functions of the ICA were later taken over by the Agency for International Development in the State Department.

and regarding the U.S. invitation to Interpol, Hoover wrote in a memorandum to the Attorney General, who had sought his views, "You are well aware of my views concerning Interpol and I have clearly and in detail explained this position to Treasury officials in the past. In connection with Treasury's proposal to invite Interpol to hold its 29th General Assembly in Washington, D.C., in the fall of 1960, Mr. Myles Ambrose of Treasury was advised by my Liaison Representative that my position on Interpol was clear; that Treasury was the U.S. member; and its dealings with Interpol were strictly its own business." Hoover ended on the curt note that, "On the basis of the past record of this organization reflecting its lack of objectivity and its use for political purposes, it appears to be far from a true international crime police organization as represented. Consequently, it is regrettable that an invitation to convene in the U.S. is contemplated,* resulting in bolstering and adding prestige to a doubtful cause."[21]

The 1960 Washington conference was an enormous success compared to the Paris meeting of the previous year. President Dwight D. Eisenhower sent a greeting and called Interpol "a splendid example" of close cooperation between law enforcement authorities. The welcoming speech was made by Secretary of the Treasury Robert B. Anderson, and the meeting was notable for its lack of dissent, but the harmony was not to last long.†

At the 1961 General Assembly meeting in Copenhagen, a large segment of the discussion had a distinctly political bite. A

---

* In the years following his withdrawal from Interpol, other nations appealed to Hoover to forgive and forget and rejoin the group, but Hoover was not a forgiving man and he seldom forgot. Sanford J. Unger, in *F.B.I.*, describes a meeting between Hoover and Interpol's Washington representative (Treasury) at a social gathering years later. ". . . Hoover seemed unpredictably eager to engage him in conversation. 'Where are you located?' the Director asked in a friendly tone. When the Interpol man replied that his office was in the basement of the Treasury Department, Hoover snorted, 'Well, that's where you belong,' and walked away."

† Interpol's Secretary General Sicot met with CIA director Allen Dulles while in Washington. It is not known what they discussed.

proposal was made to increase membership fees 100 percent to meet the cost of a new Interpol headquarters building and to finance an expanded technical assistance program.

Interpol dues are assessed on a unit system that divides its members into groups. The United States, together with the United Kingdom, France, Italy, and Germany, is a Group 1 country. Budget units are expressed in Swiss francs. According to the Interpol Annual Report for fiscal year 1975, "In September of 1974, the Interpol 43rd Assembly voted an increase in the Interpol annual dues from 4,580 Swiss francs per budget unit to 5,900 Swiss francs per budget unit. The United States,* Germany, Italy, the United Kingdom, and France each pay 60 budget units, or the equivalent of 354,000 Swiss francs. Other member countries pay correspondingly less, depending mainly on the development of the country and their utilization of Interpol."

During the 1961 debates in Copenhagen, many delegations, particularly those from the newly independent and developing countries, threatened to drop out of Interpol if the fees were increased. The Assembly voted to postpone any action on the construction of new headquarters, and the proposed technical assistance program and the budget increase were put off for reconsideration the following year.†

* Soon after it first joined Interpol officially in 1958, Treasury paid $3,000 in dues. Because of inflation and currency fluctuations, the dues have increased steadily over the years. In 1973 the United States paid $80,000, and in 1974 the dues were raised again to $120,000. In 1976 the dues rose to $138,000, and in 1977 Treasury requested $155,000 for Interpol dues from Congress. The current U.S. dues represent about 6.2 percent of Interpol's total dues. The dues, however, do not fully reflect Interpol's total cost to the United States. In 1975, for instance, the total estimated cost of the U.S. operation of Interpol, including salaries, dues, communications costs, and so on, was $528,492—a shade over half a million dollars. When viewed against Treasury's total budget request for 1977 of $2.6 *billion*, however, this is indeed a small drop in a large bucket. But money is not really the question regarding continued U.S. participation in Interpol.

† At the thirty-first session of the General Assembly in Madrid in September, 1962, the budget increases brought up at the 1961 Copenhagen conference were passed, in spite of opposition and much discussion. A resolution to purchase land for the new Interpol headquarters was also approved. In 1963

Sweden then questioned whether Interpol headquarters should remain in Paris or even in France. Delegations from Morocco and Italy agreed to a proposal for a study of where the site would be located. According to Arnold Sagalyn, chairman of the U.S. delegation,* the concern behind the debate was that "a permanent site in Paris would prevent the Secretariat of the Organization from becoming more international in character, and might tend to make Interpol a French instrument."[22]

Sagalyn said the debate alarmed some delegations "because of its political nature and ramifications and because the majority of delegations felt that any indication at this time that the headquarters site would be taken out of France might endanger the whole future of the Organization."[23] The majority voted to keep the Interpol headquarters in France.

Ten new members were elected in 1961,† among them the Republic of China. Strong opposition to the Chinese membership was expected, but "advance preparations by the United States delegation resulted in arrangements being made with the Secretariat which served to preclude any preliminary discussion or debate on China's admission. In addition, the

---

the French Government authorized a loan to Interpol of four million francs to build the new Saint-Cloud offices. The twenty-year loan resulted in a seven-story office building, complete with telex, radio, and other facilities, which was inaugurated on May 26, 1967. Another amount of almost four million francs was raised by special donations from other members.

* In 1961 the Intelligence Division of the Internal Revenue Service joined the other three Treasury investigative bureaus as a participating agency, and Sagalyn of the U.S. Treasury was elected Vice-President for a three-year period.

† At this 1961 Copenhagen Conference on the Committee on Illicit International Gold, Diamond Watch and Watch Movement Traffic, the Swiss delegation took its traditional position that international watch-smuggling was not a criminal police matter, but rather a fiscal problem. The committee members were asked to decide if smuggling per se was considered a criminal act and whether it should be considered as a competent subject of discussion and assistance within Interpol. All committee members, except Switzerland, agreed that smuggling was a crime and that member nations should furnish assistance against smugglers. The Swiss delegate conceded that assistance *after* a seizure or arrest might conceivably by considered to be within the framework of Interpol cooperation.

United States delegation solicited the support of a large number of delegates in China's behalf."[24] The Republic of China's application was approved with thirty-two votes for, five countries against, and twelve abstentions.

The issue of skyjacking came up at the 1961 conference, but the Air Police Committee decided that since skyjacking was more political than criminal in nature, there was no purpose in pursuing the topic. Nevertheless, in 1969 the issue arose again. As a result of a request at an earlier meeting of the General Assembly, a confidential report was presented to the delegates and Dickopf proposed that it be accepted without further discussion. Several delegates objected to his attempt to strangle the discussion, but he insisted that the matter had been handled.* A vote was called for and Dickopf was sustained by a narrow margin.[26] The following year, 1970, the issue was brought up again and another confidential report was issued.[27] In spite of the epidemic proportions of skyjackings and other terrorist acts, as well as pressure to act from member countries, Interpol continued to refuse to take action, quoting their Article 3.

Finally, in 1972, after intense pressure from some of its members, Interpol passed a resolution that stated in part that

Considering that certain aspects of modern international criminality, such as the holding of hostages with the intention of perpetrating blackmail or other forms of extortion, have developed to the extent of constituting a severe menace to the life and safety of persons as well as the security of property: The I.C.P.O.—Interpol General As-

---

* Interpol's attitude toward skyjacking is ironic in view of what happened after the 1969 General Assembly meeting in Mexico City. While flying from Mexico to Miami, Interpol Secretary General Jean Nepote and a deputy were among thirty-six persons hijacked to Havana, Cuba. Strangely, *The New York Times* story on the hijacking on October 22, 1969, did not mention Nepote's name but said that two "Peruvian" Interpol officials were on the aircraft.[25] A source at the International Civil Aviation Organization (ICAO) told us, "The incident was most embarrassing and was quickly hushed up."

sembly . . . recommends that member countries take appropriate measures in order to prevent or suppress these forms of criminality, and cooperate among themselves utilizing existing machinery and services of Interpol, within the limits of Articles 2 and 3 of the Constitution of the Organization.

In 1972, when hijacking was still a major flight hazard, a British newspaper reported an Israeli fear that information on potential hijackers would rapidly be sent back to the terrorists by Interpol's Arab members.[28] It was not a surprising concern, as a number of Interpol members had actually offered asylum to terrorists and hijackers in recent years.

During a special three-day Interpol conference in Paris in 1975, called at the instigation of international aviation organizations to discuss the defense of airlines and airplanes against terrorist activity, participants expressed concern at the presence of several Arab delegations. One official involved in antihijacking security commented, "How the hell can information flow if it might get back to the terrorists?"[29]

Interpol's use as an intelligence conduit has been common knowledge for some time now. More than three years ago, a confidential source said he had seen evidence which proved that information on terrorist groups had been fed back from Interpol files to the very groups it concerned. Although our source was reluctant to provide us with details, his accusation was supported a year later in a book by Yeshayahu Ben-Porat, Eitan Haber, and Zeev Schiff.[30] Regarding the rash of terrorist aircraft hijackings, the authors said, "Israel also asked Interpol to help, and forwarded secret information to their Paris headquarters, only to discover that the Arabs had gotten hold of it and they in turn had passed it on to the terrorist organizations." They went on to say that in the fight against terrorism, "Experience has shown that Interpol, the international organization of police forces, is not the tool for the job."

Interpol is not regarded highly by the Irish either, both in

Belfast and Dublin. A top Irish police officer in Northern Ireland expressed extreme disgust with Interpol's inability to forward information on the movements of firearms and explosives. The harassed policeman explained that both Catholics and Protestants received heavy shipments of arms from foreign sources, particularly Libya. "Interpol only sends us information on drug shipments which don't even come here. Besides, we have no drug problem," he said.

In Dublin, one of our researchers interviewed an official of the Republic of Ireland's civil guard. He was in a hurry, as there had been a bombing in a Dublin pub only half an hour earlier, but he did find time to condemn Interpol as incompetent, and sneered at their communiqués as being infrequent and inept. The story was similar to that in the north. "They only touch on the subject of drugs which we have no use for in Ireland," he said.

Also in 1974, the London *Sunday Times* reported that "There is a danger that the Interpol network may be strangled by its problems and its lack of a sense of immediacy—ending any hope of coordinating international policy to cope with an upsurge of thuggery of the kind practised by the Red Army, the IRA and the Palestinian guerrilla groups."[31]

Interpol's ambivalent attitude toward terrorism has placed it in the unenviable position of trying to play both ends against the middle. On one hand, terrorism is "political," and thus to act against it would violate Article 3. On the other hand, terrorist acts often involve common law crimes against persons and property.

In 1973 Interpol came up with yet another powerful resolution. Taking note of terrorist acts and how they have the effect of "creating disregard for the law throughout the world to the great detriment of the objectives of Interpol and the member states," Interpol "URGES firm and resolute opposition to interferences with due enforcement of the law and observations of international obligations."

Just as the world's main drug activity takes place under the nose of the French police, world terrorism, too, is headquartered on Interpol's front doorstep.* It has been clear for some time that Paris has been the chief transaction point for the many and active terrorist groups and "liberation movements." According to a *Newsweek* article in 1975, Paris has been a clearinghouse for numerous terrorist organizations, such as the Irish IRA, the Japanese Red Army Group, the German Baader-Meinhof Gang, Ilitch Ramirez Sanchez, alias "Carlos," the Palestinians, and the Canadian Quebec Liberation Front, to name a few.[33] Even after expelling a number of Cuban diplomats as a link to Carlos and his band, French police privately admitted that "Paris remains a center of terrorist activity" and that the connection between the terrorists and Cubans—not to mention the possibility of a role by the KGB—raised ugly new possibilities for the future.[34]

For a number of years, Interpol has refused to aid in the search for wanted Nazi war criminals. For justification, they cited their Article 3, forbidding them to intervene in political, military, religious, or racial situations. The World Jewish Congress met in Geneva in August, 1961, and passed a resolution appealing to Interpol to stop classifying Nazi war crimes as "political" offenses. Aware of Interpol's General Assembly meeting in Copenhagen in September, spokesmen for the Congress approached Secretary General Sicot and urged him to bring up before the Interpol delegates the text of the resolution they had passed. Sicot's reply was that if Interpol was to maintain its efficiency against professional criminals, it would have to resist any pressure to "meddle" in matters of a political, military, religious, or racial character.[35] Interpol has continued to remain adamant on the matter of Nazi criminals, even in the face of arguments that Nazis had fled with stolen money, gold, and paintings and were traveling with false passports, all plainly

*On May 8, 1977, the State Department announced that there was an increase in world terrorism, and that Libya, Iraq, Somalia, and Yemen had given aid to terrorists.[32] All of those countries except Yemen are Interpol members.

criminal offenses. After the capture and trial of Adolf Eichmann in 1960–61, West German police intensified their efforts to bring other Nazis to trial, and even they complained publicly that their efforts were often hampered by Interpol's refusal of assistance.

Writing in the September, 1961, issue of *World Jewry*, S. J. Roth asserted that "when it classified Nazi crimes as falling under these categories Interpol was hopelessly wrong legally and also set up a dangerous political precedent." He said that in fact Interpol was bound neither by the terms of its constitution nor by the 1951 resolution of its General Assembly, "but simply by their erroneous interpretation on the part of its Bureau."

Roth went on to make an impressive legal case to support his assertions. He pointed out that the reason asylum was given to political offenders was to protect them from the vengeance of the government *against* which they have acted. There has never been a case, as with the Nazi criminals, where a criminal has claimed, let alone been granted, the privilege of political crime because he acted *according* to the policies or under the direct instructions of his own government. Military crimes customarily relate to desertion, espionage, or treason, and religious crimes to acts directed against religion, not just against people who happen to be members of a particular religious denomination. The fourth term, racial crime, if it is to be understood as race extinction, has been covered by the Genocide Convention of the United Nations, which stipulates explicitly in Article VII that this crime should not receive protection by refusal of extradition.

"If Interpol's attitude lacks any legal basis," Roth wrote, "it certainly does not lack undesirable political consequences. First, the Nazi criminals, knowing that the international police network is indifferent to them will be encouraged to come out of their hideouts and again take part in the activities of neo-Nazi movements. Secondly, the accusation of the Communist world that the Western countries harbor Nazi-Fascist criminals will, unfortunately, be justified in some cases. And last . . .

the world will be at a loss to understand why the police should be insensitive to crimes which the governments of their countries condemn."

Ladislas Farago said in 1976 that during his pursuit of Martin Bormann in South America, he established contacts with Interpol officials in Brazil, Argentina, Peru, Paraguay, and Chile. "In connection with my project," he said, "I had ample opportunity of ascertaining that they were, with the exception of the Chilean branch, actually protecting Nazi fugitives in South America, preventing rather than facilitating and/or expediting their apprehension and extradition . . .

"The result is that Interpol's protective curtain enables fugitive Nazis, including those tried in absentia and convicted by various member-nations of Interpol, to remain at large, not only unmolested, but actually protected and guarded by local police organizations in charge of aliens. In many South American countries, these police organizations either work closely with or function in personal union with Interpol."

Farago said that the most deplorable of these cases involved Dr. Josef Mengele, a criminal German fugitive living in Paraguay, and Klaus Barbie, alias Klaus Altmann, a Nazi war criminal sentenced to death in absentia by a French court in Lyons and now living in La Paz, Bolivia.

"Even when the extradition of Barbie-alias-Altmann was demanded, not by France on war criminal charges, but by neighboring Peru on a warrant issued by the Honorable Judge Dr. Luis Carnero Checa, on such purely criminal charges as currency speculation and smuggling, Interpol intervened to thwart his extradition and in support of the refusal of the Bolivian government to extradite Barbie," Farago said. "In a similar manner, the efforts of federal judge Dr. Jorge Luque of Buenos Aires, Argentina, to obtain the extradition of Dr. Mengele from Paraguay was staved off by the Interpol organizations in Argentina and Paraguay."

According to Farago, in 1976 Interpol and the German Federal Police had attempted to suppress publication of his book. Farago said that they tried not only "to discredit my book" but to "charge me falsely with fraud and forgery in connection with my documentation of the Bormann book . . ." The German publisher, Hoffman and Campe, refused to bow to pressure and published the book, but the Editions Auguste Fayard in Paris canceled their contract to publish. "Monsieur Alexandre Gall, president of Fayard, stated to me personally and unequivocally that he had been threatened with exposure and criminal action by members of the French secret police, based on material supplied by the *Bundeskriminalamt* via Interpol, if he proceeded with the publication." Farago added that he was willing to present details under oath, "to aid efforts aimed at the exposing of this aspect of an international organization with a notorious Nazi past which it is neither willing to repudiate nor prepared to erase completely from its current operations."[36]

At the 1976 hearings before the Senate Subcommittee on Treasury Appropriations, Assistant Secretary David R. Macdonald responded to allegations of Interpol's Nazi history as a "scurrilous attack," and said, "Probably the shortest refutation of this argument is the simple fact that Israel has been a fully participating member of Interpol since 1949."[37]

A high-ranking Israeli official said in a letter to Vaughn Young in 1976, "It is inconceivable that Israel's membership in Interpol at present can be construed as an endorsement of the 'Interpol' which was under Nazi domination and was actually operating as an official agency of the Third Reich."

He went on to say that as far as Interpol's inactivity regarding the hunting down of Nazi war criminals was concerned, "it would be inaccurate to state that Israel agrees with the present policy of Interpol.* In fact, this question did not arise in the last few years, and so we did not express our agreement with

*Suddenly, in December, 1976, the press announced that Pieter Nicolas Menten, a millionaire Dutch art collector who fled war-crimes charges in the Netherlands a few weeks before, had been arrested in Switzerland. Swiss police arrested Menten after a request was filed through Interpol by Dutch authorities. Interpol has not commented on its sudden reversal of policy, but perhaps it has something to do with recent media pressure regarding their Nazi history and previous inaction on similar matters.

the policy. Perhaps the source of the misunderstanding was the fact that we did not raise the subject in Interpol, and this was misinterpreted as tacit agreement. However, the reason that we did not raise this subject was due to other causes." He would not elaborate on the "other causes."

THE CARTLAND CASE

In March, 1973, John Cartland, sixty, a Brighton school-teacher, and his son, Jeremy, twenty-eight, took a well-deserved vacation in the south of France—a trip that became a nightmare, with only one of them left alive.

On the night of Sunday, March 18, the two Englishmen were asleep in their trailer near Pelissanne when Jeremy was awakened by a noise. He shook his father awake and went outside to investigate. Someone was sitting in the front seat of their car. He walked closer and was almost level with the car when he was struck on the head.

When Jeremy Cartland woke up, the caravan was in flames, he had knife wounds in his chest and stomach, and there was no sign of his father.

A passing traveler drove him to a hospital, where he was admitted. The next day, on instructions from the police, hospital officials told him his father was injured and had also been admitted. It wasn't until late in the afternoon, during the course of a police interview, that Cartland discovered that his father had been murdered.

The next day Cartland was taken to the police station for a nine-hour interview. It was a shock to find that, instead of being treated like a bereaved son, he was treated like a criminal. The interview was conducted on traditional lines, with one policeman aggressive and one sympathetic. They accused him of killing his father. They called him a homosexual and a sadist. Then they suggested that his father was homosexual and that Cartland had killed him in a parricidal rage when he discovered it. "Most of the interview was along the lines of 'confess,

170

confess,' " Cartland said. Finally, after the help of the British Consulate and some lawyers, Cartland was released.

Cartland's ordeal did not end there. He had to return to France three times for hearings. On the third trip back he had his first experience with Interpol. Between his first and second appearance before the Magistrate, Cartland had his wounds examined in London by a Home Office pathologist, Professor Cameron. During the third hearing, just before lunch the Magistrate drew Cartland's lawyer aside and told him he had documentary evidence from Interpol confirming that Cartland was a liar and that they "shouldn't take any notice of what [he] said." Cartland tells what happened: "The afternoon session had started and Delmas [the Magistrate] reached dramatically into his desk drawer and read out the message from Interpol in which Professor Cameron was said to have described me as 'a liar who could not be trusted.' He even phoned the Interpol man in our presence to confirm the authenticity of the report."

But Cartland's lawyers had been busy during the lunch hour. "Then the news was telephoned through from London: Professor Cameron indignantly denied ever writing any such report on me. He was a pathologist, not a psychiatrist and no English doctor would dream of making such a statement."

Cartland's explanation of how the Interpol report came about is a disturbing example of irresponsibility and incompetence. Apparently a newspaper reported that Cartland had asked Professor Cameron to do a new autopsy on his father's body. Cameron saw this while he was having a cup of tea at Scotland Yard and said, "Bloody cheek. No one asked me to do anything officially. That's not true."

"Somehow that got distorted around," Cartland said. "It found its way to Interpol who telephoned it to the Magistrate and then sent a report."

How it ended up with Cameron calling Cartland a liar who could not be trusted is beyond belief.

The hearing ended with Cartland's lawyers hotly accusing Interpol and the French police of trying to frame him.

171

Although the murderers of Jeremy Cartland's father were never brought to justice, another story began to emerge.

John Cartland had worked with British Intelligence, MI-5, during World War II, with the Free French. He was also the first intelligence man to enter Gestapo headquarters in Brussels, where he found a list of French and Belgian collaborators. He claimed to have burned the list because he felt there had been enough bloodshed, but the murder opened up the possibility that the list was still in existence.

Officials admitted that Cartland's wartime activities may have been connected to his death. Also, his murder was seen by some as tied to other unsolved "political assassinations." One London paper reported that investigators were working with a theory that "an international crime syndicate with [a] political background, reaching back to the last war," was behind the murder.

John Cartland's murderers have never been found. "All researches into my father's wartime involvement with the Secret Service by lawyers and journalists have met a blank wall, which suggests to the enquirers that there is something to hide," young Cartland said. "One of my Paris lawyers was told by a former contact of my father that if he knew what was good for him he would leave it alone."

Saddened by his experience with French justice and Interpol, Cartland said, "It seems that the spirit of Vichy, the mentality of collaboration, is still a powerful force among those in authority."

If everything the FBI has is in its NCIC computer, and Interpol links with that, then the whole world has this information.
     —*The Baltimore News American,*
     March 16, 1975

Chapter Eight

THE THREAT OF COMPUTERIZATION

Along with wine and fine food and, of course, the guillotine, one of France's greatest contributions to civilization is the dossier system, a French word and a French invention that has been copied all over the world. The accumulation of data on citizens, irrespective of innocence or guilt, has long been a French police practice.

Swiss historian Dr. Herbert Luth described the attitude of the French police in his book *The State of France:* "The prefecture of police, though it has no legal right to do so, openly assumes the right of collecting dossiers of damaging material about unsuspecting inhabitants of their city who have never been in the dock or even at the police station, based on gossip and information given by concierges or informers. The existence of these dossiers remains unknown to those whom they concern, and they have no opportunity of correcting them, because they are never aware of their contents."

Philip John Stead said in his book, *The Police of Paris,* that "all the elements of the totalitarian state are present in the unlimited and impenetrable sway of this police system. . . . with its 'perennial and insatiable curiosity' and its 'passion for the dos-

sier and . . . love of the technique of surveillance . . . ,' but
'. . . the police of every country, of course, are not as concerned as are the police of France with such matters of general intelligence.' "

In 1969 the Lebanese delegation submitted a report to the General Assembly "concerning the international character of the staff of the Interpol General Secretariat" in France. The report stated that the General Secretariat's "structure has remained unchanged since those early days when all the member countries were European." It noted that the General Regulation (Article 43) required that the Secretary General "should be a national of the country in which the headquarters are situated" but also noted that most of the staff were also French. "As a result," the report said, "the General Secretariat does not really reflect the international and worldwide character of the Organization."

As a result of the Lebanese report, members proposed four amendments to the Interpol constitution. They would have required, among other things, greater representation at the General Secretariat and, significantly, diluted the power of the Secretary General by giving him more deputies of other nationalities and thus making him more answerable to the General Assembly. Of the four amendments proposed, only one passed. It was Article 30, which stated that the staff of the Secretary General "shall neither solicit nor accept instructions from any government or authority outside the Organization." It also said that members "shall undertake to respect the exclusively international character of the duties of the Secretary General" and do their best to assist him. The amendments requiring the hiring of non-French staff were killed.

In the same year the Lebanese proposal was beaten down, the Secretary General submitted an annual report that gave a statistical breakdown of the nationalities of the General Secretariat staff. Of the sixty-six police and civil servants on loan, forty-three were being paid for by Interpol. The report said that "among the police officers are one German police officer, one British, one Canadian and one Swedish. Their services are valuable to us." The report also said that the Executive Committee was studying the problem of "internationalization of Secretariat staff. It will continue its study next year."

In spite of the Executive Committee "studies" done since 1969, a more recent view shows that Interpol has done little to take on non-French personnel. The question of Saint-Cloud personnel was raised by the United States in May, 1975, during Senate hearings before the Subcommittee on Treasury Appropriations. U.S. Interpol officials sought the requested information from Nepote, who claimed that "current workload precludes compiling detailed list" of personnel.[1] However, he did send enough information to show he is still keeping Saint-Cloud and Interpol a French operation. Nepote said that "Most of the General Secretariat staff members are police officers either on active duty or recently retired from active duty . . ."[2] Of the 155 persons then employed at Saint-Cloud, 122 of them were French—about 80 percent.* In a later interview, the Secretary General explained the high number of French personnel: "We have a rather big amount of French [personnel here] because we are in France and I must say they are not more clever than others, but they are cheaper."[3]

The most striking evidence of Interpol's unique status with the French Government exists in the larger number of documents detailing an agreement that was to legalize the status of the organization in France and passed into law on December 12, 1972, although there is no public record of the final vote by the membership.

The bill's (*Projet de Loi*) wording makes it quite clear that France does not regard Interpol as the standard international, "intergovernmental" organization.

---

*Interpol's domination by, and involvement with, French officials has been studiously ignored by U.S. and British officials, publicly at least. One confidential source told us, however, that Myles Ambrose, chairman of the U.S. delegation to Interpol in 1960, "together with another Irishman, Sir Richard Jackson, head of the CID at Scotland Yard, contrived to break the Gallic stranglehold on Interpol. With Ambrose's help, Jackson succeeded in getting elected as President of Interpol."

In a "Statement of Motives," the nature of the agreement was described: "Having taken into account the special character of the organization [Interpol], this agreement provides for regulations that are slightly different from those normally applied to international institutions. It enjoys protection of its goods and assets, facilities for its reunions and for its relationships with the member countries and exonerations regarding matters of taxes and customs, *but the inviolability of its localities and archives is not a complete one to the extent that it permits agents or officials of the [French] Republic, under certain conditions, to have access to them*" (authors' italics).

This is covered in Article 3 of Interpol's agreement with the French, which states that French agents cannot enter Saint-Cloud "except after having notified, reasonably in advance, the Secretary General of the organization or his deputy, or only on their demand."

The agreement is "designed to grant nothing more to Interpol than what is necessary for its strict administration and financial functioning." The French also granted Interpol the right to "close contracts, to acquire and alienate [sell] movables and real estate necessary for its activity, and the capacity to sue, according to the first article." Personnel are not granted any sort of diplomatic immunity. In short, Interpol is a private corporation, but it is treated almost like an international governmental agency. Interpol has been given just enough freedom to avoid immediate recognition as an arm of the French Government, but not enough movement to allow any true non-French control. The French consider Interpol a part of their Ministry of the Interior under the *Directeur Central de la Police Judiciaire* in the Third Bureau. The Ministry also houses intelligence and political police.

Interpol's "international" character dissipates rather quickly when one looks beyond its membership. France's generosity since 1946 has given it what every government's police agencies dream of—a foothold and a hand in the police files of more than a hundred countries.

In 1954, the French built a radio station on government land

and gave it to Interpol. The station was operated until 1969, when Interpol acquired a new, larger facility south of Paris with sixteen transmitters that could be operated by remote control from Saint-Cloud. The new operation used circuits that belonged to the French post office.

According to an Interpol report prepared in 1956, "the amount of help provided by the French Ministry of the Interior was evaluated at 72.8% of the true working expenses" of Interpol. A footnote added that another 84,000 francs had been provided by the Paris Police. This is not surprising in view of the SDECE's manipulative activities.

Not inappropriately, the dossier system was the brainchild of a criminal. François Eugène Vidocq was recruited in 1809 by the Prefect of Paris police, Baron Pasquier, after he had served a term in prison. Like today's police, who use "reprogramed" criminals as informants, the good Baron felt that he needed a thief to catch thieves, and he saw some good qualities in Vidocq. The ex-criminal did not fail him. Vidocq created a special detective bureau and, in the process, began the dossier system. Perhaps it was premature to call him an ex-criminal, because Vidocq was later accused of instigating a crime so he could uncover it, and he was removed from office in 1833. However, his work lives on. The dossier system is still going strong and the bureau he began still exists—the Sûreté.*

Interpol's files are its pride and joy. By June, 1974, the General Secretariat's files contained 2,142,700 cards on individuals (filed alphabetically and phonetically and cross-filed to dossiers), 114,406 fingerprint cards, and 6,024 photographs of

---

* Equally ecstatic about the dossier system were political regimes such as those of the Russian czars, who adopted it as an invaluable tool for control of the population. The Okhrana, the secret police predecessor of the GPU, had developed a filing system that, if eventually carried to the extreme, would have covered the entire population of Russia. The Prussians also adopted the system, and later, when the Nazis took power, they too found it an invaluable aid in the subjugation of the population. The police and intelligence community in the United States has been compiling files on U.S. citizens for almost a century.

highly specialized international criminals. In recent years there has been roughly a 10 percent annual increase in the size of these files. The disproportionate relationship between Interpol's name cards and its fingerprint files is curious, since presumably anyone who is arrested, and thus has a criminal record, has his fingerprints on record.

As one admiring foreign policeman said of the massive dossier system, when it was housed at the Palais de Justice, "Here was the great working tool of the French police system, a kind of giant memory. French police files were supposed to be the most thorough in the world.

"Anyone who has ever come to the attention of the police had a dossier and each dossier contained all the information available about its subject. These records were kept up to date by annotations supplied by detectives on matters that might turn out to be useful at some future date."[4]

Interpol's name files are indexed both alphabetically and phonetically, as befits an international organization where the name John might be Juan or Jan. The relatively small fingerprint section consists of full sets of prints as well as a single-print file where, for instance, only a single print has been left at the scene of a crime.

Interpol has three other filing systems, the facial files system, also called the *portrait parle* or "talking picture," the analytic index file, and the punch card file.

Based on bone and muscle structure, the facial files system is designed to overcome disguises and other subterfuges. The individual characteristics of the person's face and head are assigned a numerical code that, police say, even plastic surgery cannot disguise.

The analytic index uses a system of colored tags, each of which refers to a particular factor in the description of the subject. The index is divided into seventeen groups of characteristics, such as height, face, traits of character and vices, visible scars, probable race, and so on. Between the seventeen groupings and their colored tags are forms listing 177 different characteristics. Under "face," for instance, are listed "long," "narrow," "low-browed," "high-browed," "square," "round," and so on. The idea is that Interpol can get the description of a criminal that lists only a few of these characteristics and, by pulling index cards with colored tabs and putting them together, come up with a name and dossier.

The third system, the punch card file, consists of an index of punched cards. Each card refers to one element of a crime, and each hole indicates a dossier. When several of the cards are placed on top of each other and the holes begin to correspond, the staff can come up with dossiers of possible suspects who have used the same or similar *modus operandi.*

According to Secretary General Nepote, there is a record and file purging system based on the following guidelines: "a) The records and files on persons who have died are destroyed. b) The records and files on persons involved in minor cases are destroyed ten years after the date on which the last items are entered in the files. c) The files on persons implicated in major cases are micro-filmed twenty years after the date on which the last items are entered in the files, and the paper files are then destroyed; only the micro-filmed records are kept thereafter."[5]

Forever, one must presume. No mention is made of the fact that many of the files contain either investigations that have not resulted in convictions, although Nepote does admit that "It is impossible to keep statistics on the number of convictions resulting from cases handled through Interpol channels."[6]

Interpol claims that these complicated systems of filing can be used in minutes by its well-trained staff and that they have been extremely successful.

Norman Fowler, Home Affairs correspondent of the London *Times,* wrote in 1969 that although Interpol has succeeded in getting countries to cooperate in spite of political differences, "it seems unable effectively to focus world attention on international crime or make any great impact with policies to fight it."

On September 23, 1974, journalist Peter Burden of the London *Daily Mail* wrote that "Many policemen, including several British Chief Constables, feel that Interpol's underfunded and limited resources have been left behind by the fast-moving criminal." He added that Interpol's Cannes General Assembly that year was also the site of fury over shortcuts taken by "the more efficient police forces particularly British and American police to by-pass Interpol." Burden revealed that although 30,000 Interpol messages were sent to England in 1973, 95 percent of all police enquiries between the Continent and England were handled by police officers making direct phone calls, or visiting one another. "The Interpol messages too often remained at the bottom of the action baskets in local British police stations," he wrote. "Last year [1973] many replies from Britain to official Interpol inquiries took three to four months."

However, this is far short of Interpol's known record, where it took three years for an official in South America to get an answer to an enquiry. When it came, it was the wrong answer.[7]

International Secretary General of the International Police Association,* H. V. D. Hallet, sums up his reactions to Interpol in one phrase: "The most expensive collection of filing cabinets in the world!" He went on to say that as far as the problems of illegal immigrants and drugs were concerned, "the assistance we received from Interpol was valueless."[8]

Interpol has taken the responsibility for international crime statistics by virtue of its claims of efficiency and its unique position as the only coordinating international law enforcement body.

A perusal of General Secretariat reports for the past few years indicates that Interpol is more interested in presenting quantity of cases than quality. The final results of large amounts of activity are seldom mentioned. For instance, in 1972 Kenneth Giannoules, then head of the Washington NCB, said in the NCB's annual report that the previous year Interpol

---

*The International Police Association is more of a fraternal and professional organization, much like the International Association of Chiefs of Police. It maintains no criminal files.

had sent out circulars on more than four hundred stolen paintings. "No figures on the [recovery rate] were available, but it was low," he admitted.

The Drug Enforcement Administration, FBI, Customs, and, to a lesser extent, such agencies as the Secret Service and the Immigration and Naturalization Service, have offices in major cities around the world. The General Accounting Office's 1976 report said that "The tendency of foreign police and central bureaus is to try to obtain information through these agencies because they are considered faster, more flexible than Interpol in terms of the types of cases they handle, and more effective, at least in connection with providing information relevant to immediate investigatory matters." It went on to say that Interpol channels were used when U.S. agency contacts were simply not available, or when a world-wide canvass was necessary to locate a suspect, or to determine whether arrest records existed in several countries.

On the other hand, the DEA told the GAO investigators that generally DEA agents work on important narcotics cases and refer routine drug matters to Interpol for processing.

Communication between the various NCB's is conducted through Interpol's radio, cable, and telex networks. Interpol's "antiquated Morse radio network"[9] is able to reach less than half of Interpol's member police forces—fifty-six at last count in 1976. The operators use cable circuits to operate by remote control the sixteen powerful transmitters that are located on a site 130 kilometers south of Paris. Signals are flashed out to regional stations and through them to national stations. The network is split into seven zones: three in Europe and the Mediterranean, one in Africa, and the remaining three in South America, North America, and Asia-Oceania. For example, if Paris radios Tokyo, the message can then be relayed on to Manila, Seoul, Bangkok, Djakarta, Hong Kong, New Delhi, and Saigon, as necessary. Ideally, it takes about thirty minutes for a message to go from Djakarta to Brasilia. Djakarta sends the message to Tokyo in about six minutes, Tokyo to Paris in another six minutes, Paris to Buenos Aires, which is the regional station for South America, and Buenos Aires to Brasilia. That's roughly the speed for a high priority message when all other transmission is halted to allow its passage.

Interpol also has a radio teleprinter network, installed initially to link the central station with European stations carrying large amounts of traffic. Photo-telegraphic equipment is used to transmit fingerprints and photographs. The more costly telex facilities are not frequently used. When Interpol does use telex to communicate to its NCB in the U.S. Treasury Department, it uses the facilities of the American Embassy in Paris.

As police work often involves sending long sentences in a standard form, Interpol has code words to simplify message transmission. For example, SOPEF means: "Please send all relevant information you may possess or be able to acquire about this person. (If necessary) please include his photograph and fingerprints, details of any previous convictions and, if he is wanted, please let us know whether extradition is (will be) requested and under what conditions." DUDOL means: "Should this person be found in Europe, please detain him. In any other country, please keep watch on his movements and activities." There is also a far more complicated cipher code used for secret messages, but it is not used often. A noun code similar to the one above was issued by the Nazi Interpol during World War II and used by all branches of the Nazi police.

For requesting information from any NCB, the Interpol network uses a method involving what it calls "circulations" or "international notices." These notices are categorized by a square of color in one corner—either red, blue, or green. A red circulation is sent to all NCB's and instructs them to seek and arrest a criminal wanted by police in a particular country. It also ensures them that extradition proceedings will be instituted. This is also known as a "seek, hold, and deliver" order. A green notice alerts police to the whereabouts of an individual and warns them that he should be watched, even though he may not be wanted for a crime. A blue notice, according to one writer, "is a widespread inquiry for information about an offender from any country that knows about him from past activity or that can locate him and run down new information on actual *or potential* criminal activity" (authors' italics).[10]

Interpol's dossier system poses a grave threat, particularly in view of the French attitude that everyone is a potential criminal, guilty until *they* prove *their* innocence. American businessman Leon Steinberg, for instance, ran headlong into this problem while working in Europe.

In 1973, while in Spain, Steinberg discovered that he was the subject of an international blue notice, Number 500/59-A3674, which had been circulated to all of Interpol's NCB's. Apparently he was really an alleged criminal named Marc Moscovitz and Steinberg was just an alias. At the time, Steinberg corrected the matter to the satisfaction of the relevant Spanish authorities, but in 1975 he discovered that Interpol was still circulating the notice on him. Steinberg then wrote to Nepote, informing him that he was not Marc Moscovitz and asking that the blue notice be canceled. Nepote wrote back saying that the Spanish identification in 1973 was insufficient and he would have to establish beyond a doubt that Steinberg was who he said he was. Apparently the fact that the alleged criminal Moscovitz was born in 1904 and U.S. national Steinberg was born in 1935 was not enough to prove to Interpol that they had made a mistake. After protracted correspondence, Steinberg finally straightened out the matter in July, 1976, in Los Angeles, by having the Los Angeles police take his fingerprints so that the U.S. NCB could compare them to Moscovitz's. Interpol was finally assured of Steinberg's identity and sent a notice to NCB heads informing them that Moscovitz's alias of Leon Steinberg had nothing to do with this particular U.S. national.

Since 1973, the Interpol NCB in Washington, until its physical move from Treasury to Justice in March, 1977, contained a Treasury Enforcement Communications System (TECS) terminal for its use. TECS users include the U.S. Customs Service, IRS Intelligence Division, IRS Inspection Service, and the

Bureau of Alcohol, Tobacco and Firearms. TECS users also have access to the FBI's National Crime Information Center (NCIC).

According to the U.S. NCB's annual report for fiscal year 1975, The Federal Bureau of Investigation has granted the U.S. NCB access to the National Crime Information Center (NCIC). This access is granted pursuant to the guidelines established by the Federal Bureau of Investigation for the protection of individual's rights and covers only those records containing information of the following: 1. stolen securities 2. stolen motor vehicles 3. wanted persons 4. stolen boats 5. stolen license plates 6. computerized criminal histories.*

Effective January 1, 1975, investigative requests, All Points Bulletins and Wanted Circulars received by the U.S. NCB were entered into the Treasury Enforcement Communications System (TECS). Those pertaining to stolen property, All Points Bulletins, Wanted Circulars, and certain other criminal cases in TECS have been made directly accessible to Treasury law enforcement agencies, while the remaining, approximately 80% of all TECS entries made by this NCB, are directly accessible only to this NCB. No foreign police/Interpol Bureaus have access.

Among the benefits derived from TECS are more uniform indexing, retrievability of statistics and data, a suspense system for pending cases and for purging files when no longer required, prompt entry of All Points Bulletins and Wanted Circulars, continual updating of information entered, as well as location of criminals wanted by law enforcement in the United States. Through TECS, the National Law Enforcement Teletype System was utilized to communicate with local and/or state law enforcement agencies/departments and to place nation-wide lookouts.

*Individuals indexed in NCIC are only those persons for whom arrest warrants are outstanding or persons who have had substantial involvement, supported by fingerprint records, with the criminal police system.

During the period from January to June of 1975, a total of 2341 cases were entered into the TECS system, with 5138 individual entries.

In Fiscal Year 1975, the U.S. NCB received 2406 investigative matters from 71 other Interpol Bureaus and 645 investigative matters from U.S. law enforcement agencies/departments asking for investigations. During this same period of time, the U.S. NCB sent 641 investigative requests to 77 foreign NCB's and 4572 investigative requests to U.S. law enforcement agencies/departments and certain financial and/or other commercial institutions. The U.S. NCB assisted 120 foreign and U.S. police agencies in obtaining various types of information concerning police operations, organization procedures, equipment, and special categories of criminal enforcement.

Also commencing on January 1, 1975, the U.S. NCB began keeping statistics on the number of arrests and convictions, as well as the number of U.S. citizens included in the cases handled by the U.S. NCB. Dealing only with the period from January 1 to the end of June, 1975, out of the total 5138 individual entries into TECS, 1275 had been arrested as of June 30, 1975. It is expected that many more arrests will occur as investigations are completed. Of the 1275 arrests where judicial action had been completed, 223 convictions and 23 acquittals have resulted. In a large percentage of the 1275 arrests, judicial action has not yet been completed and/or this NCB has not been advised of the final disposition. Out of the 5138 individual entries, 1015 or approximately 20% of the total caseload related to U.S. citizens.

Prior to 1973 the U.S. NCB "had been making random telephonic inquiries of CADPIN (the Customs Automated Data Program Input Network) through Customs, and NCIC through Secret Service," but at the beginning of 1973, the U.S. NCB had been "programmed to run all names referred by foreign NCB's through CADPIN and NCIC by a dial-up teleprinter" which had been recently installed in the office. Since the tele-printer necessitated "manual operation at Customs for CAD-PIN inquiries and at Treasury Communication and Secret Service for NCIC inquiries," and since the monthly charge of a TECS terminal would be "a savings to the Government in relation to the manual operation necessary for dual capabilities by Customs, Treasury Communications, Secret Service and personnel of [the] NCB,"[11] in 1973 the U.S. NCB requested and received installation of the TECS terminal.[12]

In 1975 the TECS network, hosted in San Diego, California, consisted of more than 500 terminals in the United States. A year later TECS had 600 "remote-access terminals" around the country, storing some 450,000 dossiers and containing 562,000 names.[13] In its study of TECS, the *Review* said that information was not available "as to who establishes TECS dossiers, nor as to any regulations or safeguards that may exist to control the process . . ." It concluded that TECS was subject to "almost no judicial or administrative oversight."

According to an undated (c. 1976) TECS fact sheet, the system includes data on known or *suspected* violators. Suspected individuals are defined as those with a prior criminal history, *or of current investigative interest*—an all-embracing term.

A legal document submitted by Assistant U.S. Attorney David R. Schlee to a district court in Washington on June 3, 1976, referred to Interpol as "an alien business entity," and noted that "Interpol is not physically present in, nor does it do business within the boundaries of the United States." Rick DeLano, a reporter with the *San Diego Chronicle*, followed this up at TECS headquarters in the Federal Building in San Diego. He asked Rod Johnson, the director of Customs Data Center, to explain how an alien business entity could gain access to a government computer system loaded with sensitive information. Johnson said that "Interpol as an organization does not have access to TECS." According to Johnson, only those U.S. officials temporarily assigned to represent the U.S. in Interpol were cleared for TECS access. However, according to a TECS program manager, the terminal is listed in Interpol's name. "Other alien business entities may just have to wait until they can get hold of a Treasury and/or Justice official if they want a line into TECS," DeLano wrote.[14]

But Treasury or Justice officials are not the only ones who can gain access to the FBI's computer. On March 26, 1978, *The New York Times* reported that

A figure in Cleveland crime circles was murdered last fall after alleged members of an organized crime family in that city obtained information from Federal Bureau of Investigation files indicating that he had been a Government informer, Justice Department sources have confirmed.

But some F.B.I. agents and officials familiar with the case insist that the man, Daniel J. Greene, had been targeted for murder long before the information was obtained from the bureau files and argue that his death did not result from the disclosure.

"The rumors that individuals have been killed as a result of this are absolutely false," said Joseph E. Griffin, the No. 2 official in the bureau's field office in Cleveland. "No one has been killed as a result of the attempted infiltration" of the bureau files here.

On the contrary, Mr. Griffin said, the attempt to obtain information from the files was spotted early and monitored closely, and provided additional evidence in what he describes as "probably the most successful investigation to date against any single major organized family in this country."

Whether or not the information about Mr. Greene's cooperation with the F.B.I. was a factor in his death—and some agents believe that it might have been—the disclosure has caused some consternation in the bureau, where there is concern that it might make potential informers hesitant to cooperate for fear that their own relationships might be exposed.

Because the bureau traditionally has done little undercover work of its own, it has relied heavily on informers, often criminals themselves, to help it conduct investigations, and has gone to great lengths to protect their identities.

Officially, spokesmen for the F.B.I. say that the bureau believes its system for protecting informants is sound and it is planning no special review of its records security program.

However, the incident in Cleveland marked the second time in less than a year that material from F.B.I. offices was obtained by alleged organized crime figures, and it occurred at about the same time F.B.I. inspectors were checking allegations of unauthorized disclosures from the bureau's field office in Las Vegas, Nevada.

The inspectors concluded that there had not been any unauthorized disclosures in the Las Vegas office, but in the process of their investigation learned that at least one other F.B.I. office, in Detroit, had been refusing to send information about organized crime figures to the Las Vegas office, fearing that it would be passed along to some of the persons being investigated.[15]

Another case of the system turning on itself was reported in *The New York Times* on March 11, 1978: "Two former agents of the Federal Drug Enforcement Administration were convicted [in Bridgeport, Connecticut, on March 10] of conspiring to steal and sell information from the agency's master computer and to smuggle drugs.

"The case has been considered one of the most serious in the agency's recent history, according to a spokesman in Washington, because its own personnel were involved and because of the discovery that the computer could be used as a tool by drug dealers to thwart capture . . ." There was "testimony on talks of potential murder and of obtaining information from the agency's computer on schedules for air patrols on the Mexican border."[16]

Protecting former criminals and criminals from each other, and protecting civilians from criminals and from governmental and other abuses is not an easy task, and solutions to satisfy both sides are hard to come by. At least the FBI and the Justice Department are beginning to take some steps in the right direction, as far as the civil rights of citizens are concerned. But not everyone is in agreement. On March 15, 1978, *The New York Times* revealed that the FBI, "over the objections of some of its agents but with the consent of the National Archives, has begun to destroy the inactive criminal files in its field offices . . .

"The policy, which was approved by the bureau's executive conference about four months ago, calls for the destruction of all criminal files in the fifty-nine field offices, providing that the case has been closed for five years, the subject of the file is not considered a threat to 'national security' and the subject does not have any civil litigation pending against the government."[17]

This admirable effort is still somewhat marred, however. "National security" is a fairly wide-ranging term, as evidenced by the abuses of many citizens' constitutional rights, in the interest of "national security," which were carried on in the 1960s and 1970s, not to mention the red menace of the fifties and the spy scare of the thirties. One also wonders what will become of the files of those who have civil litigation pending against the government, and whether they, too, will remain neatly indexed and watched, becoming national security risks, their files available to whoever can, by whatever means, gain access to them.

The *Times* article went on to say that

James Awe, the F.B.I. agent who supervised the management of its 7,000 file cabinets of records, said . . . that [summaries of any "substantive" information] would still be on file at bureau headquarters here in Washington and that most of the material to be destroyed would be "unfounded allegations that never resulted in Federal violations" that were proved.

A number of agents said privately, however, that agents

working on organized crime cases were concerned that information they considered important to the bureau's monitoring of criminal organizations would be lost.

"We're retreating full blast," said one, who did not want to be quoted by name. He suggested that the bureau had acted properly in deciding to limit its so-called "internal security" investigations, which often focused on fringe political groups, but then had "overreacted" to criticism of the bureau, and had decided to purge its criminal files as well.

"Five years from now, we'll have to start all over again," he predicted. "It will be like 1957. There'll be another Apalachin and nobody will know who they are." His reference was to a meeting of alleged organized crime figures at a private residence in upstate Apalachin, N.Y., in 1957.*

Others in the bureau disagree, and one senior official suggested privately that the bureau might be better off if many of its files were "burned before they're read," rather than waiting five years . . .

Several bureau sources said that a reason for the decision was that a number of persons had begun civil suits against the Government after using requests under the Freedom of Information Act to obtain information that the bureau had on file on them. [Obviously, the files on these persons will not be destroyed.]

Mr. Awe, however, said that it was more a routine management decision. "We're trying to manage these files, and it becomes a matter of cost effectiveness," he said. "It becomes a matter of using resources to maintain files, when you don't need access to them anymore."

It could not be learned immediately how many files are

---

*William Hundley, who worked in the Internal Security Division of the Department of Justice, and in 1958 became chief of the Organized Crime Section, said that the FBI at that time had to be "brought into organized crime kicking and screaming . . . [Hoover] didn't know what the hell was going on . . . I mean, how can you have the top investigative agency in the world and have all these top hoods meeting up in Apalachin and they didn't even know about it."[18]

scheduled to be destroyed under the new policy, which bureau officials said was not challenged by the Department of Justice . . .[19]

It is clear that the FBI, like Interpol, must undertake still more massive revisions of its systems if it is effectively and legally to undertake and protect the functions it is entrusted with. As far as FBI agents and officials are concerned, the recent indictments of the FBI's former Acting Director, L. Patrick Gray, and two other former high FBI officials, who were all charged with conspiring to violate the civil rights of citizens, may serve as a useful deterrent to similar activities in the future. However, other FBI agents and officials were either not charged, or the charges against them were dismissed because they were "only following orders,"[20] or because they had been granted immunity in the investigation, or because the statute of limitations had expired. "When confronted nowadays with vague assignments, Federal agents are said to be asking that the orders be put in writing."[21] Attorney General Griffin Bell, who handed down the three indictments, had stated that "following orders" will not be considered an excuse in the future. And he called for disciplinary action against sixty-eight other agents involved in black-bag operations, stirring up a new furor in the FBI.[22] It is hoped that the lesson of it being just as wrong to give illegal orders as to take them will be an enduring one.

TECS is a midget compared to the FBI's NCIC, however. A network of local, state, and federal computer systems headquartered in the FBI's Identification Building in Washington, the NCIC began operations in January, 1967. By 1971 it had stored about 2.5 million active records, handled 60,000 transactions daily and was linked to 104 law enforcement central terminals in the United States and Canada. The $11 million FBI computer system will one day, it is estimated, be linked to 45,000 terminals throughout the country. We were unable to obtain recent figures, but an earlier estimate stated that by 1975, about 95 percent of the nation's law enforcement agencies were expected to be hooked in to the system. A confidential study to plan expansion of the network, done at the Pasadena jet propulsion lab, estimates that by 1983 (one year ahead of George Orwell's schedule) most of the American public will be on file.

The NCIC system has been given information by the FBI and other Justice Department agencies; by such Treasury Department agencies as Customs, the Secret Service, IRS, and Interpol; also by the Military Police, the intelligence agencies of the Army, Navy, and Air Force, and by the Postal Service. At least, that was the case a few years ago. If an earlier estimate has proven true, the list has grown to almost 40,000 federal, state, and local agencies. The focal point of debate over the NCIC and its lack of privacy safeguards has been the Computerized Criminal Histories (CCH). It is believed to contain records today of well over 400,000 persons. However, almost 50 million Americans now have arrest records of one kind or another, and there is little doubt that sooner or later they will all reach the FBI's national data bank.

Once compiled, files take on a life of their own, in spite of time and good intentions. This was strikingly illustrated in 1971 during Senator Sam Ervin, Jr.'s U.S. Senate Internal Security Subcommittee investigation of Army surveillance of civilians. It transpired that Major General Ralph H. Van Deman, upon his retirement in 1929, started a new career in intelligence. Ervin's hearings revealed that Van Deman developed files with more than 100,000 entries on individuals he believed to be Communists, Communist sympathizers, and neo-Nazis. Although he had a national network of informants, the general was also believed to be supported by the FBI, the Army, Navy, and local police organizations. After Van Deman's death in 1952, the files were used by the Army for granting security clearances, among other things. Later, they were used during domestic antiwar surveillance activities ordered by President Lyndon B. Johnson. Although the Army now claims that the Van Deman files are secure, it is entirely possible and quite likely that the information they contained is lost to control in government data banks.

Another use of files is one such as the psychological portrait of John F. Kennedy that the CIA put together. The CIA was given access to the Kennedy family files, many of which were given to the OSS by the British Special Operations Executive (SOE) MI-5 organization in 1942. The British files contained a substantial amount of information about American citizens, politicians, and diplomats, in addition to expected information about intelligence operations and personnel.

During its heyday of illegal intelligence programs of surveillance and disruption against private citizens and organizations (between 1967 and 1970), the Army maintained files on at least 100,000 Americans. Senate investigation found that "All of the information collected by Army agents on civilian political activity was stored in 'scores' of data banks throughout the United States, some of which the Army had computerized. The reports were routinely fed to the FBI, the Navy and the Air Force, and were occasionally circulated to the Central Intelligence Agency and the Defense Intelligence Agency."[23]

Even though Army activities were curtailed, Senator Ervin noted in May, 1972, "It's going to be impossible" to destroy the information. "Our investigations show," he said, "that while the army engaged in spying on civilians, that it interchanged information that it collected with the FBI and with local law enforcement agencies throughout the United States, and there is no way we can run that down and get it out of their files."[24]

Francis W. Sargent, former Governor of Massachusetts, has been a vociferous critic of the NCIC system, and in 1973 he refused to let his state tie into the national system because of its inadequate safeguards. What particularly worried him was a 1971 Law Enforcement Assistance Administration (LEAA) study of 108 local computer systems that fed into NCIC. The study found that one-half of the collected information was on "potential troublemakers." It also concerned Sargent that arrest records could be entered into the files even if they were not followed by a conviction. However, in 1973 Congress passed an amendment to the Law Enforcement Assistance Act requiring the computer to show the disposition of arrests.

Still, in the case of Interpol, officials have admitted that dispositions are hard to come by, particularly for overseas arrests, and other law enforcement agencies face similar problems. Even if found innocent in the courts, a person's arrest record is available for checking to both governmental and private employers and is liable to haunt him for the rest of his life. More than 40 percent of all people arrested in the United States each year are either never prosecuted or charged, or else are acquitted or have charges dismissed. It is estimated that in 1974, almost 70 percent of all arrest records in the United States did not include final dispositions of the cases.

Dossiers are also compiled on citizens by scores of agencies, such as the Civil Service Commission, the Federal Communications Commission (FCC), the Department of Health, Education and Welfare (HEW), which receives the private records of hospital patients using Medicare and Medicaid, the Department of Housing and Urban Development, the Census Bureau, and the IRS, not to mention the 323 million medical histories and the more than 100 million credit files of private companies that contain information on private habits, health, and so on. Private credit departments are required to supply information in their files to law enforcement agencies and other government departments that request information for "legitimate reasons."

In other words, NCIC has access to all this information. It also receives daily input from police intelligence units (red squads) across the country. The FBI also has access to the Drug Enforcement Administration's central computerized index on Narcotics and Dangerous Drugs Information System (NADDIS), which in 1977 contained records of approximately 570,000 subjects. People indexed in NADDIS not only may not have committed crimes but may not even be suspected of doing so. The NADDIS index contains a record of drug offenders, alleged drug offenders, informants, and other persons.[25]

New York State's Identification and Intelligence System (NYSIIS) has files on more than six million people—many of whom, such as applicants for civil service jobs, do not have criminal records.[26]

All of this morass of information, and more, is available to the FBI. All they have to do is ask. Of course, the nightmare facing citizens of this country is the possibility of interfacing between the hundreds of existing data banks. However, it may be later than we think. Although this has not *mechanically* taken place yet, information is freely exchanged already. Interpol and the law enforcement bodies of more than 120 countries can now also tap into this gold mine of information.*

In 1976 the U.S. Government's General Accounting Office investigated United States participation in Interpol at the request of Congressman John E. Moss and Senator Joseph M. Montoya. The Comptroller General's report said that the U.S. NCB had not been effectively following procedures for the processing of requests for information. Almost half the sample cases the GAO reviewed involved inadequate documentation and premature action as far as checking records and initiating investigations.[27]

In most instances the U.S. NCB did not request additional, supporting data before asking other agencies to check records or begin investigations. In many cases those requesting information did not explain why the request was made, identify the type of criminal activity being investigated, precisely describe the charges, furnish evidence to support allegations that individuals had criminal backgrounds, indicate whether an individual had been arrested or was being investigated, or provide fingerprints if the subject had been arrested.[28] In spite of these violations, the U.S. NCB obtained information from state, fed-

---

*Presumably Interpol will also be able to tie into Britain's new Police National Computer System, which is under the direction of the Home Office and Scotland Yard. When completely operational, it will be the largest system of its kind in Europe.

eral, and local sources and furnished it to the requesting bureau.

According to the GAO, a serious ramification of inadequate documentation of requests is the chain reaction that takes place, including the creation of criminal information records at various agencies contacted, such as the FBI. In almost half the cases for which FBI records were established, the crimes were only vaguely described by the foreign bureau, and "the vagueness of these descriptions makes it difficult to judge the seriousness of the offenses."[29]

U.S. Interpol officials claim that although they have access to the NCIC data, they do not have access to FBI records containing data on individual private lives, friends, activities, and so on. During the Montoya hearings, Treasury Assistant Secretary David R. Macdonald was emphatic on the point, yet this was contradicted by an Interpol report on an international organization that was leaked through the German NCB to damage this organization in Germany. It was filled with hearsay, innuendo, opinion, and similar "data" from both the FBI and IRS.

At the Senate hearings on February 24, 1976, Montoya asked Louis B. Sims whether the United States had ever placed restrictions on the use or dissemination of information the United States has given to Interpol. Sims replied, "We stamp each document sent out. A resolution was passed in 1974 by the General Assembly in France. The resolution concerned privacy of information.

"This resolution in substance said that information handled within Interpol and General Secretariat channels would remain in criminal justice or law enforcement channels. Information that we provide to another NCB or the General Secretariat not only has that resolution protecting it but it also has our stamp put on each and every document, which says, 'This information will not be disseminated outside Criminal Justice or law enforcement channels without the express permission of Interpol, Washington.' "[30]

Other Interpol officials said they had conducted 446 investigative requirements in 1973 for Congressional sources, private citizens, financial institutions, commercial firms, and so on. Sims explained that these were such legitimate requests as contacting relatives overseas, lost luggage, fraud and embezzlement in the case of banks, and so on,[31] but it does set a dangerous precedent in that Interpol accepts tasks that have not come through legal law enforcement channels.

When Senator Montoya asked Sims, "How is the unauthorized use of such information prevented, other than through what you have said?" Sims answered, "I think if you consider that you are dealing with the official police agencies, normally an office within the national police and with the General Secretariat with about half of the 155 individuals being active law enforcement personnel from the various countries,* I think that is your best preventive, to keep it in official law enforcement channels."[32] In other words, the unauthorized use of such information on American citizens is not prevented at all.

This was demonstrated by a sworn deposition from a man who was a U.S. Customs patrol officer until late in 1973. For obvious reasons, he didn't want to use his real name, so we'll call him John Carter. Carter said that during his employment with Customs he observed abuses involving the processing of criminal information in the Customs Automated Data Program Input Network. The system is used to store information not only of a proven criminal nature, but also on suspected criminal activities not necessarily backed up by evidence that would hold up in court. Interpol, of course, has access to CADPIN's computerized criminal information. According to Carter: "The nature of information filed and the persons filed is solely up to the discretion of the individual law enforcement or U.S. Customs agent involved."

The specific case of abuse Carter cited occurred in 1973. He and another Customs officer arrested two Dutch nationals for

---

*Of these individuals, 122 are French.

smuggling whiskey into Florida. Both men were tried in Federal Court. One was convicted and the other was found innocent of all charges.

"A special agent for United States Customs was angry about the ruling of the one man's innocence," Carter told us. "He prepared a dossier on both of the men, composed of pictures, names, passport numbers and all information pertinent to both individuals for identification. When asked what the dossier was being used for, the agent said, 'I'm going to put them in Interpol.' I responded that I thought the man was innocent. The agent then put his finger forcefully on the man's picture and said, 'if I can't get his ass one way, I'll get it another.' I asked the agent what the effect of putting this file into Interpol would be. He stated, 'I'll see that he will never get another job anywhere in the world.' "

This is one of the "active law enforcement personnel" that Sims claims will protect us against abuse.

The recent Congressional hearings have shown an encouraging increase in awareness of the dangers inherent in the U.S. affiliation with Interpol. But sadly, no matter how zealous Congress becomes, it can only control the Washington NCB.* Interpol's central files at Saint-Cloud,† including files the United States has given them, are not subject to U.S. review. When a member police department makes a request of the U.S. NCB, a copy of the file goes to Saint-Cloud. After that, 120-plus countries are able to obtain a copy of that particular file without going through Washington.

In 1976, during additional Congressional hearings, U.S. NCB chief Sims said that his office operated exactly like any other Federal law enforcement agency, with full regard to the Privacy Act and the Freedom of Information Act.[33] A U.S. citizen, Sims claimed, has the right to request his records under

---

*Business in the U.S. NCB has increased 1,300 percent between 1969 and 1974.

†In 1972 Interpol's headquarters contained more than 1.5 million files on individuals. By 1974, the General Secretariat reported that it had files on more than two million individuals.

the Privacy Act. He said that the NCB in each country operated under the laws of that country. The files, though, are kept at the General Secretariat in Paris—a fact he neglected to point out, which means that although under the U.S. Freedom of Information Act a U.S. citizen may obtain permission to see his files, if the files are kept in France, there is no way for the U.S. law to help him.

U.S. Representative Edward Beard (D–R.I.), a strong critic of Interpol, asked the Washington NCB for access to a particular file at Saint-Cloud. He was told by the NCB: "Inquiry was made of the General Secretariat, Saint-Cloud, France, on April 18, 1975, and a reply was received on this date (April 22) from the Secretary General which related 'no information about General Secretariat files can be supplied . . .' "[34]

In 1974 the United States was a member of an eleven-nation Interpol working-group conducting feasibility studies for computerization. Secretary General Nepote first brought this subject up at Interpol's 1972 General Assembly. The studies are still continuing. Expense is a major factor, but there is no doubt at all that sooner or later Interpol will have to computerize its information systems in order to survive.

Nepote's view was that computerizing present records at Saint-Cloud only was next to useless. "But," he said, "if we have, at an international level, a system which could be compared to NCIC,* or something like this, with terminals in different countries to consult directly the computer and get a direct answer, that here is the future."[35]

In an article in the August-September, 1975, issue of the *International Criminal Police Review*, Nepote wrote that, "Data banks have been set up by various countries . . . Why not do the same on an international basis?"

Regarding the questions of national sovereignty and the rights of private individuals, Nepote said reliable safeguards could be given:

---

* Francis Sargent has called the NCIC "one of the biggest threats to our democratic system."[36]

Firstly, the data bank would store certain categories of data and certain categories only. Secondly, each country would retain responsibility for the data fed into the computer. There would be no way of "breaking through" the barrier of national sovereignty and each country would decide on its own which items of information it wished to have stored.

In addition, the data bank would only be open to those authorities authorized to consult it. And, after all, what difference is there between an item of information obtained by a letter or telegram and that printed out by a computer terminal? Lastly, the computer would supply data but any resulting action would be undertaken solely by the national authorities, with all the safeguards which each set of national laws contains.

Most countries do not have anywhere near the concern for individual rights that the United States does, yet even in the United States the various legal data banks have turned into uncontrollable monsters that frequently violate civil liberties. Nepote mentions nothing about purging incorrect records, safeguarding against false information, or needing some kind of controlling and review authority other than each country being responsible for the data it fed into the computer. Considering Interpol's membership covers the political spectrum, his eagerness to hand over responsibility is somehow disturbing.

Nepote blithely summed up his justifications by saying that, "From the point of view of ordinary criminal law enforcement, what do honest citizens have to fear?"

. . . I must draw attention to the fact that it is impossible to determine beforehand whether or not someone may become involved in some form of criminal activity.

———JEAN NEPOTE, personal letter,
November 6, 1975

Chapter Nine

THE VIOLATION OF HUMAN RIGHTS

In December, 1976, Amnesty International announced that the human rights situation around the world had deteriorated at an alarmingly fast rate. The organization's 1975–76 report claimed that in addition to the commonplace practice of torture in 60 countries, there were 112 nations with significant human rights violations that included imprisonment for religious or political beliefs, color, or ethnic origin. The majority of these nations are Interpol members. Reports of police brutality and injustice in many of these countries have been well-documented in the world press. Yet the U.S. Government, which has declared its support for human rights, seems to be perpetuating Interpol's mythical global-hero image by accepting false information as truth. This misguided stance can be seen in the statement Treasury official David R. Macdonald made to a U.S. Senate subcommittee: "Television drama to the contrary notwithstanding, Interpol has no investigative force of its own and carried on no investigations."[1]

In 1974, Interpol passed a resolution that "Urges in exchanging information the I.C.P.O.—Interpol NCB's and the General Secretariat—take into account the privacy of the individual and strictly confine the availability of the information to official law enforcement and criminal justice agencies." Such a resolution is to be commended, but as with Article 3, Interpol has no methods of enforcement.

In 1975 U.S. NCB chief Louis B. Sims testified before a U.S. Senate committee and said, in effect, that the rights of individuals could not be violated because he was "constantly on the lookout for this type request."[2] Moreover, it became perfectly clear through the course of the 1975–76 Senate hearings and through personal accounts that the NCB transmits exactly what the bureau chief wants it to transmit.

At the same 1975 hearings, Senator Henry Bellmon asked Sims: "Do you have any way of knowing whether or not the answers you get back through Interpol to the U.S. police departments are accurate? . . ."

SIMS: "We require certain information be provided with regard to the request which we hope will assist in making that determination. To answer your question can you make a determination that yes, it is or no, it isn't. That may be difficult to do . . ."[3]

Senator Montoya asked: "Have you instances where a man is charged with a crime abroad and similar information concerning his personal habits is requested from you?"

SIMS: "It wouldn't make any difference if he was charged with a crime abroad or if he was just under investigation."

MONTOYA: "You would not contact any police department to supplement information they might have on an individual?"

SIMS: "No, sir."

A Treasury Department report to Montoya flatly contradicted Sims. Under the heading "Nature of Investigative Requests," the report stated, "These investigations may include interviews with associates, suspects, witnesses, etc.; obtaining of court records, determining if certain property (securities, motor vehicles, artifacts, etc.) are stolen or missing, attempts to locate a suspect, or other usual criminal inquiries which are conducted by law-enforcement agencies countrywide."[4]

Using another hypothetical situation regarding someone who was suspected of dealing in heroin, Montoya asked: "If he had no background in narcotics traffic but they want to know something about the individual, would you send any information on the individual.

SIMS: "No. We would say, 'He has no criminal history.' "

A few minutes later, Montoya asked about a situation where an NCB in Europe wanted information on someone who was being investigated for rape. He hypothesized that there was no charge and the individual had not been arrested. "You go to his place of residence here and at your request the police department conducts a check of him, about his sex habits and so forth. There would be no charge in the foreign country. The individual has not been arrested."

SIMS: "I understand."

MONTOYA: "Would you do that and send the information back?"

SIMS: "This is a very sensitive issue which has a lot of privacy issues involved in it."

MONTOYA: "But you have handled those situations?"

SIMS: "In these situations, yes. If I could give you an example of one that fits the category."

Sims then spoke about a case where young children had been abducted and the suspect was a citizen of another country. The agency involved in the United States wanted him to request information on the criminal history of the individual in his own country and a list of the schools where the suspect had taught. Sims said that if the case was reversed and the request came from a foreign country, the NCB would handle it; " . . . there are young lives at stake," he said.[5]

In countries that do not guarantee due process of law, the citizen can be detained for indeterminate lengths of time, interrogated viciously, and denied legal assistance. Hundreds of American youths presently sit in Mexican prisons on drug charges, subjected to atrocious conditions. The publicized cases, such as the one described below, and the unpublicized cases which follow seem to show that some of them are innocent.

THE PURE WOOL SWEATER CAPER

"March 18th
Carcel Municipal
Quito, Ecuador

"Mom——

"Well, here I am again . . . in prison. Only this time more serious. I'm being held on an international smuggling charge by Interpol. Under Napoleonic law (which is like no rules or laws to follow) You are guilty and it is your burden to prove your innocence; which in most cases is practically impossible. The Special Agents from the U.S. decided to check out the Gringos residing in Ecuador and saw that I have been doing a lot of shipping to the U.S. The last shipment was two hundred pure wool hand knit cardigan sweaters with belts and hoods. Really beautiful. I bought the wool and had the entire femme population of a small town in northern Ecuador 11,000 feet up in the Andes knitting and spinning. The sweaters cost me about $7.00 U.S. each and wholesale in the state of Washington for $50.00 each with buyers offering to pay more for an exclusive. So with my record with the F.B.I. which shows two trials and a prison sentence, the agents from Interpol move in acting on information supplied from the guess work of the morons of the C.I.A.* Eight Interpol agents with guns surround our house, ransack it, literally robbed us of every item of value and my life savings of $1,600.00 in cash (I was going to use the money that day to do a banking trip necessary to get our new shipment out of the country) which makes it necessary to deposit an equal amount of money in Banco Central as the value of the shipment—like an export tax. My house was torn apart, needless to say a small quantity of drugs was found (approximately 3 grams of cocaine, and ¼ ounce of marijuana) so

*These are probably DEA officials, not CIA officials.

they took me & Bojangles & Pooka off to jail. They were sure that I was what the C.I.A. claimed and for the next three days I was hung by a rawhide cord tied to my thumbs behind my back and beaten with a wooden stick while hanging. When I would faint they would revive me with cold water and proceed with the 'interrogation.' After three days in this place, which alone was as inhumane as anywhere has ever been (hundreds of people jammed into cellars without toilets and they don't give food). If you have someone outside that knows you're in there they can bring food for you to eat, which as soon as you get it you are jumped by the rest of the people who take the food. I saw a fight over a chicken bone that someone threw on the floor. This is no exaggeration! There is no way this place can be described in which the true horror can be felt, let alone exaggerated. On the third day they tortured Pooka . . . I signed a confession they wrote in exchange for Pooka & Bo's freedom. It is completely ridiculous. They kept telling me my son was sick and was going to die (which was almost the case, they wouldn't give me any of my money to buy food or return clothes to us. We made shoes for Bo out of newspaper and plastic bags. You could see your breath but never the sun, all the time—really cold and damp!), I didn't know what they wanted me to say, I begged them to tell me what they wanted me to say. After 10 days Pooka & Bo were deported to Colombia. I was very sick with fever and malnutrition not to mention the after effects of their means of extracting information. Now almost two months later my thumbs still are numb on the ends. I have almost completely recooperated (sic) from the interrogation. I spent a total of 15 days in the dungeon. If I ever get out it will not be as easy as before not to be bitter. The American agent was totally aware of the torturing but didn't lift a finger to get them to stop. As soon as the American Consul from the Embassy got to me, I was being held incommunicado, he got the torture stopped. It's against the law here, too. The Embassy, particularly Mr. Ira Levy, has been really helping a lot. Mr. Levy knows about the police here especially Interpol. He has been through this before. He may not say anything formally but informally he regards what the police say as extremely exaggerated. Meanwhile the shipment of sweaters has finally passed customs, thoroughly searched by U.S. Customs who found it completely void of the cocaine they guessed was there. Boy are they embarrassed. The sweaters have been all sold and the money is being sent for my defense. Interpol stole 168 sweaters I had in storage here, claiming they were bought with money from drugs. They sold them and kept the money (around $1,500 U.S.). It's really amazing what they get away with, I mean really amazing! They couldn't read my record sheet from the F.B.I. (which says I was tried for posession [sic] of marijuana April 1968 and served a prison sentence, tried again for posession [sic] of marijuana June 1969 and found innocent finally) to them it meant I was busted 3 times for trafficking of drugs. That stuff isn't supposed to have even happened in the eyes of the law. Anyway, I am back to zero. For 3 years I stayed ahead of my 'record' but I knew it would catch up with me sooner or later. I'm going to write to Mr. Runyan and see if they won't quit haunting me. I had a home, family and business going well—Totally Legal. But not with a record! Nothing good ever comes from that. Now I have nothing. Can't even buy a lawyer. I'll have to stay for 6–12 years and Pooka & Bo are deported—not allowed to return and have a big red stamp 'Addicted to Drugs' stamped on her passport. I wasn't hurting a soul, they just couldn't believe that I was winning their game playing by their rules.

Love,
Gwynn"

"Dear Mrs. Lewis,

I'm sure by now you have received the telegram and perhaps a phone call from my father with the sad message . . .

. . . Gwynn is now in jail in Quito. Bo & I spent 2 months in jail also, then we were put on a bus and deported to Colombia. I have been in touch with my father who will send me money to live on till I can find a job. I have also been in touch with friends on the West Coast who I'm sure can help a little with money for a lawyer . . .

. . . Unfortunately we were taken from our house to jail and I was not allowed to return before being deported—so all is lost—clothes, furniture, refrig. all is gone.

But Bo & I are fine and concentrating all our energy on getting Gwynn out. We would greatly appreciate anything you can do to help.

Love,
Pooka"

The above letters were sent to Congressman Edward Beard by Gwynn's mother. Gwynn and Pooka's son, Bojangles, she said, was one-and-a-half years old at the time of this incident. Gwynn is now a student at the North Park College in Chicago, preparing to enter Seminary. He was released from prison in Ecuador.

THE PIERRE DUPUY CASE

In March, 1974, Pierre Dupuy, a Reseda, California, businessman, traveled to San Salvador in Central America to salvage a ship, the *Tradition*. He didn't expect stormy weather.

It began as a straight business deal. Dupuy's partner, Bob, was sailing his ship, the *Annya*, in to meet him. The remainder of the crew planned to join him there when the ship was seaworthy and help him sail her the 3,000 miles back to the United States.

"I had purchased the *Tradition* from Carlos Santiago Ruiz, known as Jimmy. We had been working on the boat a couple of days when the trouble started. When my partner, Bob, went to town, he was stopped by Secret Police at a road block. The road had never been blocked before."

The police told Dupuy's partner that his passport had expired and arrested him. There had been no problems with his passport when he had entered the country a few days before.

From that point, it was all downhill. A canoe of armed men visited the *Annya*. "They took one of my workers with them and tried to take my passport away," says Dupuy. "I indicated that I had committed no crime, but they left with one of my workers in custody."

Dupuy appealed to Jimmy Ruiz for help. His father-in-law was an important local official, and they managed to get Bob released. In the process, they discovered that the police had "received orders" to check the Americans out.

"Interpol then visited my friend, Jimmy," Dupuy said. "Jimmy gave me the card of the Interpol agent which I turned over to the American Vice Consul there, Ed Glower of the State Department."

The Interpol agent wanted information on Dupuy. He asked who had picked Dupuy up at the airport when he had arrived? How much had he paid for the boat? What kind of car was he driving? The questions went on.

"This didn't help my business relationship as I'm sure it put serious doubts into Jimmy's mind," Dupuy said. "At one stage he mentioned to me that it was okay if I had Mafia connections! I had to assume that this false information came from Interpol."

Another crew member, Paul Hunt, arrived. By now everybody was getting into the act. This time, the San Salvador Navy arrested him. They said his passport had expired. With the help of the U.S. Embassy, he was released.

Meanwhile, Dupuy's departure was being delayed. Sailing permission was denied without reason.

"Interpol boarded my partner's ship with the Port Captain. They showed me their identity cards and a photographer they brought with them tried to take my picture. Finally, I told one of my crew to take a picture of the Interpol agents and they fled the boat."

Further inquiries by Jimmy's influential father-in-law revealed that possibly the U.S. Government was behind the harassment. Supposedly they had ordered the local officials to delay sailing until they could make a full investigation of Dupuy and his partner. Finally, after a stormy visit to the

American Consulate, where he threatened to report the affair to the press, Dupuy's boat was released. No charges were filed.

"I don't profess to understand Interpol or their games," Dupuy said. "They were involved in the delay and harassment of my business in a foreign country. The harassment did not stop there but continued when I finally sailed into San Diego in the latter part of April."

Dupuy arrived in San Diego and tied up at the customs dock. A number of men tried to board the boat, several of them in plainclothes. Dupuy refused to let anyone but customs agents aboard. "In private conversations with Customs officials," he said, "I was told that the DEA was involved. After further hassles, I finally got the boat released.

"I have committed no crime, yet was hounded by Interpol agents and agents of a foreign country. My crew was held in jail for no apparent legal violations and it cost me a great deal of money and aggravation to salvage the business operation. Whatever role Interpol, the State Department and the DEA played should be examined."

Dupuy's problems probably stemmed from a 1973 incident when he and two other men were arrested south of San Luis, Mexico, and charged with trafficking in marijuana. The three spent seventeen months in Mexican prisons before being cleared of the charges. In August, 1976, Dupuy brought a $5 million suit against the Los Angeles Police Department and the DEA.

THE *DREAMBOAT* CASE

"My name is Robert Carter of San Diego, California. In about March of 1976 I was in Puerto Vallarta, Mexico, where I was offered a job on a Canadian yacht, the *Dreamboat*. The owner of the yacht, Mickey Stewart, needed a navigator and offered me a ride to San Diego if I would take the boat that far. Since I needed a way home, I agreed to this.

There was another guy and two girls that were guests on vacation aboard the boat.

We left Puerto Vallarta in the afternoon and went to Cabo San Lucas. This took about twenty-six hours. We got there early in the morning and spent the day and the next night in Cabo San Lucas.

The next day, three Mexican Coast Guard boats pulled into the bay and I talked to the skipper, Mickey, and said that I wondered what was going on, because, being from San Diego, I knew that whenever you see Mexican Coast Guard boats like that, something is happening. We went into shore and had a couple of beers and just walked around. When we came back, the Coast Guard boats were anchored about two hundred yards from the *Dreamboat* and all the doors on our yacht were closed. We thought this was rather strange, but the skipper said that maybe everybody else on board had gone into town. We rowed out to the boat—this was about three in the afternoon—and when we got on board and opened the door, we found it was just loaded with Mexican soldiers. They all had their guns cocked. There were five *Federales* from Mexico City—I spoke enough Mexican to find this out, that they were from Mexico City and that Mexico City had ordered us arrested . . .

. . . Then they started interrogating us. They asked me where the cocaine was and I told them that I was sure there weren't any drugs. I had asked the owner, Mickey, about this before I even took the job and he had assured me there was nothing, that he had a $300,000 yacht and wasn't going to take any chances with losing it by doing anything illegal and during all the time I was aboard I never saw or even heard mention of any drugs—not even marijuana . . .

. . . When they took us to the Mexican *Federale* Office in Mazatlan, two men walked in. All five of us looked at each other because these guys were obviously Americans. They were not Mexicans even though they were trying to look like it. I'm half Mexican myself and have lived in San Diego all my life, except when I was in Vietnam, and I'd stake my life on the fact that these guys were not Mexicans . . .

. . . they kept saying we had cocaine aboard—three pounds or three kilos—I'm not sure which.

Then one of them took out a cattle prod (I didn't know at this point what it was) and asked me if I knew what it was. I said no, and then he jabbed me with it. It was an extremely painful electric shock and I have some spine problems and I really didn't need anything like that. It lifted me right out of my chair and affected my whole nervous system.

I kept telling them I didn't know anything—that my name is Robert Carter and I am an American seaman, I'm a navigator on this boat and that's all I know. The guy then said I had just three minutes to tell them more or they were going to blast me again. I broke out into a cold sweat and all I could think about was, 'Wow, this is going to hurt.' He had the owner, Mickey, in there with me at this time and he told him that he was a liar and then he pulled out a gun and pointed it at Mickey's head and said, 'You're a liar and you've got cocaine and I'll find out where it is and you'll tell me or I'll kill you.'

I thought, 'Oh, wow, I don't believe this,' then he cocked the gun and pulled the trigger.

The gun was empty, but we didn't know that until he pulled the trigger and it was enough to give you a heart attack and I thought, 'Oh, my God, what's he going to do to me?'

They kept this sort of thing up all day. Mickey told them that if they didn't believe me, they had all the facilities in Mazatlan, so they could take the boat out of the water and rip it apart and they'd fine there was no drugs on it, but if they did that they had to put it together again 'cause it was worth a lot of money and it belonged to him and the Bank of Canada.

They didn't respond to this, but we found out that they had already torn the boat apart—ripping the floor up, tearing the ceiling down and things like that. They told us they had found three marijuana cigarettes and we all looked at one another and we knew they had planted them.

I didn't see it, but I was told that the owner, Mickey, was blasted twice with the cattle prod.

As far as I know, none of the others were treated this way, but we were all threatened and intimidated during the interrogation.

That night, they put all of us in a room that was all of about ten by eleven feet square that already had eighteen people in it and we were only allowed to leave to go to the bathroom. I was kept in that room for ten days . . ."

From that point on, it was the usual Mexican horror story: subhuman conditions, false charges, and corrupt lawyers. Finally, at the advice of a lawyer who said Mexican courts were lenient on women, one of the girls said the marijuana cigarettes were hers. She was sentenced and the others were freed, a few weeks after they were declared innocent. The usual horror story, except for one thing:

"The American Consul had told me that the reason we had all been arrested was because Interpol had been suspicious of our boat for some time and thought that it might be involved in drug trafficking."

All the names in this incident have been changed at the request of our informant.

THE CASE OF THE ELDERLY ENGLISH LADY

A few years ago, Mrs. Marion Wasserman, a sixty-year-old British citizen, owned a mountain chalet in a Swiss village, a shiny new Alfa Romeo, and a flourishing tourist business. It was a picture postcard life. Today she is registered as a permanently disabled person. She lives in a cramped Council flat and exists on a small Social Security allowance.

Mrs. Wasserman claims that her present situation is the result of "terrible wrongs" done to her by the dissemination of false information through Interpol.

Her decline began, she says, on a January evening in 1967,

when "I had the great misfortune, by pure accident, to discover a senior London Metropolitan Police [LMP] officer in his pajamas with two other homosexuals, also in their pajamas at midnight in a London suburban house . . ."

Mrs. Wasserman had been separated from her Swiss husband, whom she claims is homosexual, for several years. That night she visited the house where he lived with another man, to collect some housekeeping money he owed her.

When she went to the front door of the house, she says, she was chased by the man her husband lived with and another pajama-clad man, later identified as a chief inspector of the LMP. She was attacked and pulled to the ground. A neighbor, believing she needed help, telephoned the police.

Mrs. Wasserman was taken to the local police station. There the chief inspector identified himself and issued a three-day Emergency Observation Order, committing her to a nearby mental hospital. The chief inspector, a neighbor of her husband's, claimed that he had been awakened by the noise of Mrs. Wasserman shouting at her husband. He had gone next door, after putting clothes over his pajamas, to "see if he was all right."

Shortly after the police left, Mrs. Wasserman left the mental hospital and contacted her lawyer. He told her that his phone was tapped and that the police had put out a message describing her as "a dangerous escaped lunatic believed to be carrying guns."

"Frightened and helpless," she said, Mrs. Wasserman fled to Switzerland. Later she returned to England and attempted to sort out her affairs. She also instituted divorce proceedings against her husband.

In November, 1971, when she felt matters had been settled, Mrs. Wasserman went back to Switzerland, hoping to set up a new life. Within a year she owned a successful tourist business. She was well satisfied with her life until July 14, 1973, when she was arrested by five Swiss policemen on the grounds that a neighbor had seen her threaten a Dutch tourist with a gun.

It seemed to be a replay of events. Without arrest warrants or medical examination, Mrs. Wasserman was committed to another mental hospital.

Two days later her Swiss lawyer traced the Dutch tourist. The bewildered man disclaimed ever being threatened at gunpoint. That day Mrs. Wasserman was released from the hospital. As an added bonus, she was declared perfectly sane.

Her next mistake was to return to the police station to recover her car. She was immediately rearrested and sent back to the hospital. This time, when she escaped, Mrs. Wasserman returned to England.

The story doesn't end there, however. Thinking that her Swiss lawyer had handled the situation satisfactorily, she returned to start her business again.

She was arrested by the Swiss police. This time she was beaten, she claims. Fists were pounded over the lower part of her spine, and when she asked for water, "I was told to drink from the lavatory."

She was taken to the mental hospital again. And again she escaped. When she jumped out of the window, however, she fractured her spine. Although injured, she managed to escape to England with the help of friends.

Back in England, Mrs. Wasserman began to fight for the return of her property.

In November, 1973, the Federal Tribunal in Lausanne recommended that the State where the arrests took place institute an inquiry and pay substantial compensation. This was never done.

Mrs. Wasserman eventually obtained her police files and the source of her problems became more apparent. The Interpol file that was sent to the Swiss police contained false information. It claimed (a) that she had been declared insane in January, 1967; and (b) that she had a criminal record. In fact, Mrs. Wasserman had no criminal record, although she did have some civil offenses. The first item of false information explained why the Swiss police had a penchant for throwing her into mental institutions. In addition, although the Interpol report said she was no longer wanted for anything, it asked the Swiss police for her fingerprints and photograph.

In February, 1975, the Assistant Commissioner (Crime) at New Scotland Yard, wrote to Mrs. Wasserman saying, in part, "The Commissioner has asked me to say that he very much regrets that the information given to the Swiss Police at their request was in certain respects inaccurate and to assure you that this has now been corrected."

Meanwhile, "financially ruined and permanently disabled," Marion Wasserman is making, so far, futile attempts to get compensation.

THE ANTELINEZ CASE

Oakland Park, Florida—Tuesday.

Responding to a call at 7:48 P.M., police arrived at 1930 N.W. 32d Street to find a neighbor holding a gun on forty-four-year-old José Luis Antelinez.

According to Antelinez's estranged wife Mary, he had forced his way into her house, breaking the living room window, the rear screen-door, and the lock on her bedroom door. His mother-in-law, Ruth Melnick, had called the neighbor. Both mother and daughter told police that Antelinez had threatened to kill them. Antelinez was booked for breaking and entering and intent to commit murder in the first degree.

It began as a straightforward domestic case. By the time Oakland Park police had straightened it out, they had more than fifty pages of police reports, half a dozen false leads, an equal number of false accusations, evidence of Interpol's ineptitude and unreliability, and an example of how an individual could be persecuted through the use of unverified rumor.

The confusion began when Mary told police that her husband was a smuggler. He was wanted, she said, by the Royal Canadian Mounted Police, the FBI, and Interpol. And he was connected to the Canadian Mafia. The police had no choice but to check the information.

The FBI, it turned out, did not want the man. The local

agent did mention, however, that Customs was interested in him, possibly in connection with smuggling.

U.S. Customs Agent Howard Wright told police that they had a "lookout" for José put out by the Danish Embassy in connection with a child-custody case, but he was certainly not wanted.

Further checking revealed that a couple of months before, a Detective Lieutenant Robert LeBlanc of Montreal had been in touch with the Fort Lauderdale police about Antelinez. Asking for an investigation, LeBlanc had told Detective Mike Shortle that Antelinez was well connected with the Canadian Mafia, that he was probably a drug courier, and that Interpol had issued felony warrants for him. *However, the source of Le-Blanc's information was Antelinez's estranged wife Mary.* Astounding as it may seem, the policeman's actions were based on rumor.

The police wired Interpol to see what they had. At 10 A.M. on Wednesday, Detective R. Riggio of the Oakland Park police received a telephone call from Fred Douglas, then in charge of the Interpol Bureau in Washington, and the case entered the realm of comic opera.

Douglas said Antelinez first came to the attention of Interpol when he was charged in Denmark for stealing his child. Then he added, "But he is now apparently a big-time smuggler." When asked what Antelinez smuggled, Douglas replied, "Gold."

From the police report: "Douglas asked if our offense would have been a gang-revenge or gang-type murder and he was advised of the circumstances surrounding the offense, and further advised of information we'd received that José was mixed up with the Mafia in Canada to which Douglas replied that we were right, correct, and exactly right. We also advised him of the information regarding the possibility of José being an international courier for the Mafia and Douglas stated we were right and that he'd be smuggling in narcotics also, besides gold. Douglas advised he had quite a big file on José . . ."

Douglas promised Detective Riggio he would send the file.

In the meantime he would contact Denmark to see if they would extradite José Antelinez.

Three hours later Douglas called back after hearing from Interpol, Denmark. They were concerned with the whereabouts of the child involved in the child-custody case and said that a decision regarding extradition had not been made.

Meanwhile, based on the verbal Interpol report that José was a smuggler, Customs was searching his luggage. They found nothing incriminating.

Four hours later Douglas called to check on the investigation. He told the officer not to forget the "child that he's supposed to have custody of he's taken, kidnapped."

Investigation revealed that apparently Antelinez had taken the child and left Denmark after the Danish Ministry of Justice had granted custody of the child to its mother, Gladys Hermanson. She and Antelinez were divorced. Customs Agent Howard Wright had informed police earlier that the Danish Government referred to the case as child-stealing, not kidnapping. There were no criminal warrants out on Antelinez, but the Danish Consulate in New York wanted to serve *civil* papers on him to produce the child.

The officer continued the conversation with Interpol Agent Douglas: "We advised him that shortly after talking to him before, we had been contacted by Mr. Howitz of the Danish Consulate in New York City, who told us he had no interest whatsoever in José and that all he's interested in is the daughter. Mr. Douglas expressed dissatisfaction at this . . ."

By Thursday investigating officers from both Customs and the police had discussed the matter and "all agreed that we were beginning to have doubts as to the defendant José being an international courier for the Mafia and smuggling gold and narcotics, etc."

On Friday the Interpol file arrived.

From the police report: "It should be noted there is nothing in the file which would remotely indicate José was a courier or a smuggler. The entire file has to do with the child custody case in Denmark . . ."

221

The investigating Oakland Park police met the Fort Lauderdale police to get data on their investigation of Antelinez initiated by Lieutenant LeBlanc of Montreal a few months before. By that time the Fort Lauderdale police had come to the conclusion that "Mary Antelinez's main interest was to entice her husband back into the state of Florida by attempting to convince him she was interested in his welfare . . . however, her reason for this was so that her lawyer would be able to detain him for divorce proceedings and that he could be apprehended for whatever charges could be brought against him, and she could get her Cadillac back which he had been using and for which she holds the papers."

A week after his arrest, Antelinez submitted to a polygraph test. Afterward the polygraph operator advised that "José definitely did not threaten anyone and his intentions were not to kill or threaten anyone. José passed the test OK."

And what did Antelinez have to say? He claimed that his ex-wife from Denmark, Gladys Hermanson, had applied pressure through Interpol and various other agencies to harass him. Gladys's father was apparently "a very close friend of Mr. Liefer, who is an attorney in Denmark and who is also the chief or ex-chief of Interpol in Denmark." She had also contacted his wife Mary and enlisted her aid in the program of harassment.

The case against José Antelinez was finally dismissed. After it was all over, the Oakland Park police department had some disgruntled comments. According to one of the investigating officers, now a lieutenant, Interpol's false information did and could lead police on "wild goose chases." He added, "I was disgusted that Interpol could be used to forward someone's personal gain—in this case character assassination."

Interpol called the lieutenant on another matter some time later. "I hung up on them," he said. They haven't called back.

THE SAMI CASE

Dr. Mohammad Sami, an Afghan economist with the International Monetary Fund, lives in a two-story manor in prestigious

Chevy Chase, Maryland. He lives alone, although he keeps pictures of his two children in his wallet. An eleven-page Montgomery County Circuit Court ruling, giving him custody of Sophia, eight, and Iskander, six, lies uselessly in the drawer of his desk.

The tall, softspoken Sami, who holds two master's degrees and a doctorate in economics, is despondent. He no longer has his children. He feels that the U.S. Government has betrayed him. "The court gave me my children, but I no longer have them," he says. When asked why, he replies bitterly, "Ask Interpol."

Sami's predicament is common in a society where divorce is prevalent. It is a miserable situation, this vicious tug-of-war between parents, with bewildered children in the middle, but it happens every day. Local police and the FBI are usually smart enough to consider it a domestic matter and refuse to interfere. When they have been persuaded to step in and act one way or another, more often than not, they have found themselves in gray-shaded legal quicksand. Experience has proven discretion superior to valor. Not so in Sami's case, however, which is why in 1976 he sued Interpol for $3 million and punitive damages.

Court orders do not evidently hold much water in child-custody cases. The Maryland court was unable to stop Sami's wife from taking the two children back to Florida in 1973. Finally, after months of fruitless negotiations, Sami decided to take matters into his own hands. In May, 1975, he and private investigator Donald Uffinger eluded the children's armed guard in a Fort Lauderdale ice cream parlor and made it as far as Atlanta International Airport before they were stopped by police with drawn guns. Sami used his court ruling to talk his way onto the aircraft and home to Maryland with the children, where he decided he would take them back to Afghanistan with him.

Little did he know that this domestic squabble would reach the proportions of an international incident, with cable and telephone traffic running between police in the United States, England, Germany, Italy, Lebanon, Iran, the U.S. State Department, and the Afghanistan Government. Sami would soon have time to reflect upon his decision while he spent five days incarcerated in solitary confinement in a German prison. All because Interpol, "the international crime-fighting organization," had entered the case.

When Mrs. Helen Sami failed to get her husband stopped at Atlanta, she called James O. Holmes, deputy chief of the Interpol Washington NCB.

"I explained to Mrs. Sami, that unless Washington had an official request from a law enforcement agency in Florida, we could not assist in the matter," reported Holmes. "In view of the time element and possibility that the children would be taken from the United States in violation of any court ruling, I advised Mrs. Sami to contact local officers and have them in turn contact the U.S. Immigration and Naturalization officials at Miami airport as that office would be opened on the weekend."

Mrs. Sami seems to have had contacts in Florida. By 10:20 P.M., Monday, Louis Sims, Chief of the Washington NCB, was advised that arrest/extradition had been authorized by Philip S. Shailer, State's Attorney, 17th Judicial District, Broward County, Florida. It was enough, he considered, for him to act.

At 10:25 P.M. Sims used the Treasury communications center to send a message to London and a copy for information to Wiesbaden, Germany, asking that Sami be stopped. He followed this up at 10:40 P.M. with a telephone call to Detective Andrew Boardley, Interpol Scotland Yard, advising him that the message would soon arrive. At 11:10 P.M. Mrs. Sami called Sims to tell him she was leaving for London.

The next day was another busy one for Sims. At 7:00 A.M. Mrs. Sami's attorney called to say she was catching a flight to London. Sims gave him the Interpol telephone number at Scotland Yard. At 7:05 A.M. Sims sent a message to London, advising them of her arrival. By 9:20 A.M. Sims heard that London was not taking any action against Sami.

Although Sims may have been disappointed, he remained undaunted. Ten minutes later he sent another message to

Wiesbaden, reminding them of the earlier message and warning that Mrs. Sami was now enroute there. At 12:15 P.M. Sims sent another message to Wiesbaden, providing them with additional information on the warrant. By 5:30 P.M. another thought had occurred to Sims, and he sent messages to Wiesbaden (again), Beirut, Teheran, and Rome, just in case Sami took another route to Afghanistan. Finally, after a long day, Sims telephoned Interpol Wiesbaden at 10:00 P.M. to determine the status of their investigation.

By 10:30 A.M. Wednesday, the wires had begun to buzz again. Interpol Rome said they could take no action unless the mother signed a complaint there. The persistent Sims hastily worked out the details; then, at 2:30 P.M., he sent a message to the Italians saying that the mother was in Wiesbaden and would fly immediately to Rome to sign the complaint if the subject was detained. The bright boys in Rome must have puzzled over this message for a while before they realized they had made a mistake. The next day they sent a message saying that their previous message should have read, "no action can be taken against him *even if* [authors' italics] the mother of the minors brings personal action against Sami in our country," as the U.S. court order was not valid there.

Sims, however, had no cause for concern. The German police have never been noted for their scruples, and at 4:00 P.M. Wednesday, he heard from Mrs. Sami's lawyer that Sami had been arrested. The children were with their mother. Half an hour later, the Broward County sheriff's office also advised him of the arrest. Curiously, Interpol was the last to let him know. It was only at 8:30 A.M. the following day, May 15, that Wiesbaden sent Sims the following message:

. . . SAMI, MOHAMMAD BORN DECEMBER 31, 1934 IN AFGHANISTAN WAS TRACED ON MAY 14, 1975 AT 1830 HOURS AT THE FRANKFURT/MAIN AIRPORT ACCOMPANIED BY THE CHILDREN *KIDNAPPED BY HIM* [authors' italics]. THE SUBJECT WAS ARRESTED AND THE CHILDREN WERE TURNED

OVER TO THEIR MOTHER MRS. HELEN SAMI.
MRS. SAMI WAS STAYING AT THE SHERATON
HOTEL AT THE AIRPORT. THE PUBLIC PRO-
SECUTOR'S OFFICE WITH THE FRANKFURT/MAIN
HIGHER REGIONAL COURT IS GOING TO INSTI-
TUTE EXTRADITION PROCEEDINGS. PLEASE
URGENTLY SEND THE DOCUMENTS RELATING
TO THE EXTRADITION. END.

The last sentence of the message was Sims's nemesis. His
zeal had apparently overcome his wisdom. By May 16 the diplomatic channels were blazing.

After a few conversations with the State Department, the
embarrassed Sims was forced at 6:30 P.M. to send another telex
to Wiesbaden:

. . . THE USA DEPARTMENT OF STATE ADVISED
AT 1800 HOURS MAY 16, 1975 THAT CRIMINAL OF-
FENSE AS CHARGED IN FLORIDA, USA HAS BEEN
DETERMINED NOT TO BE AN EXTRADITABLE OF-
FENSE UNDER THE TREATY AND WAS NOT FOR-
WARDED THROUGH DIPLOMATIC CHANNELS.
ALSO THAT THE SUBJECT SHOULD BE RELEASED
IMMEDIATELY UNLESS AN OFFENSE HAS BEEN
COMMITTED IN YOUR COUNTRY. MESSAGE
BEING SENT VIA DIPLOMATIC CHANNELS THIS
DATE AS STATED ABOVE. PLEASE KEEP THIS NCB
ADVISED OF DEVELOPMENTS. END.

The State Department telex to its Embassy in Bonn was a
little stronger:

1. DEPT HAS BEEN ADVISED THAT SUBJECT, A
NATIONAL OF AFGHANISTAN, HAS BEEN AR-
RESTED IN FRANKFORT (sic) PURSUANT TO AN IN-
TERPOL TELEX WHICH REQUESTED SUBJECT'S
PROVISIONAL ARREST FOR EXTRADITION.
2. THIS REQUEST WAS NOT SENT THROUGH DIP-

LOMATIC CHANNELS AND DEPT WAS NOT ADVISED. AS EMB AWARE A REQUEST FOR PROVISIONAL ARREST NOT SENT VIA DIPLO-MATIC CHANNEL IS NOT VALID UNDER TREATY. MOREOVER, FROM THE INFORMATION GIVEN TO DEPT IT DOES NOT APPEAR THAT CRIME SUB-JECT IS CHARGED WITH IS AN EXTRADITABLE OFFENSE UNDER TREATY.

3. FYI, DEPT UNDERSTANDS THAT COURT IN MARYLAND HAD GIVEN SUBJECT CUSTODY OF THESE CHILDREN BEFORE THE FLORIDA COURT MADE ITS DECREE, SO THERE ARE COMPETING COURT ORDERS. DEPT ALSO UNDERSTANDS THAT SUBJECT'S EX-WIFE HAD FOLLOWED SUB-JECT AND RAN OFF WITH THE CHILDREN WHEN HE WAS ARRESTED. EMBASSY OF AFGHANISTAN HAS APPROACHED DEPT WITH CONCERN OVER CASE. END FYI.

4. DEPT UNDERSTANDS THAT EMB MAY BE AP-PROACHED BY FRG REGARDING PROVISIONAL ARREST REQUEST. EMBASSY SHOULD ADVISE FRG THAT USG DOES NOT RPT NOT PLAN TO REQUEST EXTRADITION AND REQUEST FOR PRO-VISIONAL ARREST WAS NOT AUTHORIZED. KIS-SINGER

LIMITED OFFICIAL USE.

The wheels of justice sometimes grind exceedingly slowly. According to Sami, he was imprisoned "in solitary confinement with inadequate food, clothing, sanitary facilities and comforts from 6:30 P.M. on May 14, 1975, to 10:30 A.M., May 18, 1975." When finally released, he returned to the United States, angry, bitter, and puzzled.

Meanwhile, diplomatic notes passed between Washington and Kabul. On May 22 Sims was censured by K. E. Malmborg, Assistant Legal Adviser in the State Department. "From time to time in the past," Malmborg wrote, "we have had difficulty with people being arrested abroad for extradition on instructions from Interpol. Mr. Giannoules was very helpful in screening requests through the United States representative so this would not happen.* Yet State and municipal police and prosecuting authorities still occasionally go directly to Interpol abroad with requests for extradition. Recently such a request resulted in the arrest of an Afghanistani in Germany where he was incarcerated for several days, and the offense of which he was accused isn't even extraditable." †

He went on to request Sims's cooperation in future and said, "The Department of State, before making requests for provisional arrest or extradition in State cases, assures itself that there is an extradition treaty, that the offense is covered by the treaty and that local authorities have the agreement of the Governor or Attorney General to follow through on extradition. We are also able to assist local authorities in preparing adequate documentation. None of this happens when extradition is requested by Interpol and, in addition, the State Department may be totally unaware, as in the German case, that the period for perfecting an extradition has begun to run." ‡

---

*Ken Giannoulis was Sims's predecessor as head of the U.S. NCB.

†*The Royal Canadian Mounted Police Gazette* of October, 1958, reported that as long as a country has an extradition treaty with Canada, Canadian officials would arrest a subject simply on the basis of a simple letter or telegram from Interpol stating the offense committed, the authority issuing the warrant, and assurances that extradition would be requested.

‡More than thirty years ago Interpol was having similar problems. In a special communication of November 12, 1947, sent to NCB heads, Interpol Secretary General Louis Ducloux said that on several occasions the NCB's of some countries had applied for arrests of individuals in other countries, asserting that extradition steps would follow.

"Yet," Ducloux said, "once the arrest was made, it was found in some cases that the National Central Bureaux (sic) had not contacted beforehand the judicial authorities which they are meant to assist . . ." and ". . . the police forces abroad, which had carried out the arrest, found themselves compelled to detain individuals for fairly lengthy periods, without being able to hand them over to the judicial authorities of the country they belonged to."

In stressing the importance of justifying applications for arrest, Ducloux was apparently less concerned about the rights of the individual than the fact

228

On May 30 Helen Sami sent Sims a more pleasant letter. In it she said, "I owe so much to you and Mr. Holmes, who was my first contact at Interpol. He was the one who spured (*sic*) me on to getting the various sherifs (*sic*) to change their orders. Without the two of your help I never would have gotten the children safely home. It is reasuring (*sic*) to know that even if Sami does manage to get the children out of the country again, that all is not lost.

"He has returned to Washington and is making threats about false arrest. He wanted to know who got Interpol involved. As far as I'm concerned it will remain a mystery to him . . ."

Sami is back in Washington. Of Interpol, he says, "What is this group of little men who are trying to run the world?" Meanwhile, the room belonging to his children in his plush Chevy Chase home lies undisturbed, a pathetic shrine, left exactly as it was when they lived there.

In 1976 Sami brought suit against the U.S. Government, U.S. NCB Chief Louis B. Sims, his deputy James O. Holmes, and Interpol for false arrest, imprisonment, and violation of his constitutional rights, as well as libel and slander.

The defendants argued that suit could not be brought against them since Interpol was an "alien business entity" and "is not physically present in, nor does it do business within the boundaries of the United States." Even more startling was the decision of Federal District Judge Oliver Gasch, who ruled on October 19, 1977, that "After considering the nature of Interpol and its relationship with [the] U.S. NCB, the court concludes that it lacks jurisdiction over Interpol." The complaint against Interpol was dismissed.

The United States, Holmes, and Sims had asked the court to dismiss the charges raised by Sami because the arrest and imprisonment took place in West Germany, and alleged that Sami's complaint should be lodged against the police in that

---

that mistakes could, "in the eyes of the judicial authorities of each country, cause prejudice to the international authority of our organization . . ."

country. Judge Gasch agreed that the claim arose in West Germany and could not be maintained under the Federal Tort Claims Act, and he dismissed the charges against the United States and Holmes. Gasch noted, however, that "few courts have discussed this issue and no single standard has been established for resolving it."

The charges against Sims were not dismissed. Judge Gasch concluded that "genuine issues of material fact" continued to exist. Sims had argued that Sami's arrest was lawful because it had been based not on the statement that the United States would seek extradition, but solely on Florida felony warrants that had been relayed to the West German Government. An affidavit supporting Sims had been presented to the court from a West German Interpol official. However, the court stated that the affidavit provided no evidence that the official had any personal knowledge of the circumstances surrounding Sami's arrest. It is interesting to note that Interpol's own rules forbid arrests per foreign requests unless intention to extradite is given.

"The Court concludes," Judge Gasch wrote,

> that material facts remain in dispute regarding the ground upon which German authorities provisionally arrested plaintiff. This issue is critical to a determination of defendant Sims' liability for false arrest and imprisonment, and the circumstantial evidence in the record on this issue does not conclusively resolve it. The Court also notes that facts remain in dispute regarding Sims' defense that he acted with good faith, reasonable belief in the legality of his actions. For example, the allegation that Sims made a statement to plaintiff evincing a motivation to seek plaintiff's arrest on the grounds of race or national origin bias is disputed.

Sami argued in vain that federal courts had jurisdiction over Interpol's actions, but Judge Gasch disagreed. Citing the Interpol constitution, the judge took issue with Sami's argument that the U.S. NCB was an "arm" and "office" of Interpol. "This view is clearly inaccurate," Judge Gasch wrote, "because the U.S. NCB is not controlled by Interpol and its officers are not agents of that organization. The U.S. NCB is fully controlled by the United States Government and its officers act on behalf of the United States in fulfilling this country's obligations as a member of Interpol."

Judge Gasch concluded that "Applying a standard of reasonableness and fairness, the Court must conclude that Interpol is not 'doing business' in the District of Columbia and is not subject to the Court's jurisdiction . . . Interpol does not have any 'presence' in the District of Columbia for the simple reason that it does not have any agents here acting on its behalf." He dismissed the complaint against Interpol and ended his eighteen-page opinion by saying, "Thus any liability owing by Interpol to the plaintiff is based on acts of Interpol employees in Europe, and it would be patently unjust to subject Interpol to liability in this Court for acts of its agents committed outside the District of Columbia."

Judge Gasch did not explain why he thought West German police would be Interpol employees and agents in view of his assertion that Sims and Holmes were not.

While the case against Sims was kept alive only on a technical point, the absolution of Interpol's responsibility exemplifies the concern that has prompted several Congressional enquiries.

Critics have charged that Interpol's operations are not controlled and that the organization answers to no one. If the Sami case is allowed to stand, Interpol will be given a freedom from culpability that no organization in the United States currently possesses. In future, U.S. citizens will be exposed to false imprisonment anywhere in the world without recourse or protection of their rights in the federal courts.

It is not fit the public trusts should be lodged in the hands of any, till they are first proved and found fit for the business they are to be entrusted with.

———MATTHEW HENRY

AFTERWORD

The law is a necessity in an orderly society, and generally speaking, the police have a thankless job in their efforts to enforce it. They are criticized, ridiculed, and attacked from many quarters, both law-abiding and criminal, and from all sides of the political spectrum. Their valuable contribution to society has often been overlooked, while their mistakes have made them fair game for anybody seeking a scapegoat. It is not our intention to join the army of detractors any more than is necessary, but liberty is also an essential element of a civilized, orderly society. It is as vital to life as the air we breathe and the food we eat. It is a fragile thing, supposedly protected by the law, and by some ironic twist it is often the law that is used to erode it. Police are by and large decent, well-intentioned men and women, but they have, on occasion, exhibited tendencies to overstep their responsibilities, pushed by motives ranging from enthusiasm to frustration. However, like it or not, we are as responsible for their failings as they are, for they are the servants of society, and if we are dissatisfied with their performance, it is our duty to change it. Speaking in terms of seniority and importance, justice is senior to law in any truly civilized society, and we should do all we can to make this ideal a practical reality.

There is today an antihuman element loose in the world. It is reflected in the systems of government on all continents, and it is a hungry, tireless beast, quick to sight our weaknesses and quick to take advantage of them. It could, for the sake of communication (even if a little fancifully) be called the collective consciousness of all tyrants. It has no pity, no compassion, and above all, no sense of justice. It lives to exploit life, not to glorify it, and it exists only to cheat man of the true freedom he desires and deserves an opportunity to achieve. Its main weapon, as it always has been, is our ignorance and apathy. Its enemies are our vigilance and willingness to act according to our deepest beliefs.

Interpol is not exactly a beast; nor is it the enemy of mankind. It is what it is: a tool—to be used with wisdom or with folly, but unless we accept the responsibility for our tools and exhibit a willingness to control them, they soon control us.

Interpol's activities need to be thoroughly examined, preferably by an intergovernmental investigative group that has no ax to grind except to seek justice. This disqualifies individuals affiliated with law enforcement agencies.

Although this book provides the most thorough examination of Interpol done so far, many areas need still further exploration by a group with legal rights to greater resources.

The United States Government should (a) implement a reassessment and reclassification of the United States' relationship to and cooperation with Interpol; (b) pass legislation to control the organization as far as it affects U.S. citizens; (c) implement a means, independent of the U.S. agencies involved with this organization, of enforcing this legislation. The U.S. Government should also urge the other nation members of Interpol to do the same and to take the matter up in the United Nations, so that Interpol will at least achieve an official world-wide status with its activities subject to uniform systems of regulations and enforcement. The adoption of these measures not only would allow for a fair and cooperative world-wide *informa-*

tion network, but it would also infinitely improve Interpol's efficiency, effectiveness, and credibility. We can only hope that the chaos and illegal activities Interpol has been involved with for over fifty years will finally cease and that a new, clean strength and vision will emerge with the support of the member nations around the world.

We have shown that Interpol is guilty of selective violations of its Article 3, that it contains criminal intelligence data on individuals and groups with no criminal history, that its files contain erroneous data, that individuals (law enforcement and others) have used it to further personal goals of one kind or another, that it has illegal intelligence affiliations, and that it has, on a number of occasions, violated the rights of individuals. We have shown corruption among Interpol officials and we have questioned its efficiency, but these weaknesses are only signposts pointing the way. Much deeper investigation is needed into the use of Interpol by intelligence agencies, the domination by the French, the involvement of Interpol officials with drug traffic, the actual content of Interpol's dossiers, its continuing involvement with Nazis, and its use as a conduit of "disinformation."

There are a number of immediate, practical steps that could be demanded by Interpol's dues-paying members without their investigating matters further.

They could: (*a*) Appoint an objective body to investigate Interpol, one that would afterward act as a permanent oversight body. (*b*) Enact legislation to prevent NCB's from handling information containing unconfirmed suspicions, so-called criminal intelligence. Their sole right should be to transmit legitimate criminal records. (*c*) Enact legislation enabling citizens to inspect and correct their Interpol files. (*d*) Establish harsh penalties for the transmission of false information or intelligence information. (*e*) Demand the destruction of files containing false information, gossip, innuendo, and rumors. (*f*) Institute a file purging procedure, so that individuals with past records are not prevented from present rehabilitation.

U.S. Congressional figures have privately told us that the

solution may be found by implementing a "moratorium" on the United States' participation, in other words, to halt cooperation for, say, three years and, at the end of that period, to reevaluate the worth of the organization.

Interpol supporters are apparently fearful that the United States would not return should such a plan be tried. In fact, Secretary General Jean Nepote conceded in an interview with Vaughn Young that if the United States withdrew, Interpol would die—which is probably true. For without the cooperation of the United States' law enforcement agencies and departments, and without access to the files of those agencies and departments, Interpol will have little to offer its other members, who, in turn, will reevaluate their own relationship to Interpol.

The moratorium proposed in the cloakrooms of Congress may in fact be the most judicious way to settle the question, should other steps prove too time-consuming or difficult to implement immediately. Such a measure would not in any way hinder the present capabilities of the United States' law enforcement channels. All international police communications can be sent via the State Department or through the FBI or other agencies—a system which is already in effect. In each of Interpol's member nations, arrests are made by national agencies within those countries, and not by Interpol, and thus no opportunities for proper enforcement would be lost. The institution of such a moratorium would determine whether or not Interpol actually serves any unique function and whether this function outweighs its liabilities. Nevertheless, if such a worthwhile part of Interpol's operation is indeed found, the present corruption within Interpol's ranks should still be weeded out effectively before United States' affiliation resumes.

Good government's primary concern should be related to the rights and liberties of its citizens. Positive action to prevent such abuses by Interpol as have occurred in the past and are likely to increase in the future will do much to prove government intention. In the event that Interpol proves unwilling to subject itself to reform measures, we recommend that involved countries terminate their memberships. Justice Louis Brandeis's comment is as true now as it was in 1928: "The greatest dangers to liberty lurk in insidious encroachment by men of zeal, well-meaning but without understanding." The right to justice and recourse to injustice are inalienable rights, at present violated by this Kingdom of Cops.

Appendix

INTERNATIONAL CRIMINAL POLICE ORGANIZATION

INTERPOL

Constitution

and

General Regulations

The Constitution and General Regulations of the I.C.P.O.–
Interpol were adopted by the General Assembly at its Twenty-
fifth session (Vienna, 1956).

Articles 35 and 36 of the Constitution and 45 and 50 of the
General Regulations were modified at the Thirty-first session
(Madrid, 1962).

Articles 15, 16, and 19 of the Constitution and 41 and 58 of
the General Regulations were modified at the Thirty-third session (Caracas, 1964).

Article 58 of the General Regulations was modified at the
Thirty-sixth session (Kyoto, 1967).*

*The texts of all those Articles appear here in their amended form. This edi-
tion of the constitution is dated October 3, 1967.

CONSTITUTION

GENERAL PROVISIONS

Article 1

The Organization called the "INTERNATIONAL CRIMINAL PO-
LICE COMMISSION" shall henceforth be entitled: "THE INTER-
NATIONAL CRIMINAL POLICE ORGANIZATION (INTERPOL)."
Its seat shall be in Paris.

Article 2

Its aims are:

a) To ensure and promote the widest possible mutual assistance
between all criminal police authorities within the limits of the laws
existing in the different countries and in the spirit of the Universal
Declaration of Human Rights;

b) To establish and develop all institutions likely to contribute effectively to the prevention and suppression of ordinary law crimes.

Article 3

It is strictly forbidden for the Organization to undertake any intervention or activities of a political, military, religious or racial character.

Article 4

Any country may delegate as a Member to the Organization any official police body whose functions come within the framework of activities of the Organization.

The request for membership shall be submitted to the Secretary General by the appropriate governmental authority.

Membership shall be subject to approval by a two-thirds majority of the General Assembly.

STRUCTURE AND ORGANIZATION

Article 5

The International Criminal Police Organization (INTERPOL) shall comprise:

—The General Assembly,
—The Executive Committee,
—The General Secretariat,
—The National Central Bureaus,
—The Advisers.

THE GENERAL ASSEMBLY

Article 6

The General Assembly shall be the body of supreme authority in the Organization. It is composed of delegates appointed by the Members of the Organization.

Article 7

Each Member may be represented by one or several delegates; however for each country there shall be only one delegation head, appointed by the competent governmental authority of that country.

Because of the technical nature of the Organization, Members should attempt to include the following in their delegation:

a) High officials of departments dealing with police affairs,

b) Officials whose normal duties are connected with the activities of the Organization,

c) Specialists in the subjects on the agenda.

Article 8

The functions of the General Assembly shall be the following:

a) To carry out the duties laid down in the Constitution,

b) To determine principles and lay down the general measures suitable for attaining the objectives of the Organization as given in Article 2 of the Constitution,

c) To examine and approve the general programme of activities prepared by the Secretary General for the coming year,

d) To determine any other regulations deemed necessary,

e) To elect persons to perform the functions mentioned in the Constitution,

f) To adopt resolutions and make recommendations to Members on matters with which the Organization is competent to deal,

g) To determine the financial policy of the Organization,

h) To examine and approve any agreements to be made with other organizations.

Article 9

Members shall do all within their power, in so far as is compatible with their own obligations, to carry out the decisions of the General Assembly.

Article 10

The General Assembly of the Organization shall meet in ordinary session every year. It may meet in extraordinary session at the request of the Executive Committee or of the majority of Members.

Article 11

The General Assembly may, when in session, set up special committees for dealing with particular matters.

Article 12

During the final meeting of each session, the General Assembly shall choose the place of meeting for the following session. The date of this meeting shall be fixed by agreement between the inviting country and the President after consultation with the Secretary General.

Article 13

Only one delegate from each country shall have the right to vote in the General Assembly.

Article 14

Decisions shall be made by a simple majority except in those cases where a two-thirds majority is required by the Constitution.

THE EXECUTIVE COMMITTEE

Article 15

The Executive Committee shall be composed of the President of the Organization, the three Vice-Presidents and nine Delegates.

The thirteen members of the Executive Committee shall belong to different countries, due weight having been given to geographical distribution.

Article 16

The General Assembly shall elect, from among the delegates, the President and three Vice-Presidents of the Organization.

A two-thirds majority shall be required for the election of the President; should this majority not be obtained after the second ballot, a simple majority shall suffice.

The President and Vice-Presidents shall be from different continents.

Article 17

The President shall be elected for four years. The Vice-Presidents shall be elected for three years and shall not be immediately eligible for re-election either to the same posts or as Delegates on the Executive Committee.

Article 18

The President of the Organization shall:

a) Preside at meetings of the Assembly and the Executive Committee and direct the discussions,

b) Ensure that the activities of the Organization are in conformity with the decisions of the General Assembly and the Executive Committee,

c) Maintain as far as is possible direct and constant contact with the Secretary General of the Organization.

Article 19

The nine Delegates on the Executive Committee shall be elected by the General Assembly for a period of three years. They shall not be immediately eligible for re-election to the same posts.

Article 20

The Executive Committee shall meet at least once each year on being convened by the President of the Organization.

Article 21

In the exercise of their duties, all members of the Executive Committee shall conduct themselves as representatives of the Organization and not as representatives of their respective countries.

Article 22

The Executive Committee shall:

a) Supervise the execution of the decisions of the General Assembly,

b) Prepare the agenda for sessions of the General Assembly,

c) Submit to the General Assembly any programme of work or project which it considers useful,

d) Supervise the administration and work of the Secretary General,

e) Exercise all the powers delegated to it by the Assembly.

Article 23

In case of resignation or death of any of the members of the Executive Committee, the General Assembly shall elect another member to replace him and whose term of office shall end on the same date as his predecessor's. No member of the Executive Committee may remain in office should he cease to be a delegate to the Organization.

Article 24

Executive Committee members shall remain in office until the end of the session of the General Assembly held in the year in which their term of office expires.

THE GENERAL SECRETARIAT

Article 25

The permanent departments of the Organization shall constitute the General Secretariat.

Article 26

The General Secretariat shall:

a) Put into application the decisions of the General Assembly and the Executive Committee,

b) Serve as an international centre in the fight against ordinary crime,

c) Serve as a technical and information centre,

d) Ensure the efficient administration of the Organization,

e) Maintain contact with national and international authorities, whereas questions relative to the search for criminals shall be dealt with through the National Central Bureaus,

f) Produce any publications which may be considered useful,

g) Organize and perform secretariat work at the sessions of the General Assembly, the Executive Committee and any other body of the Organization,

h) Draw up a draft programme of work for the coming year for the consideration and approval of the General Assembly and the Executive Committee,

i) Maintain as far as is possible direct and constant contact with the President of the Organization.

Article 27

The General Secretariat shall consist of the Secretary General and a technical and administrative staff entrusted with the work of the Organization.

Article 28

The appointment of the Secretary General shall be proposed by the Executive Committee and approved by the General Assembly for a period of five years. He may be re-appointed for other terms but must lay down office on reaching the age of sixty-five, although he may be allowed to complete his term of office on reaching this age.

He must be chosen from among persons highly competent in police matters.

In exceptional circumstances, the Executive Committee may propose at a meeting of the General Assembly that the Secretary General be removed from office.

Article 29

The Secretary General shall engage and direct the staff, administer the budget and organize and direct the permanent departments, according to the directives decided upon by the General Assembly or Executive Committee.

He shall submit to the Executive Committee or the General Assembly any propositions or projects concerning the work of the Organization.

He shall be responsible to the Executive Committee and the General Assembly.

He shall have the right to take part in the discussions of the General Assembly, the Executive Committee and all other dependent bodies.

In the exercise of his duties, he shall represent the Organization and not any particular country.

Article 30

In the exercise of their duties, the Secretary General and the staff shall neither solicit nor accept instructions from any government or authority outside the Organization. They shall abstain from any action which might be prejudicial to their international task.

Each Member of the Organization shall undertake to respect the exclusively international character of the duties of the Secretary General and the staff and abstain from influencing them in the discharge of their duties.

All Members of the Organization shall do their best to assist the Secretary General and the staff in the discharge of their functions.

NATIONAL CENTRAL BUREAUS

Article 31

In order to further its aims, the Organization needs the constant and active co-operation of its Members, who should do all within their power which is compatible with the legislations of their countries to participate diligently in its activities.

Article 32

In order to ensure the above co-operation, each country shall appoint a body which will serve as the National Central Bureau. It shall ensure liaison with:

a) The various departments in the country,
b) Those bodies in other countries serving as National Central Bureaus,
c) The Organization's General Secretariat.

Article 33

In the case of those countries where the provisions of Art. 32 are inapplicable or do not permit of effective, centralized co-operation, the General Secretariat shall decide, with these countries, the most suitable alternative means of co-operation.

THE ADVISERS

Article 34

On scientific matters, the Organization may consult "Advisers."

Article 35

The role of Advisers shall be purely advisory.

Article 36

Advisers shall be appointed for three years by the Executive Committee. Their appointment will become definite only after notification by the General Assembly.

They shall be chosen from among those who have a world-wide reputation in some field of interest to the Organization.

Article 37

An Adviser may be removed from office by decision of the General Assembly.

BUDGET AND RESOURCES

Article 38

The Organization's resources shall be provided by:
a) The financial contributions from Members,
b) Gifts, bequests, subsidies, grants and other resources after these have been accepted or approved by the Executive Committee.

Article 39

The General Assembly shall establish the basis of Members' subscriptions and the maximum annual expenditure according to the estimate provided by the Secretary General.

Article 40

The draft budget of the Organization shall be prepared by the Secretary General and submitted for approval to the Executive Committee.

It will come into force after acceptance by the General Assembly.

Should the General Assembly not have had the possibility of approving the budget. The Executive Committee shall take all necessary steps according to the general outlines of the preceding budget.

RELATIONS WITH OTHER ORGANIZATIONS

Article 41

Whenever it deems fit, having regard to the aims and objects provided in the Constitution, the Organization shall establish relations and collaborate with other intergovernmental or non-governmental international organizations.

The general provisions concerning the relations with international, intergovernmental or non-governmental organizations will only be valid after their approval by the General Assembly.

The Organization may, in connection with all matters in which it is competent, take the advice of non-governmental international, governmental national or non-governmental national organizations.

With the approval of the General Assembly, the Executive Committee or, in urgent cases, the Secretary General may accept duties within the scope of its activities and competence either from other international institutions or organizations or in application of international conventions.

APPLICATION, MODIFICATION AND INTERPRETATION OF THE CONSTITUTION

Article 42

The present Constitution may be amended on the proposal of either a Member or the Executive Committee.

Any proposal for amendment to this Constitution shall be communicated by the Secretary General to Members of the Organization at least three months before submission to the General Assembly for consideration.

All amendments to this Constitution shall be approved by a two-thirds majority of the Members of the Organization.

Article 43

The French, English and Spanish texts of this Constitution shall be regarded as authoritative.

Article 44

The application of this Constitution shall be determined by the General Assembly through the General Regulations and Appendices, whose provisions shall be adopted by a two-thirds majority.

TEMPORARY MEASURES

Article 45

All bodies representing the countries mentioned in Appendix I shall be deemed to be Members of the Organization unless they declare through the appropriate governmental authority that they cannot accept this Constitution. Such a declaration should be made within six months of the date of the coming into force of the present Constitution.

Article 46

At the first election, lots will be drawn to determine a Vice-President whose term of office will end a year later.

At the first election, lots will be drawn to determine two Delegates on the Executive Committee whose term of office will end a year later, and two others whose term of office will end two years later.

Article 47

Persons having rendered meritorious and prolonged service in the ranks of the I.C.P.C. may be awarded by the General Assembly honorary titles in corresponding ranks of the I.C.P.O.

Article 48

All property belonging to the International Criminal Police Commission are transferred to the International Criminal Police Organization.

Article 49

In the present Constitution:

—"Organization," wherever it occurs, shall mean the International Criminal Police Organization.

—"Constitution," wherever it occurs, shall mean the constitution of the International Criminal Police Organization.

—"Secretary General" shall mean the Secretary General of the International Criminal Police Organization.

—"Committee" shall mean the Executive Committee of the Organization.

—"Assembly" or "General Assembly" shall mean the General Assembly of the Organization.

—"Member" or "Members" shall mean a Member or Members of the International Criminal Police Organization as mentioned in Art. 4 of the Constitution.

—"Delegate" (in the singular) or "delegates" (in the plural) shall mean a person or persons belonging to a delegation or delegations as defined in Art. 7.

—"Delegate" (in the singular) or "Delegates" (in the plural) shall mean a person or persons elected to the Executive Committee in the conditions laid down in Art. 19.

Article 50

This Constitution shall come into force on 13 June 1956.

APPENDIX I.

LIST OF STATES TO WHICH THE PROVISIONS OF ARTICLE 45 OF THE CONSTITUTION SHALL APPLY

Argentina, Australia, Austria, Belgium, Brazil, Burma, Cambodia, Canada, Ceylon, Chile, Colombia, Costa-Rica, Cuba, Denmark, Dominican Republic, Egypt, Eire, Finland, France, Federal German Republic, United Kingdom of Great Britain and Northern Ireland, Greece, Guatemala, India, Indonesia, Iran, Israel, Italy, Japan, Jordan, Lebanon, Liberia, Libya, Luxembourg, Mexico, Monaco, Netherlands, Netherlands Antilles, New Zealand, Norway, Pakistan, Philippines, Portugal, Saar, Saudi Arabia, Spain, Sudan, Surinam, Sweden, Switzerland, Syria, Thailand, Turkey, United States of America, Uruguay, Venezuela, Yugoslavia.

GENERAL REGULATIONS

Article 1
These General Regulations and Appendices have been adopted in accordance with Article 44 of the Constitution of the Organization.

Should there be any differences between the two, the Constitution shall prevail.

GENERAL ASSEMBLY
PLACE   DATE   CONVENING

Article 2
The General Assembly shall meet every year in ordinary session.

Article 3
Any Member may, on behalf of its country, invite the Assembly to meet on the territory of that country.

If this is impossible, the meeting shall be held at the seat of the Organization.

Article 4
Any such invitation should be sent to the President before the beginning of the debates of the Assembly.

Article 5
If the Executive Committee considers that circumstances are unfavourable to the meeting of the Assembly in the place fixed at its previous session, it may decide on another place.

Article 6

The President shall fix the date when the Assembly is to meet after consulting the authorities of the inviting country and the Secretary General.

Article 7

The date and place having been decided upon, the notices convening Members shall be sent not less than four months in advance by:

a) The inviting country to the other countries, through diplomatic channels;

b) The Secretary General to the various Members of the Organization.

Article 8

The following may be invited to be present at meetings as observers:

a) Police bodies which are not members of the Organization;

b) International organizations.

The list of observers shall be drawn up by the Executive Committee and should be approved by the inviting country.

The observers mentioned in a) shall be jointly invited by the inviting country and the Secretary General, while those mentioned in b) only by the Secretary General, after agreement of the Executive Committee and of the inviting country.

AGENDA

Article 9

The provisional agenda of the meeting shall be drawn up by the Executive Committee and communicated to Members not less than 90 days before the opening of the session.

Article 10

The provisional agenda shall include:

a) The report of the Secretary General on the work of the Organization,

b) The Secretary General's financial report and the draft budget,

c) The general programme of activities proposed by the Secretary General for the coming year,

d) Items whose inclusion has been ordered at the previous session of the Assembly,

e) Items proposed by Members,

f) Items inserted by the Executive Committee or the Secretary General.

Article 11

Any Member may, thirty days before the opening of the session, request that an item be added to the agenda.

Article 12

Before the opening meeting of the Assembly, the Executive Committee shall form the provisional agenda and the supplement to the agenda into a final agenda in the order of the urgency and priority of the items. The items left over from the previous session shall be deemed to take priority over the items suggested for the coming session.

Article 13

In so far as is possible, Members shall receive, thirty days before the opening meeting of the session, the information necessary for the examination of reports and items on the agenda.

EXTRAORDINARY SESSIONS

Article 14

Extraordinary sessions shall be held, in principle, at the seat of the Organization.

An extraordinary session shall be convened, after assent has been given by the President, by the Secretary General as soon as possible and not less than thirty days and no more than ninety days after the request has been made.

Article 15

In principle, the agenda of an extraordinary session may only include the object for its convening.

DELEGATIONS AND VOTING

Article 16

Members shall notify the Secretary General as early as possible of the composition of their delegation.

Article 17

The General Assembly shall make its decisions in plenary session by means of resolutions.

Article 18

Subject to Article 53 of the General Regulations, each country represented has one vote.

Voting shall be performed by the head of the delegation or some other delegate. The representative of one Member may not vote for another Member.

Article 19

The decisions of the Assembly shall be taken by a simple majority, except where otherwise provided by the Constitution.

Article 20

The majority shall be decided by a count of those persons present and casting an affirmative or negative vote. Those who abstain may justify their attitude.

When the Constitution requires a "majority of the Members" the calculation of this majority shall be based on the total number of the Members of the Organization, whether they are represented or not at the session of the Assembly.

Article 21

Voting shall be done by single ballot, except where a two-thirds majority is required.

In the latter case, if the required majority is not obtained the first time, a second vote shall be taken.

Article 22

Voting shall be done by show of hands, record vote or secret ballot.

At any time a delegate may request a record vote to be taken except in cases where a secret ballot is required by the Constitution.

Article 23

Persons composing the Executive Committee shall be elected by secret ballot. If two candidates obtain the same number of votes, a second ballot shall be taken. If this is not decisive, lots shall be drawn to determine which shall be chosen.

Article 24

Resolutions may be voted on paragraph by paragraph on the request of any delegate. In such a case, the whole shall subsequently be put to the vote.

Only one complete resolution shall be voted on at one time.

Article 25

When an amendent to a proposal is moved, the amendment shall be voted on first.

If there are several amendments, the President shall put them to the vote separately, commencing with the ones furthest removed from the basis of the original proposal.

CONDUCT OF BUSINESS

Article 26

Meetings of the Assembly and the committees shall not be public, unless otherwise decided by the Assembly.

Article 27

The Assembly may limit the time to be allowed to each speaker.

Article 28

When a motion is under discussion, any Member may raise a point of order and this point of order shall be immediately decided by the President.

Should this be contested, any delegate may appeal to the Assembly, which shall immediately decide by a vote.

Article 29

If, during the discussions, a speaker moves the suspension or adjournment of the meeting or the debates, the matter shall immediately be put to the vote.

Article 30

A delegate may at any time move the closure of the debates. Two speakers opposed to the closure may then speak, after which the Assembly shall decide whether to accede to the motion.

Article 31

The Assembly may not vote on a draft resolution unless copies of it in all the working languages have been distributed.

Amendments and counter-proposals may be discussed immediately unless a majority of Members request that written copies of them shall be distributed first.

When a draft resolution has financial consequences, the Executive Committee shall be requested to give its opinion and the discussions postponed.

Article 32

The Secretary General or his representative may intervene in the discussions at any moment.

SECRETARIAT

Article 33

Summary records of the debates of the Assembly in the working languages shall be distributed as soon as possible.

Article 34

The Secretary General shall be responsible for the secretarial work of the Assembly; for this purpose he shall engage the necessary personnel and direct and control them.

COMMITTEES

Article 35

At each session, the Assembly shall form such committees as it deems necessary.

On the proposal of the President, it shall allocate work relative to the various items on the agenda to each committee.

Article 36
Each committee shall elect its own chairman.

Each committee member shall have the right to vote.

Meetings of the committees shall be subject to the same rules as the plenary sessions of the Assembly.

Article 37
The chairman of each committee or a reporter nominated by it shall render a verbal account of its work to the Assembly.

Article 38
Unless otherwise decided by the Assembly, any committee may be consulted between sessions.

The President, after consultation with the Secretary General, may summon a committee to meet.

THE EXECUTIVE COMMITTEE

Article 39
At the end of the ordinary session the Assembly shall fill such vacancies on the Executive Committee as exist, by election of persons chosen amongst the delegates.

Article 40
At the beginning of each session the General Assembly shall elect three heads of delegations who will form the "Election Committee." They shall scrutinize the nominations they receive to determine whether they are valid and submit the list of these nominations in alphabetical order to the Assembly.

They shall also act as tellers.

Article 41
If, for any reason whatsoever, the President can no longer perform his duties either during or between sessions, his place shall temporarily be taken by the senior Vice-President.

Should the three Vice-Presidents be absent, the duties of President should provisionally devolve upon a Delegate of the Executive Committee designated by the other members of the Executive Committee.

GENERAL SECRETARIAT

Article 42
The Assembly shall elect a Secretary General by secret ballot for a term of office of five years.

The candidate for the post of Secretary General shall be proposed by the Executive Committee.

Article 43

The Secretary General should be or have been a police official.

He should preferably be a national of the country in which the seat of the Organization is situated.

Article 44

The Secretary General's term of office shall commence at the end of the session during which he has been elected and terminate at the end of the session held in the year when his term of office expires.

The Secretary General shall be eligible for other terms of office.

Article 45

Should the Secretary General be unable to carry out his duties, these shall be performed in the interim by the highest-ranking official in the General Secretariat provided the Executive Committee has no objection.

THE ADVISERS

Article 46

Advisers may be individually or collectively consulted on the initiative of the Assembly, the Executive Committee, the President or the Secretary General. They may make suggestions of a scientific nature to the General Secretariat or the Executive Committee.

Article 47

At the request of the General Assembly, the Executive Committee or the Secretary General, reports or papers on scientific matters may be submitted to the Assembly by Advisers.

Article 48

Advisers may be present at meetings of the General Assembly as observers and, on the invitation of the President, may take part in the discussions.

Article 49

Several Advisers may be nationals of the same country.

Article 50

The Advisers may meet when convened by the President of the Organization.

BUDGET—FINANCE

Article 51

The General Assembly shall:

a) Establish the basis of subscriptions of Members on an equitable basis,

b) Approve the budget according to the estimates provided by the Secretary General.

Article 52

The financial administration and the accounts of the Organization shall be checked in accordance with the procedure set forth in the Financial Regulations.

Article 53

If a Member constantly fails to fulfil its financial obligations toward the Organization, the Executive Committee may suspend its right to vote at General Assembly meetings and refuse it any other benefits it may claim, until all obligations have been settled.

The Member may appeal against such a decision to the General Assembly.

Article 54

The financial year shall begin on 1st January and end on 31st December.

Article 55

The Executive Committee may authorize a greater expenditure than that decided upon by the Assembly with the provision that this be accounted for to the latter.

Article 56

The financial administration of the Secretary General may be checked at any time by the Executive Committee.

Article 57

Should any state or Member give to the Organization permanent direct or indirect aid which is above its normal contribution, an agreement relative to such aid shall be drawn up and submitted for approval to the Executive Committee.

LANGUAGES

Article 58

The working languages of the permanent departments of the Organization shall be: French, English and Spanish.

The working languages of the General Assembly shall be: French, English and Spanish.

During General Assembly sessions, any delegate may speak in another language provided he makes arrangements for the interpretation of his speeches into one of the official languages.

Any request submitted by a group of countries for simultaneous interpretation of a language other than the official language must be sent, at least four months before the opening of the General Assembly session, to the Secretary General who will state whether such interpretation will be technically feasible.

Countries wishing to apply the special conditions in paragraphs 3 and 4 of Article 58 may do so only if they have undertaken the responsibility to provide adequate administrative facilities and to meet all expenses involved.

MODIFICATION OF THE GENERAL REGULATIONS

Article 59

These Regulations and their Appendices may be modified at the request of any Member so long as the suggested modification has been sent to the General Secretariat at least 120 days before the opening of the following session. The Secretary General shall circulate this proposal at least 90 days before the session of the General Assembly.

The Secretary General may propose a modification to the General Regulations or their Appendices by circulating his proposal to Members at least 90 days before the session of the General Assembly.

During the session, in case of urgent necessity, any modification of the Regulations or their Appendices may be placed before the Assembly provided a written proposal to this effect be submitted jointly by three Members.

Article 60

The General Assembly shall take a decision on the proposed modification of the Regulations or their Appendices after consultation with an "ad hoc" committee composed of three delegates elected by the Assembly and two persons appointed by the Executive Committee.

This committee shall also be consulted on any proposal for the modification of the Constitution.

MEMBER NATIONS

The following is a list of 126 countries that belonged to Interpol in 1977. The political situations (as of 1977) of countries on this list cover a wide spectrum.

ALGERIA   Dictatorship. Supports terrorists. Relies on secret police with extraordinary powers. Soviet advisers to army.

ARGENTINA   Totalitarian. Haven for Nazis. Political murder every ninety minutes in 1976. No civil rights.

AUSTRALIA   Democracy. (The Australian Security Intelligence Organization, which works closely with police, is under federal investigation for abuses of individual rights—a luxury, it must be pointed out, that a totalitarian government could not afford.)

AUSTRIA   Socialist democracy. Haven for former Nazis.

BAHAMAS   Socialist democratic government.

BAHRAIN   Constitutional monarchy. No civil rights. Political torture.

BELGIUM   Democratic state. Heavily infiltrated by KGB agents.

BERMUDA   Colony with representative government. Politically unstable.

BOLIVIA   Dictatorship. No civil rights. Political torture. Corrupt police.

BRAZIL   Brutal police. KGB infiltration.

BRUNEI   Sultanate dictatorship. Police guarantee rule.

BURMA   Socialist dictatorship. Heavy internal security. No civil rights.

BURUNDI Dictatorship. Genocide. Torture.
CAMEROON Dictatorship. Political prisoners. Torture.
CANADA Democracy.
CENTRAL AFRICAN REPUBLIC Individual rights and democracy suspended since 1966. Crime suppressed by amputations of limbs.
CHAD Dictatorship. Persecution of Christians.
CHILE Police state. Political torture. Haven for former Nazis.
CHINA, REPUBLIC OF (TAIWAN) Dictatorship. Widespread torture.
COLOMBIA Dictatorship. Torture. Corrupt police.
CONGO (BRAZZAVILLE) Run by army. Close relations with Soviet Union.
COSTA RICA Haven for internationally accused criminal Robert Vesco from 1972 to 1978, who loaned the government money to stay. Republican form of government with strong President.
CUBA Communist dictatorship.
CYPRUS Politically unstable. Wide police powers. Republican form of government embroiled with Turkey.
DAHOMEY Military dictatorship. Communist principles.
DENMARK Democracy.
DOMINICAN REPUBLIC Dictatorship. Political assassination, torture.
ECUADOR Dictatorship. Corrupt police.
EGYPT Totalitarian. Police forces trained by former Nazi SS men. Support of terrorists.
EL SALVADOR Republic supported by police power. Torture.
ETHIOPIA Totalitarian, in process of nationalization. Marxist.
FIJI Democracy.
FINLAND Parliament. Close cooperation with Russia.
FRANCE Democracy. Strong corrupt police.
GABON One-party dictatorial government.
GERMANY Democracy. Many former Nazis in police.
GHANA Military government since 1972. Soviet assistance. Torture of dissidents.
GIBRALTAR Small, important naval and air base.
GREECE Democracy returning. Not fully stable.
GUATEMALA Banana republic rife with political murder.
GUINEA (EQUATORIAL) Dictatorial government supported by Russia and China. Reign of terror. One vast concentration camp.
GUYANA Dictatorship, in process of nationalization.
HAITI Dictatorship. Torture common practice.
HONDURAS Dictatorship. Police brutal.
HONG KONG British colony. Major spy and drug center.

265

ICELAND Democracy.
INDIA On-again, off-again democracy. Extensive police powers.
INDONESIA Dictatorship. About 55,000 political prisoners detained without trial.
IRAN Dictatorship. Ruthless secret police.
IRAQ Dictatorship. Supports terrorists.
IRISH REPUBLIC Democracy. Terrorist and espionage playground.
ISRAEL Democracy.
ITALY Democracy. Unstable.
IVORY COAST Right-wing parliamentary government patterned after French. Police torture.
JAMAICA Parliamentary state. Left wing.
JAPAN Democracy. Terrorist activity.
JORDAN Monarchy. Political repression.
KENYA Dictatorship.
KHMER REPUBLIC (CAMBODIA) Oppressive Communist regime. Civilians massacred. Political opponents jailed.
KOREA (REPUBLIC OF) Suspension of liberties and an amended constitution. Torture of dissidents.
KUWAIT Sheikdom. Supports terrorists.
LAOS Communist. Major opium producer.
LEBANON War-torn country. Has supported terrorists. Rulers must be chosen along religious lines.
LESOTHO Dictatorship. Torture by police.
LIBERIA Democracy. Dominated by foreign industrial interests.
LIBYA Military dictatorship. Financial and political support to terrorists. Police torture.
LIECHTENSTEIN Miniature democracy.
LUXEMBOURG Democracy.
MADAGASCAR Police state.
MALAWI Totalitarian. Torture. Religious persecution.
MALAYSIA Confederation of Sultanates. Heavy police powers.
MALI Military dictatorship. Russian supported.
MALTA Former democracy.
MAURITANIA Dictatorship.
MAURITIUS Police state.
MEXICO Democracy. Brutal, uncontrolled police.
MONACO Monarchy. Gambling haven.
MOROCCO Dictatorship. Major drug-producer.
NAURU Country of less than 7,000 population. Former Pacific trust territory.
NEPAL Dictatorship. Drug-producer.

NETHERLANDS Democracy.
NETHERLANDS ANTILLES Political unrest. Governor appointed by Dutch government.
NEW ZEALAND Democracy.
NICARAGUA Dictatorship. Brutal treatment and torture by police.
NIGER Military government.
NIGERIA Military government. Strong ties to Soviet Union.
NORTH BORNEO Member of Federation of Malaysia. Wide police powers.
NORWAY Democracy.
OMAN Sultanate. Torture. Slavery common till 1970.
PAKISTAN Semi-democracy. Major drug producer. Corrupt police.
PANAMA Military dictatorship. Torture by police.
PERU Police under a military government. Haven for ex-Nazis.
PHILIPPINES Dictatorship. Political arrest and torture.
PORTUGAL Strife-torn country moving toward democracy.
QATAR Dictatorship.
RUMANIA Communist police state.
RWANDA Totalitarian regime, dominated by military.
SARAWAK Member of Federation of Malaysia.
SAUDI ARABIA Monarchy. Public floggings and executions. Supports terrorism.
SENEGAL Corrupt administration. Elected President has full powers.
SIERRA LEONE One-party rule. Ties with Soviet Union.
SINGAPORE Dictatorship. Has Russian naval base.
SOMALIA Dictatorship. Had Russian naval base. State security police trained by KGB.
SPAIN Fascist monarchy now relaxing totalitarian rule.
SRI LANKA Socialist-Marxist police state.
SUDAN Totalitarian regime.
SURINAM One-party government.
SWEDEN Socialist democracy with good civil liberty record.
SWITZERLAND Democracy. Neutral state.
SYRIA Totalitarian rule. Army and police trained by Russian soldiers and intelligence experts.
TANZANIA Police state. Torture by East German-trained police.
THAILAND Totalitarian.
TOGO Military government.
TRINIDAD and TOBAGO People's National Movement Party in power. British ministerial-type system.
TUNISIA Police state. Supports terrorists.
TURKEY Limited democracy. Drug-producer. Brutal police.

267

UGANDA Totalitarian regime under vicious dictator Idi Amin.

UNION OF ARAB EMIRATES Totalitarian. Said to support terrorists.

UNITED KINGDOM Democracy. Growing police powers. Secretive government.

UNITED STATES OF AMERICA Democracy.

UPPER VOLTA Military dictatorship.

URUGUAY Military government.

VENEZUELA Right-wing democracy.

VIETNAM Communist totalitarian police state.

YUGOSLAVIA Communist totalitarian police state.

ZAÏRE Totalitarian state. Torture and brutality.

ZAMBIA One-party government upheld by police and military.

LEGISLATIVE HISTORY OF THE UNITED STATES' MEMBERSHIP IN INTERPOL

June 1938: U.S. Code, Title 22, Section 263A.

The Attorney General is authorized to accept and maintain, on behalf of the U.S., membership in the International Criminal Police Organization . . . the total dues to be paid for the membership of the U.S. shall not exceed $1,500 per annum.

(June 10, 1938, ch. 335, 52 Stat. 640)

August 1968: Public Law 85-768 authorized the Attorney General to designate departments and agencies which may participate on a pro-rata share basis, in the U.S. representation with the International Criminal Police Organization, and increased from $1,500 to $25,000 per annum the amount of expenses which may be incurred by reason of U.S. membership.

(Aug. 27, 1958, PL 85-768, 72 Stat. 921)

Nov. 1967: Public Law 90-159 increased from $25,000 to $28,500 per annum the amount of expenses which may be incurred by reason of U.S. membership.

(Nov. 28, 1967, Public Law 90-159, 81 Stat. 517)

Aug. 1972: Increased U.S. membership fee authorization to $80,000 from $28,500.

(Aug. 10, 1972, Public Law 92-380, 86 Stat. 531)

Oct. 1974: Increased U.S. membership fee from $80,000 to $118,000 per annum.
(*Oct. 24, 1974, Public Law 93-468*)

1976, 1977: Attempts made to lift the $118,000 ceiling entirely and allow any amount of dues money to be paid. Both bills have died with objections from Congressional figures. In 1978, the U.S. Interpol office was slipping behind in membership dues (which was raised above the $118,000 figure which is all the U.S. can legally pay) and no one is interested in helping.

April 1978: Minnesota becomes the first state to prohibit agencies from working with Interpol. Addendum to a privacy bill prevents state agencies from cooperating with Interpol effective 1980. This is the first such ban by any governmental body in the world. A similar bill began to move successfully in the Florida legislature and was being introduced in other states as well.

SYNOPSES OF FOREIGN AND U.S. INVESTIGATIVE REQUESTS

The following synopses of cases handled by the U.S. NCB* exemplify the types of requests received from law enforcement at all levels in the United States that require investigations abroad. They also show the types of requests received from foreign law enforcement for investigation within the United States.

FOREIGN REQUESTS TO THE UNITED STATES

Interpol Rome, Italy, notified the U.S. NCB of the arrest of two British nationals, suspected of being members of a large-scale narcotics ring also involving Italians and U.S. nationals. They were found in possession of passports in the names of several British and American citizens. Photographs and fingerprints were sent to this Bureau for identification, and one of the alleged British suspects was identified as a U.S. national wanted since 1973 by the Drug Enforcement Administration. Another of the U.S. nationals suspected in the case was identified as the former wife of a notorious LSD advocate, known for her involvement with narcotics and wanted in the United States in connection with a narcotics investigation.

Interpol Wiesbaden, Germany, initiated investigations of a U.S. national in December of 1972 for fraud. The suspect had rented a house

*From U.S. NCB (Washington) annual report for fiscal year 1975.

in Germany and had subsequently reported the theft of numerous valuable items. Investigations in the United States and other Interpol member countries revealed that the suspect had a history of making fraudulent insurance claims and was wanted by the Austrian authorities. The suspect and his female accomplice were later arrested in Denmark for attempted insurance fraud and were deported to Austria for trial.

Interpol Wellington, New Zealand, requested the criminal history check on three American brothers and two of their wives, who had been arrested as illegal immigrants in New Zealand when their residence permits expired. A check with NCIC revealed that they were wanted in Indiana for possession of a large amount of marijuana. They were voluntarily deported to the United States, where the three brothers were arrested, tried, and are currently serving sentences.

Interpol Wiesbaden, Germany, advised the U.S. NCB of the arrest of a U.S. national for robbery and attempted sale of thirty kilograms of hashish. Inquiry in TECS and NCIC determined that the suspect was wanted by Louisiana authorities for robbery and attempted murder. He was deported from Germany to the United States in March and was taken into custody upon his arrival.

Interpol Paris, France, initiated investigations on a Greek national for use of counterfeit and forged documents and swindles committed through marriages to wealthy women. The suspect was found to have been using numerous aliases, and when he was definitely identified it was found that he was the subject of an Interpol International Wanted Notice, wanted in Germany for fraud and drug-trafficking. We received information that the suspect intended to marry a U.S. citizen and attempt to claim refugee status in the United States. He was located in New York, where he was taken into custody for extradition to the Federal Republic of Germany.

An All Points Bulletin was received from **Interpol London, United Kingdom,** concerning a U.S. national wanted there for encashment of stolen bank drafts. The General Secretariat of Interpol further advised that the same subject was also wanted by the authorities in the United Arab Emirates for uttering approximately $250,000 in stolen checks. The suspect was using an alias, but it was determined that he was identical with a person wanted by a California Police Department for uttering stolen checks. In cooperation with the Drug Enforcement Administration, the suspect and an accomplice were arrested by Thailand authorities for smuggling two kilos of heroin. The U.S. NCB advised the United Kingdom and the United Arab Emirates of this fact. It was discovered that the suspect had been committing frauds in various countries, using as many as twenty-six different passports, and that he was simultaneously under investigation by four government agencies in the United States for fraud and drug-trafficking. At present, the suspect is in custody in Thailand. Upon completion of his sentence, his extradition will be considered by the United States, British, and United Arab Emirates authorities.

UNITED STATES REQUESTS ABROAD

A New York police department requested the U.S. NCB to issue an international lookout for a Mexican national wanted for grand larceny by the New York State Supreme Court. With the help of Interpol Madrid, the suspect was located in Barcelona, Spain. The New York authorities were advised and are requesting extradition of the subject to the United States.

The U.S. NCB was informed by a California police department that a Malayan national, who was wanted there on two counts of murder, was to be traveling between Japan and Canada to visit a brother. Canada and several Far Eastern Interpol countries were alerted and the suspect was traced to Singapore through a check he had written there. He was arrested by the Singapore authorities and following his extradition through diplomatic channels, he was handed over to the authorities in California for trial.

The sister of a U.S. national wrote directly to the U.S. NCB requesting aid in locating her brother, who had disappeared in February, 1971. A general radio All Points Bulletin was sent out to all Interpol bureaus with a description of the brother. His passage had been noted in Peru and Chile, and he was finally traced to Germany, where he was located in West Berlin.

Investigation was initiated with this Bureau by a New Jersey district attorney's office concerning a suspect wanted on seventy felony counts for grand larceny, involving swindle of approximately $10 million. Information had been received that the suspect had departed for London. Interpol London reported that he had passed through London but had continued on to Sweden. The Swedish Interpol authorities were notified, and the suspect was subsequently arrested in Stockholm.

Police authorities in Florida advised the U.S. NCB that a Spanish sailor from a Danish ship had been robbed and beaten to death in Florida. Two suspects had been arrested in connection with the case, and both had entered a plea of guilty to second-degree murder. However, before the case could be brought to trial, fingerprints and other materials were needed for positive identification of the victim. Since the Danish ship had left and was not scheduled to return for several months, no such identification could be made. Assistance was requested from Interpol Washington. At our request, Interpol Madrid promptly furnished the necessary identifying documents and the suspects were brought to trial.

In March of 1975, this Bureau [the U.S. NCB] was advised that a subject claiming to be an Interpol agent, using various different aliases, had cashed worthless checks in department stores in several states. Based on this information, the U.S. NCB sent out a nationwide All Points Bulletin alerting possible victims of the subject's *modus operandi*. The suspect was subsequently identified by a photograph on an identification card used to cash a check, and it was found that he was a Cuban citizen in exile, on record with the FBI for passing unlawful checks, and named in several outstanding warrants in Georgia, Minnesota, Oregon, and Florida.

As a result of a report received from a police department in Massachusetts concerning a burglary involving twenty-two valuable oriental rugs, Interpol Wiesbaden, Germany, was advised that one of the rugs had been shipped to Hamburg. The German authorities were able to trace the rug through several middlemen and seize it. The rug, valued at approximately $45,000, has now been returned to its owner in Massachusetts.

At approximately 11:30 P.M. on April 18, 1975, one of the federal agents assigned to the U.S. NCB received a call from the U.S. Secret Service that a person who had previously threatened the President of the United States, and who had recently been released from a mental institution, was preparing to board a plane for London to see Queen Elizabeth. Medical authorities considered this person to be a danger to the Queen. This information was forwarded via the U.S. NCB to Interpol London. When the person arrived at Heathrow Airport in London a few hours later, he was interviewed by Scotland Yard and was subsequently committed to a mental institution in London.

In January 1975, this Bureau was contacted by a police department in New York concerning the murder and robbery of a U.S. national, believed to have been committed by a Swiss national. This Bureau contacted Interpol Berne, Switzerland, and on the same date, the suspect was identified and arrested by Swiss police in Zurich as he left an international flight originating in the United States. A photograph of the suspect sent by the Swiss police was shown to a witness to the murder and a positive identification was made. The Swiss national later confessed to the crime. At the time of his arrest, the suspect had $16,000 in undeclared dollars in his possession, which has since been returned to the United States. Another $46,000 had been turned over to the police in Texas, and investigations are continuing in Texas concerning this drug-trafficking ring.

REFERENCE SOURCES

INTRODUCTION

1. Robert Walters, "Does Interpol Threaten Your Privacy?" *Parade*, November 9, 1975.
2. William Corson, *The Armies of Ignorance*.
3. The London Sunday *Times*, September 22, 1974.
4. Jean Nepote, "The Role of an International Criminal Police in the Context of an International Criminal Court and Police Cooperation with Respect to International Crimes," from *A Treatise on International Criminal Law*, edited by M. Cherif Bassiouni and Ved P. Nanda, Charles C. Thomas, Springfield, Illinois, 1973.
5. *International Criminal Police Review* (hereafter referred to as *I.C.P.C. Review*), 50th anniversary edition.
6. *Interpol* brochure, January, 1958.

CHAPTER ONE

1. Letter dated November 7, 1974, from Interpol Berne to Interpol Washington regarding Interpol Washington radiogram 409121 of October 2, 1974, regarding Dickopf.
2. Curt Reiss, *The Nazis Go Underground.*
3. Letter of March 14, 1975, from Simon Wiesenthal to NCLE researcher Heber Jentzsh.
4. Ladislas Farago, *Aftermath: Martin Bormann and the Fourth Reich.*

CHAPTER TWO

1. William Corson, *The Armies of Ignorance.*
2. *The Times* (London), October 9, 1926.
3. Harry Soderman, *A Policeman's Lot.*
4. *Ibid.*
5. Baron Collier, "International World Police," *Journal of Criminal Law and Criminology*, September–October, 1932.
6. Memorandum of June 1, 1933, U.S. Department of State, Division of International Conferences.
7. Collier, "International World Police."
8. *Ibid.*
9. Soderman, *A Policeman's Lot.*
10. Ovid Demaris, *The Director.*
11. *Ibid.*
12. Letter of December 4, 1924, to the Assistant Attorney General for the U.S. Department of State from the Assistant Attorney General.
13. Note of April 14, 1935, from unnamed Austrian Minister, Austrian Legation, Washington, D.C.
14. Letter of April 17, 1935, from Assistant Secretary of State Wilbur J. Carr to Attorney General Homer Cummings.
15. Letter of April 10, 1935, from Acting Attorney General Stanley Reed to the Secretary of State Cordell Hull, regarding communication from the Minister of Austria.
16. Demaris, *The Director.*
17. Robert Payne, *The Life and Death of Adolf Hitler.*
18. Harry Soderman, *A Policeman's Lot.*
19. Records of the Reich Ministry for Public Enlightenment.
20. National Archives, Records of the Third Reich.
21. Letter of March 28, 1936, from the Assistant Secretary of State Wilbur J. Carr to Attorney General Homer Cummings.
22. Letter of April 3, 1936, from Attorney General Homer Cummings to the Assistant Secretary of State, Wilbur J. Carr.
23. Report of June 13, 1936, from John L. Calnan, Vice-Consul, Yugoslavian Consulate, to the Department of State.
24. Note of April 9, 1937, from the British Ambassador Rt. Hon. Sir Ronald Lindsay to the Secretary of State, Cordell Hull.
25. Letter of April 19, 1937, from the Secretary of State Cordell Hull to President Roosevelt.
26. Letter of April 20, 1937, from Assistant Secretary of State Wilbur J. Carr to W. H. Drane Lester, Assistant Director of the FBI.
27. Report of July 21, 1937, to the State Department from W. H. Drane Lester, Assistant Director of the FBI.

28. Corson, *The Armies of Ignorance.*
29. Sanford J. Unger, *F.B.I.*
30. Proposed recommendation to be submitted by Attorney General Cummings to the Congress, March, 1938.

CHAPTER THREE

1. Trial of the major war criminals before the International Military Tribunal, Volume 16, p. 182. June 13, 1946, Nuremberg. Published 1942 by the IMT.
2. Nuremberg document #3282, Archives of the *Institut für Zeiteschichte.*
3. Memorandum of May 26, 1938, U.S. Department of State.
4. Note of June 1, 1938, from Secretary of State Cordell Hull to the Minister of Rumania.
5. William Corson, *The Armies of Ignorance.*
6. *Ibid.*
7. Soderman, *A Policeman's Lot.*
8. Letter of July 26, 1939, from W. Fleischer, Third Reich Criminal Police Commissioner, to J. Edgar Hoover, Director FBI. Memorandum of July 26, 1939, from FBI official N. H. McCabe to FBI Assistant Director Louis B. Nichols.
9. Note of July 5, 1939, from the German Embassy to the Department of State.
10. Letter of July 21, 1939, from the Assistant Secretary of State Francis B. Sayne to the Attorney General Frank Murphy.
11. Letter of July 28, 1939, from FCC Acting Chairman Frederick I. Thompson to the Secretary of State Cordell Hull.
12. Memorandum of July 31, 1939, U.S. Department of State.
13. Letter of August 21, 1939, from the Attorney General Frank Murphy to the Secretary of State Cordell Hull.
14. Division of International Conferences memorandum by Dr. Warren Kelchner, 1939.
15. *I.C.P.C. Review,* No. 9, June 20, 1938.
16. *I.C.P.C. Review,* No. 4, May, 1941.
17. Reinhard Heydrich quote.
18. *I.C.P.C. Review,* No. 4, May, 1941.
19. Soderman, *A Policeman's Lot.*
20. David Littlejohn, *The Patriotic Traitors.*
21. *Ibid.*
22. "The German Police," report of November 22, 1941, by G-2 (Counter-Intelligence Sub-Division), Evaluation and Dissemination Section, Supreme Headquarters of the Allied Expeditionary Force.

23. Memorandum of November 22, 1941, from FBI aide J. F. Buckley to J. Edgar Hoover, Director FBI.
24. Payne, *The Life and Death of Adolf Hitler.*
25. Louis Decloux, *From Blackmail to Treason, Political Crime and Corruption in France 1920–1940.*
26. Jacques Delarue, *The Gestapo: A History of Horror.*
27. Delarue, *The Gestapo.*
28. Delarue, *The Gestapo.*
29. Alexander Mitscherlich (head of the German Medical Commision at the Nuremberg trials), *Doctors of Infamy.*
30. Delarue, *The Gestapo.*
31. Michael Elkins, *Forged in Fury.*
32. Don Cook, the *Los Angeles Times,* July 26, 1976.
33. "The German Police," G-2 report of November 22, 1941.

CHAPTER FOUR

1. Soderman, *A Policeman's Lot.*
2. Sir Ronald Howe, *The Story of Scotland Yard.*
3. Soderman, *A Policeman's Lot.*
4. Paul Levy, *Affair Stavisky—Justice Pourrie;* Horace de Carbuccia, *Le Massacre de la Victoire, 1914–1934.*
5. Soderman, *A Policeman's Lot.*
6. Letter of September 20, 1946, to the Head of the Secretariat of the Allied Control Authority in Berlin from Louis Ducloux. The file on this matter was declassified on January 27, 1973, at the Federal Record Center in Suitland, Maryland.
7. John Macklin, "World Police Files Found," *P.M.*, August 2, 1945 (© 1945 by the *Chicago Sun*).
8. Letter of September 1, 1945, from FBI agent Frederick Ayer, Jr., to J. Edgar Hoover, Director FBI.
9. Memorandum of October 10, 1945, from Clyde A. Tolson to J. Edgar Hoover, Director FBI.

CHAPTER FIVE

1. Telegram of May 15, 1946, from Under Secretary of State Dean Acheson to the American Embassy in Brussels.
2. Telegram of May 17, 1946, from "Kirk" to Under Secretary of State Dean Acheson.
3. Ovid Demaris, *The Director.*
4. *Ibid.*
5. *Ibid.*

6. Letter of April 22, 1947, from Under Secretary of State Dean Acheson to Attorney General Tom Clark.
7. Letter of May 26, 1947, from Attorney General Tom Clark to Under Secretary of State Dean Acheson.
8. Justice Department memorandum of May 22, 1961, from Foley to Miller.
9. Sanford J. Unger, *F.B.I.*
10. *Ibid.*
11. *I.C.P.C. Review*, No. 50, September, 1951.
12. Report from the American Ambassador in Lisbon, Lincoln McVeagh, to the Justice Department, June 25, 1951.
13. *I.C.P.C. Review*, report on Twenty-first General Assembly.
14. *Ibid.*
15. Interview with Vaughn Young, 1975.
16. Public Law 806, 81st Congress, approved September 21, 1950.
17. Letter of May 7, 1954, from Assistant Secretary of State David McKay to Secretary of the Treasury George M. Humphrey.
18. Letter of June 1, 1954, from Assistant Secretary of the Treasury H. Chapman Rose to the State Department.
19. *Ibid.*
20. Memorandum of April 22, 1954, from Malachi L. Harney (the Assistant Commissioner of the Bureau of Narcotics who had attended Interpol's 1951 meeting) to Mr. John P. Weitzel.
21. Memorandum of November 5, 1954, from Chief of the Secret Service U. E. Baughman to Assistant Secretary of the Treasury, H. Champan Rose.
22. Interview with Vaughn Young, 1975.
23. *Ibid.*
24. Memorandum of December 24, 1957, from Administrative Assistant Attorney General S. A. Andietla to Frank Chambers, Chief Legal and Legislative Section.
25. Memorandum of February 13, 1958, from Acting Assistant Attorney General Rufus D. McLean to the Deputy Attorney General.
26. Letter of February 26, 1958, from Deputy Attorney General Laurence E. Walsh to Assistant Secretary of Treasury David W. Kendall.
27. Letter of April 19, 1958, from Interpol Secretary General Marcel Sicot to District Supervisor of the Bureau of Narcotics (Rome) Charles Siragusa.
28. Memorandum of August 1, 1959, from the State Department to the Justice Department.
29. Demaris, *The Director.*
30. Memorandum of May 5, 1961, from Assistant Attorney General

Herbert J. Miller, Jr., to Nicholas Katzenbach of the Department of State.

31. Letter of July 14, 1961, from Attorney General Robert F. Kennedy to Secretary of the Treasury Douglas Dillon.

32. Demaris, *The Director.*

33. Memorandum of October 9, 1963, from U.S. Attorney Joseph D. Tydings to Assistant Attorney General Herbert J. Miller, Jr.

34. *Ibid.*

35. Memorandum of October 18, 1965, from Assistant Attorney General (Criminal Division) Fred M. Vinson, Jr., to Deputy Attorney General Ramsey Clark.

36. Memorandum of November 12, 1965, from Herbert E. Hoffman, Chief, Legislative and Legal Section of the Justice Department, to Deputy Attorney General Ramsey Clark.

37. Letter of August 22, 1966, from Assistant Attorney General (Criminal Division) Fred M. Vinson to J. Edgar Hoover, Director FBI.

38. Memorandum of May 1, 1969, from chief of the U.S. Interpol NCB Andrew Tartaglino to chief of the Department of Justice's General Crime Section Carl Belcher.

39. Memorandum of May 13, 1969, from chief of the Department of Justice's General Crime Section Carl W. Belcher to file.

40. Interview with Vaughn Young, May 21, 1975.

41. Hearings of the Senate Committee on Treasury, Postal Service and General Government Appropriations, February 24, 1976.

42. Richard Starnes, Scripps-Howard News Service, July 9, 1976.

43. Jack Anderson, United Features Syndicate, March 14, 1975.

44. U.S. Interpol NCB Chief Louis B. Sims in testimony before House Subcommittee on Treasury Appropriations, U.S. Congress, House of Representatives, March 4, 1977.

45. *Ibid.* March 3, 1977.

46. *Ibid.* February 23, 1977.

CHAPTER SIX

1. Thomas W. Braden, "I'm Glad the C.I.A. Is Immoral," *Saturday Evening Post,* May 20, 1967.

2. Alfred W. McCoy, *The Politics of Heroin in Southeast Asia.*

3. *Ibid.*

4. The Staff and Editors of *Newsday, The Heroin Trail.*

5. Alain Joubert, *Dossier D . . . Comme Drogue.*

6. *Newsday, The Heroin Trail.*

7. *Ibid.*

8. Joubert, *Dossier D.*
9. *Newsday, The Heroin Trail.*
10. *Ibid.*
11. *Ibid.*
12. *Ibid.*
13. McCoy, *The Politics of Heroin in Southeast Asia.*
14. *Ibid.*
15. *Ibid.*
16. *Ibid.*
17. *Ibid.*
18. Interpol General Secretariat report, 1974.
19. U.N. Commission of Narcotic Drugs, Eighteenth Session, draft report, 1964.
20. Harry Anslinger, *The Protectors.*
21. Bureau of Narcotics, "Traffic in Opium and Other Dangerous Drugs for the Year Ending December 31, 1965." U.S. Government Printing Office, Washington, D.C., 1966.
22. John Ingersall, Director, Bureau of Narcotics and Dangerous Drugs.
23. "Interpol Methods Criticized," *The Guardian* (London), March 16, 1977.
24. "The French Connection Stays Dominant in Market Here," *The New York Times*, April 23, 1975.
25. Interpol General Secretariat report of 1972, "International Illicit Drug Traffic in 1971."
26. Interpol General Secretariat report of 1973, "International Illicit Drug Traffic in 1972, Some Cases of International Cooperation."
27. Progress Report by the Secretary General, Interpol General Assembly, Frankfurt, September, 1972.
28. Statement of David R. Macdonald, Assistant Secretary of the Treasury (Enforcement, Operations and Tariff Affairs), to the Senate Subcommittee of the Committee on Appropriations, February 24, 1976.
29. U.S. Senate Hearings, Committee on Appropriations, 1975.
30. "Herreras Among Biggest Cocaine Organizations," *The New York Times*, April 12, 1975.
31. *Ibid.*
32. Interview with Vaughn Young, December 12, 1975.
33. Nicholas Gage, "Latins View Leaders of Hard Drug Trade," *The New York Times*, April 21, 1975.
34. *Ibid.*
35. Report of the Drug Law Enforcement Sub-Project of the USAID Public Safety Program, by David R. Powell and Jess A. Ojeda, April, 1970.

36. Gage, "Latins View Leaders of Hard Drug Trade."
37. "Ecuadorians Oust a Reporter Over Narcotics Issue," *The New York Times,* January 15, 1976.
38. Frank Browning, "An American Gestapo," *Playboy,* February, 1976.
39. *Ibid.*
40. Jack Anderson, "CIA Linked to Other Agencies," *The Washington Post,* February 19, 1975.
41. Jack Anderson, "CIA Has Black Book for Sexual Playmates," *Miami Herald,* June 22, 1976.
42. McCoy, *The Politics of Heroin in Southeast Asia.*
43. "C.I.A. Using Drug Agency Cover," *Long Beach Independent Press-Telegram,* March 16, 1975.

CHAPTER SEVEN

1. *France-Soir,* October 28, 1976.
2. *Herning Folkeblad,* Copenhagen, Denmark, May 21, 1976.
3. *The London Evening Standard,* April 29, 1974.
4. Report of the Special Subcommittee on the International Court of Justice and the International Criminal Police Organization, the House Judiciary Committee, April, 1959.
5. *Ibid.*
6. U.S. Senate Subcommittee of the Committee on Appropriations, February 24, 1976.
7. Letter of May 4, 1975 to Interpol Washington, from Secretary General Jean Nepote, Interpol Paris.
8. Interview with Vaughn Young, Paris, December 12, 1975.
9. Memorandum of February 26, 1975, from Acting Assistant Commissioner of the IRS John F. Hanlon to the Commissioner of the IRS, Donald C. Alexander.
10. Interview with Vaughn Young, London, January, 1977.
11. *Børsen,* Stockholm, Sweden, October 25, 1973.
12. *Aftonbladet,* Vienna, Austria, September 1, 1977.
13. Interview with Vaughn Young, February 3, 1977.
14. Interview with Vaughn Young, February 4, 1977.
15. Memorandum of November 24, 1959, from FBI Director J. Edgar Hoover to Attorney General William Rogers.
16. Report by Edward F. Penaat, Brigadier General, Provost Marshal, U.S. Army, Europe, to Major General Hayden L. Boatner, on December 29, 1959.
17. *Ibid.*
18. Report of Myles Ambrose, Chairman of the U.S. Delegation to Secretary of State, Christian A. Herter, dated February 4, 1960.

19. Brigadier General Penaat report of December 9, 1959.
20. Memorandum of July 20, 1959, to Deputy the Provost Marshal General.
21. Memorandum of November 24, 1969 from FBI Director J. Edgar Hoover to Attorney General John Mitchell.
22. Report of December 15, 1961, to the Department of State from Treasury official Arnold Sagalyn.
23. *Ibid.*
24. *Ibid.*
25. "Pan American Jet with 36 Hijacked to Cuba by Youth," *The New York Times*, October 22, 1969.
26. *I.C.P.C. Review*, February, 1970, Issue No. 235.
27. *I.C.P.C. Review*, December, 1970, Issue No. 243.
28. "Terror: Why Interpol Is Handcuffed," *Daily Mirror* (London), September 18, 1972.
29. *The Times* (London), February 2, 1975.
30. Yeshayahu Ben-Porat Zeev Schiff and Eitan Haber, *Entebbe Rescue.*
31. "Why Interpol Can't Help," *The Times* (London), September 22, 1975.
32. "World Terrorism on the Rise?" *Florida Times Union*, May 9, 1977.
33. "All Roads Lead to Paris," *Newsweek*, July 21, 1975.
34. *Ibid.*
35. *World Jewry*, October, 1961.
36. Letter of March 31, 1976, from Ladislas Farago to Vaughn Young.
37. February 24, 1976, U.S. Senate Hearings Before the Committee on Appropriations, Subcommittee on the Treasury, Postal Service and General Government Appropriations for Fiscal Year 1977.

CHAPTER EIGHT

1. Radio Message of May 13, 1974, to Interpol Washington from Secretary General Jean Nepote, Interpol Paris.
2. *Ibid.*
3. Interview with Vaughn Young, December 12, 1975.
4. Harry Soderman, *A Policeman's Lot.*
5. Dispatch letter of May 14, 1975, to Interpol Washington from Secretary General Jean Nepote, Interpol Paris.
6. *Ibid.*
7. Ladislas Farago: *Aftermath: Martin Bormann and the Fourth Reich.*
8. Letter of August 4, 1976, from International Secretary General of

the International Police Association H. V. D. Hallet, to Vaughn Young.

9. "Our Policemen Don't Impress Interpol . . . ," *Daily Mail* (London), September 23, 1974.
10. Michael Fooner, *Interpol.*
11. Memorandum of December 20, 1972, from Kenneth Giannoules, chief of U.S. Interpol NCB, Washington, to Treasury official Eugene T. Rossides.
12. Memorandum of May 2, 1972, from Kenneth Giannoules to Jack McKenzie, Director, Office of Central Services.
13. *Boston University Law Review*, November, 1976.
14. Rick Delano, "Interpol in San Diego Drug Scene," *San Diego Chronicle*, December 1, 1977.
15. Anthony Moro, "F.B.I. Worried on Abuses of Files in Aftermath of Informer's Slaying," *The New York Times*, March 26, 1978.
16. Diane Henry, "Two Former Federal Agents Convicted in Drug Case," *The New York Times*, March 11, 1978.
17. Anthony Moro, "F.B.I. Is Destroying Criminal Files on Cases Closed for Five Years," *The New York Times*, March 15, 1978.
18. Ovid Demaris, *The Director.*
19. Moro, *The New York Times*, March 15, 1978.
20. "Rough Justice for the F.B.I.," editorial, *The New York Times*, April 12, 1978.
21. *Ibid.*
22. *Ibid.*
23. Supplementary Detailed Staff Reports on Intelligence Activities on the Rights of Americans, Book III, Final Report of the Senate Select Committee to Study Governmental Operations with respect to Intelligence Activities, U.S. Senate, April 23 (under authority of the order of April 14), 1976.
24. Paul Cowan, Nick Egleson, and Nat Hentoff, *State Secrets.*
25. *Justice Department Watch*, newsletter published by the Committee for Public Justice, November, 1977.
26. Cowan, Egleson, and Hentoff, *State Secrets.*
27. Comptroller General's Report, General Accounting Office, December 12, 1976.
28. *Ibid.*
29. *Ibid.*
30. Hearings of the U.S. Senate Committee Hearings on Appropriations, February 26, 1974.
31. *Ibid.*
32. *Ibid.*
33. *Ibid.*
34. *Ibid.*

35. Interview with Vaughn Young, May, 1975.

36. Cowan, Egleson, and Hentoff, *State Secrets.*

CHAPTER NINE

1. Statement to U.S. Subcommittee by Treasury official David R. Macdonald, May 6, 1975.

2. U.S. Senate Hearings, Committee on Appropriations, May 6, 1975.

3. *Ibid.*

4. U.S. Senate Committee on Appropriations Hearings, February 24, 1976.

5. *Ibid.*

RESEARCH RESOURCES

Because Interpol is not a governmental agency but a private company which leased services to police agencies, it is not a difficult group to examine. Information for this book was gleaned from governmental documents, informed sources and officials, including some from Interpol itself, and personal observations. We personally visited eight countries, and others in four more nations gathered information which was included.

In some cases information was freely available as in the National Archives where Interpol's Nazi background was discovered with such relative ease it was apparent no one had ever bothered to walk in and ask. In other cases, notably in Europe, people were afraid to talk and had to be coaxed, often over several meetings, to even provide leads or the names of others to see for the information we sought.

In the United States we were able to use the Freedom of Information Act successfully to obtain thousands of pages of documents detailing Interpol activity from a number of agencies, e.g., Department of the Treasury, Department of Justice, U.S. Army, Central Intelligence Agency (which refused to release their documents but provided some information when the matter was taken to court), Department of State, Drug Enforcement Administration, Bureau of Customs, and, after delaying the matter for two-and-one-half years, the FBI.

Thus the vast bulk of information obtained for this book was gained from original documents and interviews. We also relied on Interpol's magazine *The International Criminal Police Review*, which can be found in a few libraries in the United States. Earlier books and articles about the group proved to be of little value because the authors relied solely upon Interpol and their assumed credibility as the total source of information, much as writers used to rely on J. Edgar Hoover for stories about the FBI and thus helped to perpetuate the myth.

An unknown quantity of documents was withheld even under the Freedom of Information Act. In many cases documents were heavily censored—with words, sentences, paragraphs, and even whole pages struck. When, as in the case of the CIA, nothing at all was released, and the matter seemed worthwhile, the agency's refusal was taken to court under the FOI Act, but such litigation is lengthy and no results were forthcoming.

In order to assist those who might want to obtain the documents from the respective agencies, we are providing citations in this section as to the sources used for each chapter. In the case of interviews, the source is cited in the footnotes. In some instances, our resource clearly requested anonymity, for very obvious reasons.

CHAPTER ONE

Dickopf's personnel file can be found (at last word) in the Berlin Document Center, although we cannot guarantee its present condition, let alone that it still exists. Information on how the Nazis searched for missing persons was taken from Nazi records in the Modern Military Branch of the National Archives in Washington, D.C. Information about Ajax was obtained almost entirely from former Ajax members who were laboriously traced down in France and personally interviewed. We were able to see very briefly some Ajax records.

CHAPTER TWO

In addition to the sources cited in the footnotes and bibliography, we relied upon the National Archives for the documents detailing Interpol's early years and the role of Collier.

CHAPTER THREE

Again, files in the hands of the U.S. National Archives in Washington, D.C., provided much of this information. Some is also in their extension in Suitland, Md. The G-2 report, which is an excellent exposition of the Nazi police system, can be found in the Modern Military Branch (13W) of the National Archives. The Nazi Interpol magazines are on microfilm there. The Hoover material was obtained under an FOIA request that took two-and-one-half years to complete and even then the FBI refused to tell all. The Dressler book can apparently be found in only one place in the U.S., the Library of Congress.

CHAPTER FOUR

Some of the information on Interpol's post-war activity came from Justice Department and U.S. Army records obtained under FOIA. Material regarding Interpol's Nazi funding was found both in the Nazi Interpol magazine which is on microfilm in the U.S. National Archives and Allied Control Authority documents at the Suitland Record Center just outside Washington, D.C. Knowledge of Hoover's interest in the files was obtained from some of his correspondence requested under FOIA from the FBI. The names of persons who collaborated can be found in the Nazi Interpol magazine.

CHAPTER FIVE

U.S. reinvolvement after the war was found in documents obtained from the Justice Department through an FOIA request. Treasury's involvement came from the same material as well as from documents obtained from Interpol Washington and from the Treasury Department. Other information was gained from dissident agency officials who must remain unnamed.

CHAPTER SIX

For two years before, various sources had hinted to us, often in the strongest of terms, that Interpol officials were involved directly in the trafficking of narcotics, but it took a trip into Europe to discover evidence. Documentation detailing such involvement has been made available to U.S. officials, but none of this material has turned up in any FOIA request and is apparently also being withheld from the Congress. Cocaine traffic out of Bolivia is coordinated by Interpol there, primarily out of Santa Cruz, Cochabamba, and La Paz, but our resources there, who were understandably frightened and preferred to remain anonymous, would not allow any copying of the materials. The AID report, however, can be found in the AID library on the first floor of the State Department in Washington, D.C.

CHAPTER SEVEN

Information about IRS involvement with Interpol came from IRS documents obtained under FOIA. These were heavily censored and unusually scarce. The 1959 meeting was found in Justice Department materials, which also provided the bulk of the information about the 1960 General Assembly meeting in Washington. The latter meeting was also documented by the U.S. Army's files. Additional information about terrorism and Interpol's alleged role stemmed from personal interviews and correspondence with officials in several nations.

CHAPTER EIGHT

Unfortunately the only place we could find copies of the agreements between the international headquarters of Interpol located just outside Paris and the French government was in France itself. Apparently other member nations have not been supplied copies of the full text but have seen only what the Saint-Cloud office wanted them to see. Cartland's case was well covered in the British media, but we interviewed him as well.

CHAPTER NINE

Because Interpol operates as a "middle man" and is seldom identifiable, it is as difficult to find victims of its actions as it would be to find them of the CIA's. These cases were found by the National Commission on Law Enforcement and Social Justice (NCLE). One other group that is familiar with abuses by Interpol Bolivia is the Committee of Concerned Parents representing parents whose children are locked in Bolivian prisons. The CCP can be reached at 4920 Piney Branch Road, N.W., Washington, D.C.

BIBLIOGRAPHY

ALAIN JOUBERT. *Dossier D . . . Comme Drogues.* Paris: Editions Alain Moreau, 1973.

ANSLINGER, HARRY JACOB WITH J. DENNIS GREGORY. *The Protectors.* New York: Farrar, Straus and Company, 1964.

BERNART, PHILLIP. *Roget Wybot et Bataille la DST.* Paris: Press de la Cité, 1975.

CAEBERT, HANS WALTER. *Interpol aut Verbrecherjagd. Die Internationale Kriminalpolizeiliche Kommission in Einsatz.* Würzburg: Arena, 1968.

CLARK, EVERT AND HORROCK, NICHOLAS. *Contrabandista!* New York: Praeger, 1973.

CONTRERAS PÉREZ, HECTOR. *La Organización Internacional de Policia Criminal, Interpol.* Santiago, 1966.

CORSON, WILLIAM. *The Armies of Ignorance.* New York: Dial Press, 1977.

CRAMER, JAMES. *The World's Police.* London: Cassell, 1964.

CRANKSHAW, EDWARD. *Gestapo, Instrument of Tyranny.* New York: Putnam, 1956.

DECLOUX, LOUIS. *From Blackmail to Treason, Political Crime and Corruption in France, 1920–1940.* London: Deutsch, 1958.

DELARUE, JACQUES. *The Gestapo, A History of Horror.* New York: Dell, 1967.

DEMARIS, OVID. *The Director.* New York: Harper's Magazine Press, 1975.

DRESSLER, OSKAR. *Die Internationale Kriminalpolizeiliche Kommission und ihr Werk*. Berlin-Wannsee, Hrsg. fur den Dienstgebrauch von der Internationalen Kriminalpolizeilichen Kommission. Vorwort, 1942.

DULLES, ALLEN. *The Secret Surrender*. London: Wardenfeld & Nicolson, 1967.

EISENBERG, DENNIS. *The Re-emergence of Fascism*. London: McGibbon & Kee, 1967.

ELKINS, MICHAEL. *Forged in Fury*. New York: Ballantine, 1971.

FARAGO, LADISLAS. *Aftermath: Martin Bormann and the Fourth Reich*. New York: Simon & Schuster, 1974.

FOONER, MICHAEL. *Interpol, The Inside Story of the International Crime-Fighting Organization*. Chicago: Henry Regnery Company, 1973.

FORREST, A. J. *Interpol*. London: A. Wingate, 1955.

GISEVIUS, HANS BERND. *Wo Ist Nebe? Erinnerungen an Hitler's Reichskriminaldirektor*. Zurich: Droemer, 1966.

HAGEN, LOUIS. *The Secret War for Europe*. London: McDonald, 1968.

HILBERG, RAUL. *The Destruction of the European Jews*. London: W. H. Allen, 1961.

HOEVELLER, HANS J. *International Fighting of Crime*. Hamburg: German Police Publishing House, 1966.

HÖHNE, HEINZ. *The Order of the Death's Head: The Story of Hitler's S.S.* New York: Coward-McCann, 1970.

HOWE, SIR RONALD. *The Story of Scotland Yard: A History of the C.I.D. from the earliest times to the present day*. London: A. Barker, 1965.

KRAUSNICK, HELMUT; BUCHHEIM, HANS; BROSZAT, MARTIN; JACOBSEN, HANS-ADOLF. *Anatomy of the SS State*. London: Collins, 1968.

LITTLEJOHN, DAVID. *The Patriotic Traitors: The history of collaboration in German-occupied Europe, 1940–45*. New York: Doubleday, 1972.

LÜTHY, HERBERT. *The State of France: A study of contemporary France*. London: Secker & Warburg, 1955.

MCCOY, ALFRED W. *The Politics of Heroin in Southeast Asia*. New York: Harper & Row, 1972.

MITSCHERLICH, ALEXANDER AND FRED MIELKE. *Doctors of Infamy: The story of the Nazi medical crimes*. New York: H. Schuman, 1949.

Newsday STAFF AND EDITORS. *The Heroin Trail*. New York: Holt, Rinehart and Winston, 1974.

NEIER, ARYEH. *Dossier: The Secret Files They Keep on You*. New York: Stein and Day, 1975.

NOBLE, IRIS. *Interpol: International Crime Fighters*. New York: Harcourt Brace Jovanovich, 1975.

——. *Polizei der BRD; Polizei der Monopole*. Berlin: Autorenkollektiv unter der Leitung von P. Köhler Deutscher Militärverlag, 1972.

PAYNE, ROBERT. *The Life and Death of Adolf Hitler*. New York: Popular Library, 1974.

REISS, CURT. *The Nazis Go Underground*. Garden City, N.Y.: Doubleday, Doran & Co., 1944.

REITLINGER, GERALD. *The Final Solution*. London: Vallentine Mitchell, & Co. Ltd., 1953.

RUSSELL, CORD. *Return of the Swastika*. London: Robert Hale Co., 1968.

SICOT, MARCEL. *A la barre de l'Interpol*. Paris: Productions de Paris, 1961.

SMITH, JUAN CARLOS. *La organizacion internacional Interpol y la extraterritorialidad de la ley penal*. La Plata: Ediciones Libreria Juridica, 1970.

SODERMAN, HARRY. *A Policeman's Lot*. New York: Funk & Wagnalls Company, 1956.

STEAD, PHILLIP JOHN. *The Police of Paris*. London: Staples Press Ltd., 1957.

TULLET, TOM. *Inside Interpol*. New York: Walker, 1965.

UNGER, SANFORD J. *FBI*. Boston: Little, Brown and Company, 1975–76.

VON SCHUSCHNIGG, KURT. *The Brutal Takeover*. New York: Atheneum, 1971.

WHEELER, BENNET, J. W., *The Nemesis of Power*. London: Macmillan, 1953.

WIEDMER, JO. *Interpol-Fälle* Falschgeld, Checkfälschung, Rauschgift, Ein Tatsachembericht, Bern, 1969.

WIESENTHAL, SIMON. *The Murderers Among Us*. London: Heinemann, 1967.

INDEX